BATTLESHIP BARHAM

BATTLESHIP BARHAM

Geoffrey P. Jones

WILLIAM KIMBER · LONDON

First published in 1979 by
WILLIAM KIMBER & CO. LIMITED
Godolphin House, 22a Queen Anne's Gate,
London, SW1H 9AE

© Geoffrey Jones, 1979
ISBN 0 7183 0416 0

Set by Jubal Multiwrite Limited, London SE13
and printed and bound in Great Britain by
Redwood Burn Limited, Trowbridge & Esher

Contents

List of illustrations

Photographic acknowledgements

Copyright pictures from Imperial War Museum (pages 52, foot, 66, foot, 213, 236), A & J Pavia (pages 105, foot, 150, foot, 226, 240, foot), H. D. Frhr von Tiesenhausen (pages 230, 252), Wright & Logan (pages 156, top, 163, foot, 175). Other photographs were kindly supplied by H. C. Bourdillon, E. J. Bush, E. Eustance, S. Haines, L. Horner, Mrs A. Jones, Mrs E. Rogers, E. A. Rowles, J. L. Wynne.

Acknowledgements

I am very pleased to acknowledge the help I received in varying degrees from several kind people. First I will mention those that served aboard *Barham* at various times. H. W. Adamson, J. H. Baddeley, E. J. Bush, A. J. Cobham, H. Cowley, E. Eustance JP, O. Gordon, J. C. Gregory, L. Horner, J. H. A. Lewis, F. Loy, E and J Rowles, C. R. Stratton-Brown, W. S. Walters, T. White, J. Wright and J. L. Wynne.

Others include: Commander H. C. Bourdillon (grand-nephew of Admiral Sir Hugh Evan-Thomas), A. Britton, Lieutenant B. V. Drew RM, T. P. Gorst (grandson of Edward Phillips) E. J. Grove, H. Hodgkinson, G. Lovell, S. F. Paris, Mrs E. Rodgers, Mrs B. Strickland, H. D. Freiherr von Tiesenhausen. Public Records Office at Kew and the US Navy Department in Washington.

My brother Ted, in Australia, contributed a sketch and a map.

A small part of Ted Eustance's story first appeared in *Ark Royal* by Kenneth Poolman, published by William Kimber and Co Ltd 1956, and part of Oliver Gordon's story first appeared in his book *Fight it Out* published by William Kimber and Co Ltd 1957.

Len Horner is Secretary of The Barham Survivors Association and lives at 10 Astbury Road, Peckham SE15.

Hugh Hodgkinson is the author of an excellent book, *Before the tide turned,* published by George G. Harrap and Co Ltd 1944.

Glossary of abbreviations and terms

ADC	Air Defence Control
ADP	Air Defence Platform
A/S	Anti-Submarine
Burberry	Naval Raincoat
DF	Direction Finder
DOS	Department of Supply
Dutchmans Log	A piece of wood, thrown over ships side at the bow, whose passage between two fixed markes on the side of the ship can be timed to give the speed of the ship. Developed and used by the Netherlands in the 17th Century.
Guzz	Devonport
HA	High Angle
HACS	High Angle Control Sector
HE (shells)	High Effect
HE (submarines)	Hydrophone Effect
NAAFI	Navy, Army & Air Force Institute
Oppo	Friend or best friend
PB	Picket boat
RNVR	Royal Naval Volunteer Reserve
Rocky	Sailor in the Royal Naval Reserve
SBT	Submarine Bubble Target
SP (telephone)	Sound Powered telephone
Townie	Somebody from the same area
TS	Transmitting Station

Introduction

There remains an historic piece of celluloid showing the end of the only battleship ever sunk at sea by a U-boat. Every now and again this old film is taken out, dusted down, and shown on television. It records the sinking of HMS *Barham* by *U-331* on 25th November 1941 and was shot from HMS *Valiant*. It shows the drama from the moment the great ship was torpedoed, how she continued to steam ahead, heeling over fast as she went. Men are seen scrambling over the anti-torpedo bulges into the water, then comes the terrific explosion which shatters the ship and hides the last act of the tragedy in a huge cloud of black smoke.

The most memorable past of *Barham*'s career is her end, but, what I have attempted to achieve in this book is to recreate her story, to show life on board during her twenty-seven great years' service with the Royal Navy.

When I was serving in the Navy I was pleased to have my draft chit to HMS *Anson* cancelled at the very last moment. To me, then, a battleship was a floating gun platform made of steel, with its crew on board regimented by a bugle call. Now, all these years later, I bitterly regret not having the unique experience of serving in a battleship; there will never be another. Meeting all the fine sailors and marines that served aboard *Barham* has convinced me that I have missed something.

Battleship Barham is about these men; it is not a technical book full of statistics. Indeed some statistics are still ambiguous — for instance, the survivors from *Barham* were rescued only by the destroyers *Hotspur* and *Nizam*, who took 186 and 168 men respectively; yet the Admiralty state there were 396 survivors; similarly the number of officers and ratings killed or died of wounds is variously given as between 862 and 879. But this book is more concerned with the thousands of men who served in *Barham* from before Jutland until after the Battle for Crete, their lives and conditions under which they worked.

Barham had two badges. This came about because in the early days tompion badges were made aboard, based on the design of the ship badges supplied by the builders, John Brown, of Clydebank, and then in 1919–20 the Admiralty issued an official

badge incorporating the coat of arms of Admiral Lord Barham,
First Sea Lord at the time of the Battle of Trafalgar.

Through the columns of *Navy News* I found a good many 'old
salts' who served aboard the ship and remember her with affection.
These men have been most helpful and I have been able to weave
their contributions into the framework of the story. They are
acknowledged separately.

The most prolific writer was John Bush, now of Walsall, who
kept a record of his early days aboard; I only regret I could not
include his full story, poems and photographs.

After some detective work I located a sea-salt stained diary
recording the Battle of Jutland and before, which belonged to
Gunnery Instructor Edward Phillips. His relatives kindly loaned
this priceless work for my use.

I finally located Hans Dietrich Freiherr von Tiesenhausen after
a long search. It was he, as commander of *U-331*, who sank
Barham. He was kind enough to check my story of the sinking and
provide some photographs. At the end of the war he lost most of
his possessions, including a record of his broadcast of the sinking
on the German radio. He would be pleased to hear from anybody
who may still have a recording.

Admiral   A. B. Cunningham,   Commander-in-Chief   of   the
Mediterranean at that time, described the sinking as a 'most
distressing calamity', but praised the 'most daring and brilliant
performance on the part of the U-boat'. The sinking of a battleship screened by destroyers should not have occurred, though
there were extenuating circumstances. Yet it is a coincidence
that *Barham* was *twice* torpedoed while so screened, and the
commander of *U-331* tells me that before the war he briefly met
the notorious Fritz-Julius Lemp, who as captain of *U-30* also
torpedoed *Barham*.

When I finished writing this book, I was left wondering whether
it was solely of a tragedy that I had written. It was tragedy that
860 men or more lost their lives in appalling circumstances; but
the battleship herself was spared an inglorious end in a breaker's
yard, and the spirit that was fostered amongst those who served
aboard her during her twenty-seven years of service lives on still,
amongst the survivors who gather each year to remember the
past and their fallen friends from *Barham*. And it is to these men,
the living and the lost, that I offer this book in tribute.

PART ONE

THE WAR TO END ALL WARS

1914–1918

CHAPTER ONE

'A nipping and eager air'

When war was declared with Germany on 4 August 1914 it was exactly a hundred years since any adversary had successfully disputed Britain's right to the title of 'Mistress of the Seas'. This position, after the Napoleonic wars, had been maintained by a succession of squadrons of ships whose weight and numbers kept command of the seas of the world.

At the outbreak of war Winston Churchill was First Lord of the Admiralty, a position he had held for the previous three years — throughout her life *Barham* was to be closely linked with the politician, who at this time was forty years old.

Two weeks before the commencement of hostilities King George V had paid a visit to his fleet assembled at Spithead. The gathering of ships was the greatest ever known; Spithead had overflowed for the first time in the history of the Navy. The weather was as always windy and grey, with choppy seas and scudding clouds, then sunshine, a calm and blue skies, all within the same half-hour. The wind and the greyness suited best the endless lines of black ships that stretched in lines that ran for forty miles. No fewer than 232 ships and submarines, manned by over 70,000 men and thirty aeroplanes and seaplanes with two airships, were gathered to greet the 'Sea King', while others were necessarily despatched for want of room to other anchorages. There were twenty-four vessels of Dreadnought type, from the first of the class to *Iron Duke* and *Marlborough*, frowning monsters, thirteen of which mounted 13.5 in guns, thirty-five older battleships, twenty armoured cruisers, thirty-five protected cruisers, seventy-eight destroyers (most notable were the lean black hulls of the new 'X' class), sixteen submarines, seven minelayers, six auxiliaries and eleven minor craft.

An observer, a guest on a ship of the Second Battle Squadron wrote:

As one passed down the avenues made by these numberless
fortresses there came the feeling of being in a vast town of iron
castles, each standing alone and independent of the other. But
they were not silent castles by any means. One saw the cluster
of life in all of them, heard the sound of bugles, had one's
eyes turned constantly this way and that by the ceaseless
coming and going of picket-boats, so commonplace a business
of the sea, and yet so fascinating. My first impression of a
battleship is always, 'How small it looks!' That is a deception
due to the harmony and completeness of all its details. And it
is a deception quickly corrected when, from a picket-boat, one
sees the seamen like ants upon the decks of some great levia-
than. And the fancy is dispelled even more effectively when
one goes aboard one of these huge ships of the line, and finds
oneself wandering over seemingly illimitable expanses of deck.

They seem so vast and so complex to be run by such young
men. For youth is the next overpowering impression on such a
day. In the ship where I was I saw not a man who looked
over twenty-five, except the flag-captain and the rear admiral,
and neither of them looked over forty. One found oneself talking with apparent lads of twenty-two, who, one discovered
presently, were commanders, and had seen every corner of the
globe. And the youthfulness of aspect was reflected in the
gaiety of spirits, genuine and remarkable when, looking back,
one remembers that many there, for all their apparent outward
carelessness, must have had some intuition that behind this
pageant there lurked a shadow of what was to be. The night
cut into a thousand glistening searchlights from the ships;
and the early morning, with its Portsmouth steamers crammed
and jammed and packed with liberty men; and the singing in
the ward-room on Saturday night, the sound of which still
remains in my ears, and is like a knife in my heart; and Divine
service on the quarterdeck on Sunday morning, so touching
in its simplicity and sincerity.

On Monday 20 July King George V led his ships to sea in the
forenoon, and the following days were spent in tactical exercises
in the Channel. At the end of the week the ships put into their
home ports prior to midsummer leave. By Wednesday 29 July

the fleet was informed that there could be no leave and there was to be no dispersal of ships; indeed for many their leave was long delayed.

A week later, the day after war had been declared, 54-year-old Admiral Sir John Jellicoe was appointed Commander-in-Chief of the Home Fleet and hoisted his flag in HMS *Iron Duke*. Rear Admiral Sir Lewis Bayly commanded the First Battle Squadron and had as his second-in-command Rear Admiral Hugh Evan-Thomas. Sir David Beatty was Rear Admiral Commanding First Cruiser squadron; this remarkable man became a captain at twenty-nine and reached flag rank before he was forty. An outstanding leader, he was liked by all.

In March, earlier that year, Winston Churchill had announced that every ship in the fleet would be put on a war footing in July and that 30,000 men of the Royal Fleet Reserve would be called for service between 15 and 25 July. When the reserves were discharged to their civilian duties again, after their call-up, they were told that they were likely to be required again shortly; and so it proved, for on 2 August they were recalled to the flag. At the outbreak of war the British Home Fleet consisted of the *Iron Duke* as flagship and four battle squadrons:

First Battle Squadron, Dreadnought type, 10 guns: *Marlborough, Collingwood, Colossus, Hercules, Neptune, St Vincent, Superb* and *Vanguard*.

Second Battle Squadron, Super-Dreadnought type, 10 guns: *Conqueror* and *Monarch* and 6 Dreadnought type, 10 gun ships, *King George V, Ajax, Audacious, Centurion, Orion* and *Thunderer*.

Third Battle Squadron, pre-Dreadnought type, 8 guns: *King Edward VII, Africa, Britannia, Commonwealth, Dominion, Hibernia, Hindustan,* and *Zealandia*.

Fourth Battle Squadron, Dreadnought type, 10 guns: *Dreadnought, Bellerophon, Temeraire* and *Agamemnon* a pre-Dreadnought type ship with 14 guns.

The Dreadnought type, 8-gun battle-cruisers were *Lion, Princess Royal, Queen Mary* and *New Zealand*. There were 85 destroyers and dozens of lesser ships.

Barham was to belong to a Fifth Battle Squadron; at this time the squadron was still being built, but the enemy would encounter its might at the Battle of Jutland, still twenty months hence.

The 1912 building programme had allowed for a new class of battleship, a ship armed with eight 15-inch guns and sixteen 6-inch guns. The ships were to be powered by oil-fired boilers, and the weight saved, as compared to coal in bunkers, allowed for an extra protection thickness on the torpedo bulkheads to 2 inches and the belt at the waterline to 13 inches. The main protection belt was 13 feet deep, 5 feet of this was the 13 inch belt which tapered down to 8 inches at the bottom edge and the top 4 feet, tapering to 6 inches at the top edge.

The four battleships originally envisaged were named *Barham*, *Queen Elizabeth*, *Valiant* and *Warspite* but the Federated Malay States offered to pay for an additional unit and this ship was appropriately named *Malaya*.

It is *Barham* in which we are interested: she was the fourth to carry the name. The first was a 74-gun ship of 1,761 tons built by Perry, Wells & Green at Blackwall and launched in July 1811. At the end of 1826 she was reduced to a 50-gun ship and was finally broken up in 1839. The second was a wood-screw frigate of 21 guns with a 3,027 ton displacement which was ordered in 1860 and later cancelled. The third *Barham* was a 3rd-class cruiser of 1,830 tons carrying six 4.7-inch and four 3-inch guns. This ship was launched in September 1889.

Like so much else in the Navy, the name *Barham* is associated with Nelson. Sir Charles Middleton was born in 1726 and in April 1805 was First Lord of the Admiralty; when raised to the peerage a month later he took the title of Lord Barham. He was still at the Admiralty when the Battle of Trafalgar took place on 21 October 1805 and died in 1813.

Barham, and the rest of the class of ship, was designed by the Director of Naval Construction Sir Eustace Tennyson D'Eyncourt who in 1912 succeeded Sir Philip Watts. *Barham* was built by John Brown & Co on the Clyde from 24 February 1913 to December 1914. Winston Churchill suggested the ships be armed with 15-inch guns and this idea was greeted with enthusiasm by the 'big-gun' men, led by Lord Fisher. At this time no 15-inch gun had ever been manufactured, and it says something for Winston Churchill, even at this early stage of his career, that he risked all by ordering the guns without any prototype being manufactured and tested. However, all was well and the twin turret 15-inch guns proved successful. The maximum range of fire was 23,400 yards. A 15-inch director control tower was fitted on the fore-top; the whole of the 15-inch armament could be controlled from 'B' turret. In the original design the 6-inch guns were planned six each side forward on the upper deck and two each side aft on the main deck, but in the event the four guns aft were not fitted on *Barham*.

Barham was launched on 31 December 1914 and commissioned on Thursday 19 August 1915 by Captain A.W. Craig as flagship of the new Fifth Battle Squadron. Captain Craig became known to his crew as 'Trunky' on account of his big nose, and his ship carried an initial complement of over 1100 men.

Most of the crew, from Portsmouth Depot, arrived at Clydebank before the ship was completed and some of them were billeted in the local police station. Two of the new arrivals were Petty Officer E. Phillips and Able Seaman John Baddeley. Both these men were from Brighton; in fact John says a good number of the crew were from the Sussex town, and he was called 'Brighton' as at this time many of the crew were identified and known by their hometown. Also on board was Able Seaman Berger, son of the paint manufacturer, for which he often had his leg pulled. Among the first of many sporting personalities *Barham* accommodated was Able Seaman Buggs, the heavyweight boxing champion of the Fleet.

The crew joined *Barham* at 1000. The remainder of the day was occupied in a general look around the ship by the crew under their officers who included Commander Charles R. Blane (later to die at Jutland) and 'Jimmy the One' Creighton.

The ship, all 600 feet of her, lay alongside the dockyard wall as the morning sun filtered in through the scuttles. The white painted deckhead was intersected by closely spaced beams studded with hammock-hooks, each one at precisely the same distance from its neighbour. Everything was literally as bright as new paint, accentuated as it was by the electric lights that burned throughout the day below deck. The administrative staff were settling in and soon station cards were ready for all the crew, containing essential information with the man's name, rating, mess, and number on

the ship's book. The card signified the holder's part of watch by
its colour and was handed in whenever he went ashore. The 'commissioning card' duplicated this information, and contained also
his part of the ship, part of the watch, and stations for action,
fire, collision, going in and out of harbour and the like.

In the days following the commissioning, action and collision
stations were exercised and later defence and abandon ship stations. On Sunday the crew prayed for their sins and one watch
was allowed a run ashore in the evening. The crew were settling in.
For those on a capital ship for the first time it was a new experience. Marines were carried on board, as was evident by the sound
of bugles, and the Marine band played at the Divine service on
Sunday.

Gradually the geography of the ship began to register; places
like the sick bay, galley, canteen and mail office became known.
Odd holes and corners were utilised for amateur, though officially recognised, 'snobs' who repaired their shipmates' boots,
'barbers' cut their colleagues' hair and 'tailors' did their 'jewing'
with sewing machines — all, of course, for a small consideration.
Petty Officer Phillips had a 'jewing' concession and with a few
yards of serge he ran up a 'tiddly' suit for seven or eight shillings.

On the Monday after commissioning the ship took in some
ammunition, and this was followed by drill at all guns in the ship.
Those that had not already experienced it were soon made aware
that guns were the only thing that mattered in the Royal Navy.
'Guns', the gunnery officer on board a battleship, carried out
practice at every opportunity, working his Whale Island 'graduates'
hard, and he also gave the First Lieutenant plenty of work getting
the paintwork cleaned up after him. The gunnery officers were
some of the keenest in the service, but were seldom popular due
both to the hard work they handed out and because they thought
they were the élite of the service.

The ship was a hive of activity; all was on topline when she
weighed and proceeded down the Clyde for a short trial, everything worked splendidly. Eight days after commissioning *Barham*
got underway again and tested the 6-inch guns and mountings,
firing four rounds from each gun. At 1000 *Barham* proceeded to
sea; she steamed to Liverpool; arriving next day the ship put into
Gladstone Dock and evening leave was granted to the off duty

watch. There were plenty of pretty girls ashore waiting to meet the sailors from Britain's newest battleship. Pay day came on 1 September and most of the crew went ashore and took in a good cargo of beer; there were plenty of fat heads the next morning which didn't help the sailors who had to take in another cargo — for now the ship was being properly ammunitioned. The loading went on from Thursday right round until Sunday evening, during which time a thousand 15-inch shells and over 18,000 cases of 15-inch cordite were taken aboard together with ammunition for the smaller calibre guns. Later in the week the turrets were tested for tilt; then *Barham* left the dry dock and moored to a buoy.

There was a scare a week or two later when a lookout reported a submarine and blew his whistle. It turned out to be a false alarm — what he had seen were two lights ashore; it certainly put the dockyard workers aboard in a panic. When the sailors were off duty and not ashore many of them played the card game Bezique, which was all the rage at the time; others engaged in yarn-spinning competitions, adjudging the winner between themselves.

The good life in Liverpool was coming to an end; although some were not sorry to get away, no doubt in the weeks to come they would regret being away from the bustle of the busy seaport as they spent weeks in the desolate Scapa Flow. On Friday 1 October the guns were sponged out and later in the day Rear-Admiral Hugh Evan-Thomas was piped aboard. It will be remembered that he had been second in command of the First Battle Squadron; now he joined the ship with his staff and hoisted his flag, for *Barham* was first flagship of the newly formed Fifth Battle Squadron. Hugh Evan-Thomas was a popular choice, a personal friend of Sir John Jellicoe, and was liked by officers and men. An unassuming man, he had progressed well in his Naval career.

Hugh Evan-Thomas had joined *Britannia* at Dartmouth as a thirteen-year-old in January 1876, being advanced to sub-lieutenant in 1882. He was appointed to *Sultan* on the China Station, and within less than three years was promoted to lieutenant on the last day of 1884. Two years later he returned but in 1887 was at sea again, this time in *Bellerophon*, as flag lieutenant to Admiral Lyons, commander-in-chief on the North American and West Indies Station. On returning to England he went through a course in gunnery and torpedo, and in 1889 was lieutenant of *Camper-*

down for the naval manoeuvres. As a young officer he recognized the unreadiness of the Navy for its serious responsibilities, but he embodied the new spirit which was abroad in the fleet, wherein sea experience and efficiency in the practical duties of the profession were predominant. In December 1889, he was appointed to *Victoria*, flagship of Sir Anthony Hoskins, in the Mediterranean, where he remained for two years, and, after a period in the royal yacht *Osborne*, proceeded again to the same station as flag lieutenant to Sir Michael Culme-Seymour, commander-in-chief, in *Ramillies*. For three years he continued to serve in one of the finest and best disciplined ships in the fleet, and, in association with a chosen band of officers, nearly every one of whom afterwards became a renowned admiral. The ship was a veritable nursery of flag officers. Her captain was the future Sir William May, her commander was John Jellicoe, her torpedo lieutenant was Sir Leopold Heath, her gunnery lieutenant was Sir Arthur Leveson.

From this notable brotherhood of officers Lieutenant Evan-Thomas was promoted to commander in the January list of 1897, and was appointed to *Victory* for a posting to the Signal School at Portsmouth. Methods of signalling were receiving ever-increasing attention, and the commander took a practical part in training and development. His work there made very fruitful progress. Promotion was rapid, and, after commanding *Pioneer* in the Mediterranean, he was advanced to the rank of captain in June 1902, and was the flag captain to Lord Charles Beresford in *Majestic* and *Caesar* in the Channel in 1903–4. Afterwards for a short time he commanded the Admiralty yacht *Enchantress*. His service had been almost wholly at sea, in the East, the Atlantic, the Mediterranean, and in home waters, and he became known as one of the most capable and progressive captains in the Navy.

He was concerned in the execution of some of the manifold changes which Lord Fisher introduced when he came to the Admiralty in October 1904, and a year later himself joined the Admiralty as private secretary to Lord Cawdor, continuing in the same office with the next two incumbents until December 1908. It was a period of reorganisation which affected every part of the naval structure, including the entry and training of officers and men, the redistribution of the fleet, the institution of the system

Battleships old and new. HMS *Victory* was under the command of Commander Hugh Evan-Thomas and HMS *Royal Sovereign* was manned by Portsmouth ratings to join *Barham* at Devonport in 1935

Barham spreading anti-range sails in Scapa Flow

of nucleus crews, changes in the dockyards, and much else. Very responsible and exacting duties fell to the private secretary to the First Lord in those momentous years, and Captain Evan-Thomas, who had now become acquainted with every side of naval organisation and administration, left the Admiralty with enhanced reputation, and was clearly marked out for the most responsible duties of the fleet. After being captain of *Bellerophon* in the Home Fleet, he was from July 1910 to August 1912 in command of the Royal Naval College at Dartmouth, having the important charge of directing the education of young officers under the new scheme.

The retirement of officers from the flag list under new rules brought him rapidly to the head of the captains' list, and he was promoted to rear-admiral in July 1912, at the age of 50, vacating thereupon his appointment as aide-de-camp to the King, which he had held since February 1911. His first flag appointment in December 1913 was as Rear-Admiral Second in Command in the First Battle Squadron, with his flag in *St Vincent*, and he was holding that command at the outbreak of the Great War. A year later he received a letter from the Admiralty in Whitehall signed by James Balfour who had been Prime Minister from 1902 to 1905 and was now serving as First Lord of the Admiralty having succeeded Churchill in May. The letter, dated 22nd July 1915, read:

I have much pleasure in offering you the command of the new battle squadron about to be formed with *Barham* as flagship. The uncertainty as to the lines on which this squadron will be developed makes it difficult to promise a definite period of command.

And so Rear-Admiral Hugh Evan-Thomas became the first admiral to serve in *Barham*, the battleship chosen as flagship of the new battle squadron

With the Admiral and his staff aboard, Captain Craig ordered *Barham* to sea and the flagship was underway in the first dogwatch; she headed for Scapa, arriving early the next morning. Two days later the battleship put to sea again for gunnery trials, each 15 inch gun fired four rounds. The trials were satisfactory, but one or two men in the turrets couldn't stand the noise. Further practices were carried out in harbour the following week, during which time there was some fog. By 12 October the weather was roughening up and the sailors started wearing their chin stays but old hands said it wasn't blowing as it used to! Next day the fleet proceeded to sea at 1600 for exercises; the sea was still rough and the hands took defence stations in watches. There was not much sleep for anybody; the turrets were wet, and there was plenty of seasickness but all recovered in time to claim their rum ration. Later the ship was darkened and action stations were exercised before *Barham* arrived back in harbour during the middle watch. Later in the day she put to sea for more firing. *Canada* arrived while *Barham* was sponging out her guns.

The system of messing in *Barham* will be described later; Petty Officer Phillips however makes occasional references in his diary to meals, such as 'rabbit pie and marrow for dinner', 'in the evening had a nice supper of chop off a horse, it was too tough for mutton'.

One afternoon there was a sailing regatta, in which *Royalist* took the honours with *Temeraire* just beating *Faulknor* to second place. Back to sea again *Barham* went for more exercises and to carry out 15-inch gun firing. It was choppy and she took in a good deal of water as she ploughed through it at 20 knots. The destroyers were seen to be dipping their noses. Two runs at ranges of 13,000 yards proved satisfactory especially considering the state of the sea.

Back at Scapa *Barham* oiled ship; refuelling by the simple expedient of just screwing on hoses was considered to be a modern miracle by the stokers, others were surprised that the oil didn't come aboard in bags! The flagship also took on 63 tons of solid fuel, for the galley was coal fired. As October ended the hands painted ship and sorted out their winter clothing to wear from the beginning of November. *Albemarle* and *Africa* arrived. S.7 won the 6-inch loading competition with 20 rounds in 75 seconds and practice torpedoes were fired without any losses. Practice followed practice.

On the first Sunday of the month *Zealander* and *Hindustan* came in while the hands were at morning service on the upper deck. Later in the day *Albemarle* returned from patrol with her

fore bridge carried away by a sea; the commander and one rating
had been washed overboard and her captain was seriously injured.
In fact, the sea was so rough and boisterous that *Barham* set
anchor watch. The weather continued bad and it was snowing
hard when *Minotaur* arrived. It continued to snow as *Barham* and
Canada got underway with two light cruisers; arriving at Cromarty
it took seventy minutes to moor the ship in the bad conditions.
Both ships later completed two runs for a 12,000 to 15,000 yards
shoot before returning to Scapa and anchoring with the fleet; they
received congratulations from the Admiral on their fine shooting.

Towards the end of the month *Warspite* arrived, and another
sister ship, *Queen Elizabeth*, left to refit.

On Wednesday 1 December *Barham* prepared for sea and got
underway with the fleet just before the dog-watches. The weather
was cold and the next day the sea became so rough that the flagship shipped water; it was not comfortable for those aboard.
By Friday the sea had moderated a little although it still remained
cold.

At 1015 Petty Officer Phillips was in a store chatting when a
colleague burst in saying, 'Come out quickly, and see the sight of
your lives. *Warspite* is going to ram us!' They tumbled out just in
time to see her hit *Barham* on the starboard quarter. Her port
anchor went through the ship's side into the captain's cabin, then
carried away and ran out, losing anchor and cable. 'Close all
watertight doors' was quickly piped; collision mats were put out.
Barham did not stop but kept her engines running. *Warspite* was
taking in water for'ard.

Barham was ordered to Scapa and started off at 10 knots,
later this was raised to 15 knots. All this time the damage control
party had been in action; fortunately the inner casing held, so
although a good deal of water had been taken in, it was confined
to the wing passages. When the hands arrived in the captain's
cabin they started putting all his bedding and mats into the hole.
Captain Craig came in and said, 'Don't put my bedding in there!
Send for some of the men's hammocks,' which they did — but
his bedding went in as well!

Fortunately the weather moderated and *Barham* left *Warspite*
behind as she was not able to match the speed of the flagship.
The hands remained at defence stations all night, reaching the

Pentland Firth at 0700 the next morning and Scapa Flow four hours later. Divers were sent down to assess the damage. It was difficult trying to clear all the water from the ship, even with the pumps going flat out; the carpentry staff were busy boarding up the hole above the waterline.

Warspite arrived six hours after *Barham* and immediately started unloading her shells to lighten ship. This turned out to be an all night job. *Barham* pumped all day on Sunday and the divers were continually on the go. By Tuesday the collision mat was able to be taken off. A storeship arrived and took away the lower booms and all spare gear in the ship, including boxes of ship's biscuits. On the same day a Court of Enquiry into the collision took place on board. Later it was learned that the reason given was that *Warspite* had misread a signal for eight knots as eighteen knots, and as she increased speed her port bow struck *Barham's* starboard quarter. Several officers in both ships were blamed. Fortunately the damage in both ships was not too severe and *Warspite* sailed to her home port.

On Wednesday *Barham* prepared for sea early and was underway after breakfast. The hands on the upper deck were looking to see which way the ship turned, when they found they were passing by Pentland Firth they knew they were bound for Cromarty. Half-an-hour out to sea, trawlers were seen with their sweeps out and were firing at something, probably mines. Snow was falling as *Barham* moored in Cromarty Firth in the early afternoon, joining four battleships of the 2nd Battle Squadron and three cruisers of the Shannon class. There was a lecture in the first watch on the Battle of the Falkland Islands, which had taken place in 1914; the snow continued to fall and everything froze hard. During the middle watch the marine sentry fell overboard from *Ajax*; the picket boat from *Barham* made an unsuccessful search for him. Petty Officer Phillips recorded in his diary: 'No doubt he is walking home on the bottom, he had a big coat on so he will be nice and warm.'

Preparatory to going into the floating dock, *Barham* pumped out 2,000 tons of oil into a tanker that came alongside. Workmen came aboard as more snow fell and started burning out rivets from the ship's side, round the hole, so that the plate could be removed. On Saturday the flagship *Iron Duke* arrived, just as

Queen Elizabeth came out of dock.

It was still snowing on Sunday 12 December as Captain Craig had the hands mustered aft to tell them the good news that long leave would be given and that in the meantime he wanted them to work hard on boat-pulling and sports, to give the ship (and indirectly him) a good name. In the afternoon *Barham* unmoored and went into dock and soon working parties were cleaning the ship's bottom.

Admiral Jellicoe came on board the following day; as soon as he saw the damage he allowed seven days' immediate leave. The Captain gave the crew the good news and there was a great cheer. The next morning hands were employed holystoning the deck but their thoughts were all of home. Leave commenced in the afternoon with the west coast line men first away at 1330 and the remainder two hours later; they caught the 1645 from Invergordon and arrived at King's Cross at 1055 the following morning.

The first party arrived back on board a week later and the second party departed the next day; they had been unfortunate enough to suffer the privations a crew suffers when their ship is in dock, but were compensated by being able to spend Christmas at home. After they left, *Barham* undocked and moored next to her sister ship *Queen Elizabeth* where she refuelled before the ship's side was repainted; there were now no signs remaining of the collision.

After the enforced stay in harbour Captain Craig was pleased to receive orders to proceed to sea. *Barham* weighed anchor in the forenoon of 23 December and proceeded out of harbour with *Queen Elizabeth* and an escort of destroyers. As soon as they were clear and hit the open sea *Barham* started to roll a bit. The escorting destroyers were sent back as it was too rough for them. *Barham* increased to 23 knots and soon ran into trouble; she shipped big green seas over the starboard side and they swept everything before them. One sea lifted the captain's galley, and both skiffs out of their crutches standing them up against 'X' turret before breaking them up. Another sea hit the 6-inch gun on the starboard side of the upper deck and opened out the shields like an umbrella, breaking the sights and carrying away the projectiles' stowage rack. 'A' turret was swamped and 'Y' turret was nearly as bad. Three feet of water swilled round the casemates on the battery deck and outside as well; all the storerooms were flooded and mess lockers were concertinaed and the trappings were awash. So much for big ship comfort! The clothes in the slop room were ruined and sacks of flour contaminated. The messtub was used for paddling. Four of the starboard 6 inch guns were put out of action and the shells were floating. It is not often that 6-inch shells float, but they did on this December day. Upper and lower deck alike were pleased to arrive at Scapa during the first dog watch and once again get on an even keel. It was a black and dirty night so the anchor was dropped and the watch on deck kept an eye on it and the two mud-hooks that were down.

Next morning, Christmas Eve, the wind still blew strongly, bringing with it snow, hail and rain. There was a strong sea running as *Barham* shifted her billet; *Warspite* arrived and *Queen Elizabeth* went to sea. All the crew were engaged in cleaning up their ship and attempting to put the pieces together again.

On Christmas Day the messdecks were decorated and Sunday routine was carried out. The petty officers' mess had a party in the evening, even though rum had been flowing during the day. The hands were allowed to carry on smoking and singing in the messdecks until 2300 while the petty officers cracked nuts and spun ditties for another hour.

By Sunday 26 December the wind had dropped, the sun shone over the now calm sea as the provision boat came alongside. Among the 'goodies' it brought was a parcel for an 'oppo' of Petty Officer Phillips. He thought it was a piece of wedding cake until he opened it and discovered it to be a rotten piece of gorgonzola cheese, and it 'didn't talk well' he says.

The weather had turned bad again by the time the second party arrived back from leave at the end of the month.

The old year ended with the news of *Natal* blowing up with heavy loss of life following an internal explosion. There was a party in progress on board at the time and many civilians were killed. On New Year's Eve there was too much wind for *Barham* to carry out a proposed sub-calibre shoot at a floating target. At midnight a 'clown party' somehow obtained the big drum and all the side drums and tin gear they could lay their hands on and proceeded round the ship making an infernal noise for half-an-hour.

In her first four-and-a-half months *Barham* had proved herself seaworthy and more than capable of taking care of herself at sea. The sea crew had shaken down well, all were on top-line; all that was wanted now was a sight of the enemy. Since the war began more ships had joined the Fleet. In November 1914 the powerful battle-cruiser HMS *Tiger* joined Admiral Beatty's force and another coal-burning battleship that was being built in a British yard for the Chilean Navy was taken over by the Royal Navy and named HMS *Canada*. She, as already mentioned, was at Scapa with *Barham*.

CHAPTER TWO

The Year of Jutland

As 1916 opened, the men in *Barham*, in fact in the whole of the Grand Fleet were yearning for action. Where was the High Seas Fleet?

The Battle of Coronel, the Battle of the Falkland Islands and the Scarborough raid had taken place in 1914, the Dogger Bank action and the Dardanelles in 1915; now in 1916 the Grand Fleet were impatient for action.

It was thought in some quarters that the Royal Navy lacked offensive spirit, but this was not the case. Earlier, Winston Churchill had proposed sending a squadron of the Queen Elizabeth class ships into the Baltic to contain the High Seas Fleet. This idea was turned down as the limited space in the Baltic would be more conducive to destroyers, submarines and smaller craft rather than large fast battleships, and the advantage would be very much in the favour of the Germans. In fact, Admiral Beatty was on record as saying that the Germans would only fight on their own terms.

A proposal towards the end of 1915 suggested that a half-hour bombardment of Heligoland might well provoke the enemy to send a squadron out for a confrontation, but this was not implemented on the grounds that submarines could get among our capital ships or they could get caught in minefields. There was some apprehension among the British top brass that Zeppelins might make a decisive contribution in any sea battle, since they would be able to spot and report the British dispositions, flying high enough that the high angle guns and seaplanes would not be able to ward them off while the Grand Fleet would be firing blind; this however was to be in the future.

The bad weather continued at Scapa; to the sailors based in the Flow, cold winds, misty hills, rough seas, snow and boredom were always associated with the Grand Fleet anchorage. During the first week of the year *Barham* continued with sub-calibre firing, range firing tests and practising breakdown procedures. Despite the rough weather *King Edward VII* left harbour during the forenoon of 6 January; she was mined and sank with the loss of eleven lives thirty miles off the Pentland Firth. The mines were laid by the disguised raider *Moewe* four days earlier. The weather in the Flow continued bad, blowing hard and raining; it rained particularly hard as the Marines coaled ship for the galley fires. In the middle of the month a 6-inch gun-loading competition took place with two men per gun; a Marine crew won. Later, *Barham* sailed with *Iron Duke* to carry out base range findings but due to a fault in *Barham's* condensers she had to return to harbour where she moored with the cruisers at the opposite end, on the other side of her usual station. *Barham* had two anchors down, as it was still blowing hard. Twelve new ratings joined the ship, just in time to receive a box of chocolates which was presented to each member of the crew as a gift from the Colonies, and much appreciated.

On Monday 17 January as the hands were painting ship a signal was received to raise steam for full speed and be prepared for action. This was probably to act as distant cover for Commodore Tyrwhitt's Harwich Force which was attempting a seaplane raid on the airship bases at Hage, north of Emden, on the Schleswig coast. Unfortunately, before the flying off position had been reached a dense fog came down and the operation was cancelled.

Toward the end of the month an epidemic of measles broke out on board keeping the medical staff busy in the sick bay.

In marked contrast to the rest of the month the dawn of the last day heralded the reappearance of the sun as *Barham* weighed anchor at 0630 and proceeded out of harbour with *Queen Elizabeth*, *Warspite* and *Canada* to carry out a full calibre shoot with four rounds per gun. The ships rolled as they raised steam for 22 knots and *Canada* had difficulty keeping up; she was the sole coal-burning ship, and the only one making smoke as her stokers below laboured hard shovelling coal. *Barham*, increasing to 23 knots, entered Moray Firth; later in the day the full charge firing took place at 16–17,000 yards. Both 'X' and 'Y' turrets misfired due to the lock insulation being broken, so that the current went to earth through the withdraw sleeve. The rest of

the guns fired successfully and were cleaned out as *Barham* returned to Scapa at 20 knots.

On 7 February there had been a heavy fall of snow in the
night, and the cold weather continued during the forenoon when
Barham left harbour with the 2nd Battle Squadron as the 3rd
Battle Squadron came in from Queensferry. During the first watch
a whirlwind passed over the Fleet and as it came across *Barham*
took the screen from the bridge and dumped it on top of the
marine sentry on the foc's'le. It also dislodged a tampion on one
of the guns.

Four days later the watch below were turned out at 0230 after
the signal to prepare for sea had been received. Action was delayed
until 0500 when the 5th Battle Squadron proceeded out and
steered a south-easterly course; *Barham*, ahead of *Iron Duke*,
escorted by light cruisers and destroyers, was zig-zagging at
16 knots. Despite the snow-covered hills the sea remained calm.
On the previous day Vice-Admiral Scheer, the new German
Commander in Chief, ventured out with a destroyer sweep near
the Dogger Bank and sank a British sloop engaged in sweeping
mines. When this became known ashore the Grand Fleet and the
Harwich Force were ordered to sea. By the time the cruisers
and destroyers from Harwich arrived the enemy had withdrawn
back to base. When returning, Commodore Tyrwhitt's flagship
Arethusa struck a mine and had to be abandoned after breaking
in two on a shoal. *Barham* anchored early the next morning,
filled up with oil and remained at four hours' notice for sea.

A nasty accident occurred in the middle of the month when a
seaplane that had been flying low over the fleet came to grief
passing over Kirkwall pier. The propeller broke off and decapi-
tated a petty officer from the *Benbow*. The seaplane landed
without further damage and the pilot and passenger were rescued unhurt. A couple of days later the measles quarantine ban
in the ship was lifted. There was a further mishap the following
week. Both cutters left *Barham* under sail in mid-morning; as
darkness approached a drifter was sent to bring them back. She
picked them up and secured one on each quarter, each cutter
having a skiff in tow. While they were coming through the Fleet
another drifter came down and somehow the skiffs were over-
turned and their two occupants drowned. A search was made for

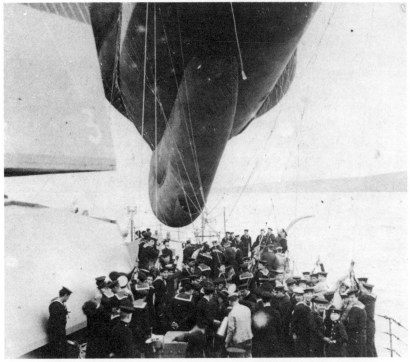

The Pussers Zep'—Kite balloon carried on *Barham* for spotting

Topmen holystoning deck of *Barham*

their bodies the next day but they could not be found; a Court of Enquiry into their disappearance was convened on board *Barham*.

A couple of days later *Barham* weighed at the beginning of the morning watch. All the Fleet were out and made an impressive sight. *Barham*, with *Iron Duke*, closed to action stations in the evening as information had been received that an air raid was expected, but in the event it was too windy. *Barham*, in company with *Marlborough* and *Superb*, headed for base the following day just as it came on to blow in the evening. As she arrived at day-break the steering gear gave out just as she entered harbour but luckily she managed to keep clear of the remainder of the fleet and proceeded to her anchorage.

Loading trials that far surpassed any previous ones took place next day when 16 rounds of 15-inch shells were loaded in 7.31 minutes by the fastest gun's crew, *Barham* was given a thorough clean up and painted as Russian officers were expected for a visit; they duly arrived next day and were described as 'a rough looking lot with one having whiskers like von Tirpitz'. The ship's concert party made a successful debut the same day.

Early in March *Valiant* arrived in heavy snow to complete the Fifth Battle Squadron. A day or two later a party of petty officers left *Barham* in the picket boat to test *Valiant's* director. They had almost reached the newly arrived ship when they saw a recall signal being hoisted. Arriving back on board they learned that a German squadron was out. *Barham* went with *Iron Duke* at full speed through the choppy sea in a south-easterly direction but returned to harbour when a signal arrived to say that the enemy had returned to base. Back in harbour the aerial guns crew remained on duty as word had been received that a German seaplane ship was at sea; the crews remained on duty night and day. On 9 March the 6-inch gun crews of *Queen Elizabeth* came on board *Barham* for a loading competition and the guns crews of each ship had two runs before they all went aboard *Queen Elizabeth* for a return match. The outcome was that *Queen Elizabeth* performed the fastest loading time, but the best average loading time was achieved by *Barham*. It was agreed to call the result an honourable draw.

Four days later SS *Borodino* came alongside *Barham*; some of the petty officers went aboard and purchased forty haddock and what was described as a 'frozen, rotten fowl'. On the following Saturday French and Russian officers were embarked to observe a firing practice; two rounds were due to be fired from the 15-inch guns, but just as *Barham* had prepared for sea a thick fog came down, so the event was postponed for a couple of days. *Barham* weighed at first light on Monday and proceeded to sea with *Queen Elizabeth* and *Warspite* and fired six rounds per turret with reduced charge; she returned to anchorage and ammunitioned ship the following day.

Barham had two casualties the following weekend. On Saturday a steaming signal put the battleship at four hours' notice; during the evening Petty Officer Fisher fell out of the sailing pinnace while working the main derrick and fractured his skull. He was immediately rushed to hospital. The watch were called at 0230 the next day; *Barham* weighed and proceeded to sea with all the fleet following suit. *Barham* shipped a great quantity of water in the rough sea and just before the end of the last dog a Marine was washed overboard and drowned; after this nobody was allowed on the upper deck. Altogether a total of 15 men were lost from the fleet due to the weather. The fleet had expected to meet the enemy at dawn on the Monday, but were again disappointed. *Barham* enjoyed a short diversion escorting *Undaunted*, who had her bow pushed in, to Newcastle before returning to the fleet anchorage.

Pay day came again on the first day of the month when a collection was made for the family of the man lost overboard.

Petty Officer Phillips recorded in his diary: 'It is just beginning to get exciting', for the previous day *Barham* had been under six hours' notice for sea and the day before that a submarine had been reported. On 2 April the fleet were told to expect an air raid; high angle gun crews were posted night and day but nothing materialised.

Humour had its place too: in the middle of the month a midshipman, exercising ratings, told one man to keep still while marking time! There was more the next day when *Gourko* came alongside to give the sailors a cinema show; there was a comedy among the films which was described as 'quite humorous'.

The following day *Barham* was at sea carrying out long range torpedo firing. On Easter Sunday *Barham* was at sea, taking station eight miles ahead of *Iron Duke* as the Fifth Battle Squadron made 16 knots. Later it became foggy as the squadron proceeded back to base.

During the first dog on Easter Monday steam was raised for 22 knots. The Admiralty knew the enemy were at sea and an intercepted signal indicated that their objective was a bombardment of Yarmouth. At 2000 *Barham* and the rest of the Fifth Battle Squadron and the Battle Cruiser Fleet put to sea and headed due south. At 0600 on Tuesday news was received that the German raiding force were bombarding Lowestoft, so the squadron increased speed despite the fog which cut down visibility to 1,200 yards. The Harwich Force, although not being ordered to sea until almost too late, drove off the attacking Germans. The attackers had too good a start for the Grand Fleet to chase and catch them before they returned to Kiel. This escape caused a furore and the Admiralty were blamed for not co-ordinating the forces at its disposal. *Barham* returned disappointed to Scapa; she topped up with oil while the fleet remained at two hours' notice.

Early in May light cruisers and destroyers left Rosyth to escort the seaplane carriers *Vindex* and *Engadine* to a position off the island of Sylt from which a bombing raid on the Zeppelin sheds was intended. It was hoped that the raid would provoke the High Seas Fleet to sea where the Grand Fleet was lying as distant cover to the attackers. *Barham* proceeded to sea in the early hours of 2 May. The hands were called and closed-up for action at 0330. For a change the water was calm as the fleet made its way across the North Sea. However, the raid failed; the Germans were not quite sure of the situation and sent up a Zeppelin which was spotted from *Birkenhead*. *Barham* prepared shrapnel and it was later learned that the First Light Cruiser Squadron brought him down. Because of the bad weather the Germans remained at anchor so the Fleet turned back, arriving at Scapa at noon on 5 May.

A week later *Royal Oak* arrived in the Flow. The Fleet regatta commenced at 0900 on 11 May although the sea was a little choppy. *Queen Elizabeth* won most of the races on the first day. Next day *Barham* won the launch race and came second and fourth in the cutter and gig in the all-comers' race, giving her second place among the Fifth Battle Squadron.

On the following Monday the Commander-in-Chief was due aboard to present the prizes. There was plenty of red tape and everything that shone was given a polish. Unfortunately it then came on to rain. The Commander was most upset, but he rigged an awning, so that the prizes and cup could be presented to *Queen Elizabeth* in the dry.

Two days later *Borodino* came alongside for the benefit of the crew who had earlier taken in 60 tons of coal from a collier as well as sand and water. The following day a U-boat was reported, so fluorescent nets were put out; those ships with no nets had a collier secured along each side.

Sunday 21 May turned out to be a glorious day; there was not a ripple on the water as *Barham* and *Achilles* left the Flow early in the afternoon with a strong escort of destroyers and proceeded at 20 knots. Early the next morning the force arrived in the Firth of Forth to find thick fog; it had to reduce to 12 knots and proceed cautiously. The fog lifted in mid-morning. *Barham* passed under the girdered bridge and moored just before noon when the clocks were advanced by one hour. The Commander addressed the ship's company, telling them that although the scenery was much better than at Scapa there was little likelihood of any leave; they should remember that they were still at war! Just to cap it all, the officers went ashore in the afternoon! Later in the day *Queen Elizabeth* entered dock for a refit and the crew were sent on leave. Next day *Barham* shifted billet and tied up to a buoy; the Commander relented and there was afternoon leave for chief and petty officers, they could go anywhere except Edinburgh. The following day leave was allowed for the whole ship's company, one watch each afternoon. The beer allocation at the shore canteen was one pint per man.

After a day of painting ship *Barham* raised full steam to go to sea, and stood by all night and all the next day. On Sunday the ship reverted to four hours' notice and leave was again granted but those that went ashore came back drenched due to a thunderstorm in the afternoon. Then came the calm before the impending storm. On Monday 29 May there was just the usual routine, and on Tuesday there were training classes. At eight bells in the afternoon *Barham* was ordered to prepare for sea and slipped at 2208.

The first entry in Petty Officer Phillips' diary for Wednesday 31 May is 'Today was the day'. Indeed it was, the day that the British Navy had long awaited, the day that would give them the chance to act as part of the team of the Fifth Battle Squadron which in turn was part of the Grand Fleet — yes, today was the day, the Battle of Jutland day!

Admiral Reinhard Scheer had succeeded the mortally ill Admiral Hugo von Pohl as Commander-in-Chief of the High Seas Fleet at the end of January 1916. Scheer had been commanding the 2nd Squadron of the High Seas Fleet at the time of his appointment. A vigorous personality, he determined to pursue a bolder line than his predecessor.

After two sorties further out to sea than anything previously in the war, the High Seas Fleet received an important signal on 30 May to assemble outside Wilhelmshaven, in the Jade Roads, at 1900. This measage was picked up by the listening British, and Admiral Jellicoe was notified that the Germans were planning an operation to take place the following day. The message could not be deciphered in its entirety, but the information was sufficient for the Commander-in-Chief to order the Grand Fleet to sea.

In the late evening of Tuesday 30 May 1916 the Fifth Battle Squadron left Rosyth. *Barham* passed the outer gate at 2253 and four mintues later she was making 18 knots. In the early hours of the next morning six boilers were lit up and speed was increased while the squadron zig-zagged two points on either side of course. At 1440 *Barham* was making 22 knots and hands were piped to action stations.

At 1530, when the Battle Cruiser Fleet, formed line of battle, the Fifth Battle Squadron, consisting of *Barham*, *Valiant*, *Warspite* and *Malaya* in single line in the order named, was five miles from the Battle Cruiser Fleet, bearing from the latter north-north-west and conforming to its movements. Twenty minutes later the enemy's battle cruisers and light cruisers were sighted to the eastward and then south-south-east; fire was opened six minutes later when *Barham* was making 25 knots. After two or three salvos these enemy light cruisers turned away eight points and disappeared out of sight. At 1602 the British battle-cruisers altered course gradually to the south-eastward; the enemy battle-cruisers also turned to the south-eastward. This turn enabled the Fifth Battle Squadron to gain, and four minutes later fire was opened by pairs concentrating on the two rear ships at a range of approximately 18,000 yards.

Some minutes later enemy battle cruisers were sighted and *Barham* engaged the rear ship, *Von der Tann*, at 19,000 yards. Though but dimly seen she was straddled and forced to zigzag to avoid the salvos. Shifting to the second ship, as she overhauled her, the action became more general but only one or two ships could be seen in the haze.

The enemy replied at 1621 and straddled *Barham*. Two minutes later she received her first hit, but no serious damage occurred. At 1640, by which time the Fifth Battle Squadron was heavily engaged with the enemy battle cruisers, enemy destroyers were observed to be attacking, and were driven off by light cruisers and destroyers attached to the Battle Cruiser Fleet. The squadron was turned away by preparative flag, and torpedoes were observed to cross the line, one ahead and one astern of *Valiant*. At 1650 the British battle-cruisers, having previously turned to the northward, crossed the line of fire. Admiral Jellicoe wrote:

> The Fifth Battle Squadron were closing on an opposite course and engaged the enemy battle cruisers with all guns. The position of the enemy battle fleet was communicated to them, and I ordered them to alter course 16 points. Led by Rear-Admiral Hugh Evan-Thomas in *Barham*, this squadron supported us brilliantly and effectively. At 1657 the Fifth Battle Squadron turned up astern of me, and came under fire of the leading ships of the enemy battle fleet.

At 1655 the German battle fleet had been sighted, bearing south-south-east, steering to the northward, at a distance of about 17,000 yards. *Barham* opened fire with her starboard battery and with *Valiant* continued to engage the enemy battle-cruisers while *Warspite* and *Malaya* fired at the head of the enemy's battle fleet.

The rest of the story of the Battle of Jutland will be taken from the diary of Gunnery Instructor Phillips who recorded his impressions shortly after the battle. Obviously the story is not complete in every detail but it is the honest contemporary story of the battle as seen by a crew member of *Barham*. In his preamble he speaks rather disparagingly of *Queen Elizabeth* as a *Daily Mirror* ship, that is, a ship that receives all the publicity and praise while other ships, carrying out the same tasks, are scarcely mentioned. It struck him as rather ironic that *Queen Elizabeth* missed the battle due to her refit — as already mentioned.

'At sea Wednesday 31 May, enemy submarines sighted in forenoon, battle-cruisers five miles ahead of Fifth Battle Squadron, excepting *Queen Elizabeth*. We went to action stations in the forenoon and loaded all cages before going to dinner, after which the night defence crews closed up. Nothing much doing until at 1555 we sighted enemy cruiser. *Barham* went to action stations and brought all guns to the ready. *Lion* opened the engagement and we followed at 19,400 yards range. We opened fire at 1655 but our first salvo, by director, fell short. We first fired at a light cruiser then shifted to the battle cruisers and opened fire on *Derfflinger*. The enemy did not reply at once, the range being too great. We put in some good salvos by director, and then they started; a 13.5 inch shell came in through the starboard side, alongside the first 6 inch gun down through the deck in the reading rooms and through the bulkhead into the danger space where all the sick and medical staff were, killing or wounding them all.

'Things were pretty lively now and we set *Derfflinger* on fire. Then we shifted to *Seydlitz* and after a few salvos she caught fire; at the same time we had another shell explode in the 6 inch magazine, killing a seaman. A further shell aft wrecked the gun room and another the officers' WC, completely shattering it. There was also one through the admiral's cabin which wrecked everything. The German cruisers now were more or less all on fire, while we were burning in places. *Queen Mary* had been sunk, *Majestic* blown up and *Indefatigable* dipped as well. *Warspite* dropped out and had to return to harbour so it was left to the Sixth Battle Cruiser Squadron and three of us to carry on the scrap.

'By this time the whole of the German Fleet had arrived; there were about thirty of them out and we were getting a warm time of it. We had got in behind their cruisers so that they would not get back, and so when their fleet arrived we were between the two.

German 'overs' photographed from *Barham* during Battle of Jutland

Things looked very bad for us, although they were not hitting us now; we opened out to 20,450 yards and then closed in to 8,300 yards and gave them a few 15-inch salvos. Just then our Grand Fleet arrived and so the situation was saved as they opened fire at once and the Germans started to run but not before they had suffered. *Malaya* was badly hit but *Valiant* wasn't hit and she had no casualties, we had 26 killed and 37 wounded. We buried 20 at sea and took the remainder back to harbour.

'Well, we have had our day, the day that we had been looking forward to and I can't say that I particularly want to see another sight like it. On board here the poor devils that were killed were lying about, some had their heads blown off, some had no legs or arms and the pieces of shell that were found all had picric acid on them so all the men that were wounded were poisoned and that caused more deaths. I went down to where the first shell came in and I picked up a large piece of — well it looked like gristle and it smelt awful so I put it out of sight.

'We carried on with the Fleet looking for the ships that had run away and during the night three more actions were fought. It looked lovely in the dark; three ships blew up. It was a pretty sight watching the illuminations in the sky. We kept at our guns all day Thursday so by the evening we were beginning to feel a bit weary but everybody worked well and all the fires were put out. The Admiral called the Fleet together for muster and found we had the *Queen Mary*, *Indefatigable*, *Invincible*, *Black Prince*, *Defence*, *Warrior* and five destroyers away sunk and six more did not answer the call.

'We searched everywhere for any of the Germans that were skulking and one of our battle squadron came across one of the cruisers we had put out of action and sank her. Then we all proceeded to base, *Valiant* going to Rosyth with the battle cruisers as she was not damaged at all. *Malaya* went to Scapa so that Admiral Jellicoe could come on board and see the damage. We arrived at Scapa at about noon on Friday and put the clock back one hour, then we had all the admirals and captains of ships on board. We started to take on cordite and got out all the empties. The hospital ship came alongside and took all the wounded. The remainder of the dead were put on board a tug and then she collected three from *Malaya* and steamed down the lines as all ships half-masted and sounded the last post. We received the signal not to take in ammunition, so packed up about midnight and turned in. I needed it, it was the first sleep since Tuesday and it didn't take long to go off.

'On Saturday morning the oiler came alongside and we took in 200 tons. All hands were set to work clearing up the vast quantities of debris. Admiral Jellicoe came on board again at 1300; our Admiral left the ship and went on board *Malaya* from where he made a signal wishing us good luck and a pleasant and well-deserved leave after our hard work. At 1600 *Malaya* left for Cromarty floating dock and the Admiral went on to Rosyth by train, taking over *Queen Elizabeth* until our return. Two hours later we weighed and proceeded through the Pentland Firth on our way down to refit, but as yet we didn't know where. We spent Saturday night at sea and a notice was put on the board that *Barham* was going to Devonport to refit. Everyone is beginning to look their old selves again after recovering from the effects of the engagement and looking forward to a few days leave, which will be welcome.'

Now that the men of *Barham* are happily looking forward to a little rest and relaxation, despite the wind coming up, let us go back to the early evening of 31 May at the point at which Edward Phillips took up the story.

It is now known that the Battle of Jutland, fought 75 miles off the Danish coast, was the largest and most decisive naval engagement of the war. In the early period the light was very much in favour of the Germans. The horizon to the eastward was entirely obscured by haze, and when the Fifth Battle Squadron engaged, only the flashes of the guns could be made out. On the other hand, a strong light to the westward enabled the British ships to be distinguished by the Germans.

With the arrival of the Grand Fleet a contest of high naval strategy began; by means of brilliant manoeuvres Admiral Jellicoe forced the High Seas Fleet into a 'V' formed by British ships. Elements of the two fleets engaged each other intermittently throughout the late evening but due to a series of mishaps, including confusion of orders, poor intelligence reports and a skilful retreat by Admiral Scheer, the German Fleet escaped under cover of darkness.

We now return on board *Barham*, with Edward Phillips:

'On Sunday we were getting down the west coast a bit escorted by *Noble* and *Nonsuch*; it came up a bit rough so the Captain sent the two destroyers into the Clyde and we proceeded on our own; after getting down a bit farther we ran into calmer water so we sent a wireless message to our escorting destroyers to return and we turned back to meet them. As soon as we turned everyone said the German Fleet was out again and we were going back to meet them, but no such luck; as soon as the two boats picked up again we turned and proceeded south once more. The sea by now was quite calm and we passed some merchant ships making for the Mersey. News was received that leave would start on Tuesday and the ship's company would go in two watches, the length of leave depending how long it took for the repairs.

'This morning the Captain read prayers and said a few words; he was crying all the time. He had taken it to heart seeing all the dead and wounded.

'On Sunday we saw a merchant ship that acted strangely and started to turn away from us so we fired a shot across her bows. One of our destroyers sent a boarding party aboard and examined

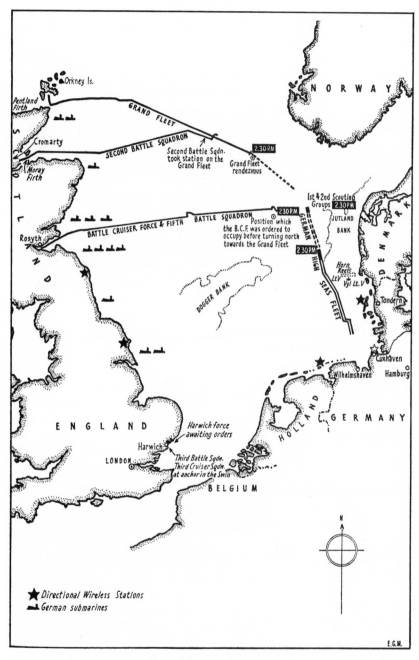

Dispositions at Jutland

AFTERMATH OF JUTLAND — in dry dock at Devonport showing (above)
ship side damage (below) damage to deck

her. She turned out to be British and had mistaken us for Germans! When we picked up again the weather turned a bit rough, our northern escort left us and we picked up the southern patrol. The sea really became rough during the night and was the same the next morning as we rounded Land's End at 0900.

'*Barham* steamed up Channel tying up at the buoy in Devonport in the early afternoon. The Commander-in-Chief came aboard and looked round the ship and then we cleared lower deck for him to give us a speech and didn't he let it go. He said he represented the nation in saying that they were proud of the way we fought and the victory we attained. We gave him three cheers and he had a tear in his eye and so did a good many of the ship's company. We slipped the buoy and proceeded up harbour to dock. The first people to give us a cheer were the destroyers lying against the breakwater, then all the way up river the ships' companies cheered and it seemed as if the whole population had come down on the beach to see us. There were bands playing and flags waving, they were there by the thousand. There was no doubt about the warmth of our reception, everyone seemed to go batchy. We arrived in the basin in the evening and went straight into dock.'

As *Barham* went into dock the Germans too were trying to save their ships. After the last engagement, during which the German battle-cruisers covered the second 'turn away' of the High Seas Fleet, *Seydlitz* was badly damaged forward by several salvos from the Grand Fleet. Fire broke out in both handing rooms of the magazine of the two foremost turrets, and, thanks to the safety devices employed in the construction of their magazines, the flashes from the cordite were prevented from immediately spreading to the magazines themselves, which had been the cause of the blowing up of *Queen Mary* and *Indefatigable*. Nevertheless, it was realised by the officers that the heat of the fires in the magazine handing room and gun houses would eventually ignite the cordite in the magazine proper, and in spite of every effort they could not get the fires under control.

The situation was indeed critical, and at all costs Admiral Hipper, commanding the German battle-cruisers, had ordered the ship to be saved. The Captain decided then to flood the whole part of the ship forward, including the magazines, handing rooms, gun houses and passages, and to do this by closing all watertight doors forward before flooding, so that the flooding process was confined to the fore part only. The men had, of course, to do this themselves from the inside, and, led by their officers, they closed all the hatches, doors etc and then opened the Kingston valves. Altogether there were about 400 men concerned who thus voluntarily sacrificed their lives and saved the ship for the sake of the Fatherland. Those of the crew outside the forepart could hear the terrible screams of death agony. The ship was finally grounded in the Amrun Channel drawing 42 feet of water forward; the effect of this appalling experience on the survivors nearly drove them all mad. The German authorities later disbanded these survivors and spread them in different parts of the country, with a pension and certificate of exemption of service for the remainder of the war, on the condition that they were under honour never to relate their experience.

Barham came out of dock on 1 July and left Devonport four days later calling in at Greenock where she carried out full speed trails in Bute Sound before proceeding on to Scapa Flow where a delighted Admiral Hugh Evan-Thomas returned on board. *Barham* was back at sea with the Fifth Battle Squadron for three days during the middle of the month but then for the next few months became a curiosity for visitors. The Bishop of London, His Eminence Cardinal Bourne, Colonial and Dominion representatives, journalists and many other Admiralty guests visited the ship.

John Baddeley, who had commissioned the ship, said the time on board after Jutland was boring; after the battle he had to sleep on the mess deck itself as all the mattresses were stuffed in the holes. He said that Admiral Hugh Evan-Thomas always said a cheery 'Good Morning' when passing the ratings holystoning the quarterdeck. John once received seven days' punishment for failing to salute the quarterdeck and says that at this time there was still a punishment in which a rating had to stand close to and facing a wall for half-hour morning and evening. John remembers playing cricket on Lord Rosebery's estate. He says there was a good schoolmaster on board who taught many of the hands to count, write and spell; in fact he says there was more education on board than there was ashore, especially at the voluntary night classes. He was confirmed by the chaplain, Reverend Harcourt, at

South Queensferry; he said that going for confirmation lessons was a good way of getting ashore. John remembers the large clock being mounted for spacing out distance of gun ranges; he says *Barham* was the first ship to be fitted with one. When he was ill he was sent down from Scotland in a small boat to Haslar hospital at Gosport where even though it was a very cold winter, he received treatment under canvas!

The rest of the year of Jutland was taken up with occasional days at sea followed by swinging round the buoy at Scapa or Cromarty. The last months of 1916 were very much an anti-climax for the crew of *Barham*.

CHAPTER THREE

Becalmed

When, finally, the detailed statistics of the Battle of Jutland had been assessed, it was found that the Germans lost 11 of their 110 ships and 2,545 men while the Royal Navy lost 14 of their 149 ships but 6,274 men. Although the material and human losses of the Royal Navy were greater, the High Seas Fleet made no further attempts to break the Allied blockade of the coast of Germany. Allied supremacy of the North Sea remained unchallenged for the duration of the war.

At the beginning of 1917 criticisms of the handling of the British ships at the battle began to appear in book form and have done so regularly ever since, long after the chief characters were dead. The game was not confined to English writers alone. A general consensus of opinion of the principal protagonists was:

Jellicoe: super cautious; had excellent opportunities to take action that would have resulted in a decisive success.
Evan-Thomas: the most effective tactical leader on the British side.
Beatty: committed numerous errors and did not show tactical skill. Despite spirited and aggressive leadership, distinctly inferior as a technician to both Jellicoe and Scheer.
Scheer: executed an excellent conception of war poorly.

Admiral Hugh Evan-Thomas, and indirectly *Barham*, came out of Jutland well; during the three hours' engagement the ship was hit by six large projectiles and although a good deal of structural damage was done, her fighting efficiency was never impaired. After Devonport had finished with her. *Barham* was almost as good as new, as was proved at her speed trials in Bute Sound when the mean average recorded was 23.9 knots.

While *Barham* was being underused at the end of 1916 things were happening at the Admiralty. The submarine war was threatening Britain and it was thought that the First Sea Lord, Sir Henry Jackson, was not a strong enough character to co-ordinate all the forces that would be required to deal with the menace. The First Sea Lord himself suggested that John Jellicoe should take over and he did so eventually at the beginning of December. It was with heavy heart that the Admiral, beloved by all the sailors of the Grand Fleet, struck his flag in *Iron Duke* in the Firth of Forth at the end of November and headed for London.

Although he was junior to most of his contenders Admiral Beatty was the logical choice for Commander-in-Chief of the Grand Fleet and he was appointed. A further change at the top took place when, rather surprisingly, Sir Edward Carson, one of the best legal brains in the country, took over from James Balfour as First Lord of the Admiralty. Britain certainly changed horses in mid-stream, from Fisher and Churchill to Jackson and Balfour, to Jellicoe and Carson.

During February 1917 *Barham* underwent a short refit in the Invergordon dock. On 22 June King George V again visited the ship and took the salute at a march past of officers and ships' companies of the Fifth Battle Squadron in the first dog watch.

Nearly three weeks later, while at Scapa, the crew on board *Barham* rushed on deck when they heard a huge explosion in the direction of B4 and B5 berth. A minute later there was another big bang and dense smoke as burning debris thrown up from the scene of the magazine explosion marked the end of HMS *Vanguard*, with the loss of over 800 lives.

In the middle of July the new Commander-in-Chief, his cap at a rakish angle, came aboard *Barham* to distribute prizes to the Fifth Battle Squadron for events won at sports. In September Admiral May, Commander-in-Chief of the American Atlantic Fleet, visited *Barham*. During October Admiral Hugh Evan-Thomas became ill and struck his flag for fifteen days while he was away. At the beginning of November *Barham* was at sea with the Fifth Battle Squadron again and arrived at Scapa in the middle of the month. The crew on board were pleased to return to the Firth of Forth, much nearer the centre of civilisation, just a week before Christmas.

At this time Boy Seaman John Bush, unknown to him at the

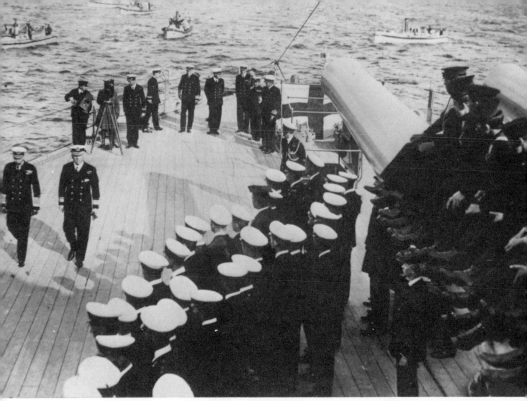

H. M. King George V on board *Barham* accompanied by Rear-Admiral Hugh
Evan-Thomas at Invergordon June 1917

HMS *Barham* and fleet at anchor

time, was about to join *Barham*, and it is he who continues with the story of life aboard the battleship until the end of the war. His narrative is probably unique in that it shows the day to day workings, in a battleship, of men who received a pittance for the dangerous tasks they could be called upon to perform, yet served happily together sharing the camaraderie and simple shipboard pleasures of life.

'On 19 December 1917 about a hundred of us left Devonport in a tug for Mill Bay pier and station on our way to the Grand Fleet. We had completed our training in HMS Impregnable, a collective name for three hulks, *Lord Howe*, *Inconstant* and *Black Prince*, the latter being a sister ship of Britain's first ironclad HMS *Warrior*.

'I was among a group for the Fifth Battle Squadron and our draft was labelled for Inverness. The duffle coats we wore were on loan, as no overcoats were issued in our kit. We breakfasted at Taunton, where the department girls gave us each a mug of tea and a packet of sandwiches. I remember looking out at Burrobridge Mump, one of my home county landmarks en route. Our next meal hand out came from the girls at Crewe; while we were waiting there we met a couple of ex-Impregnable boys who had gone on draft before us. They wore HMS cap ribbons and were naturally cagey about the name of their ship but as their eyelids were full of coal dust we gathered that they were 'hard' ships that burned coal.

'At Crewe a petty officer selected me and another hefty looking chap to travel in the guards van to Carlisle. A message had been received that the Fifth Battle Squadron would be at Rosyth so the baggage for twenty of us had to be sorted out. The train appeared to stagger along wagging its tail and as we were in the last coach we were flying around with the bags and hammocks. It was good to arrive at Carlisle for another mug of tea. Around midnight we passed through Edinburgh and a little later puffed up to the Forth bridge. In the dim light we saw a Scotsman with a fixed bayonet in a sentry box at the entrance to the bridge; passing on we glanced up and saw the girdered pattern overhead and guessed the Fleet were somewhere below. Finally we stopped and our coaches were diverted to Rosyth dockyard. Once the train had been unloaded we found it was quite a walk from the siding to HMS *Crescent*, the depot ship where we were to spend the rest of the night — if indeed it could be called rest. We staggered along untidily under the load of a full kitbag, a hammock lashed to it with a cap box and ditty box on the top of it. There was a bit of light above as we walked past a battleship, close up, lying alongside the jetty, the size was somewhat frightening.

'*Crescent* was packed with kit and sleeping ratings though the sound of coins jingling suggested there were a few gamblers playing cards at the far end of the messdeck. Lukewarm pussers kye was available when one could borrow a basin, and then a few hours sleep. In the morning we took our kit to the Fleet's ferry pontoon and boarded *Triton*, a maid of all work known as a 'puffer' as it was a useful craft with a hold, a derrick and a slow speed engine that chugged around the fleet; one by one the big ships loomed up out of the misty Firth and we could hear distant bugles, pipes and shouted orders. At length the puffer slowed down and we saw ahead of us the stern and two after turrets of a big 'un. Then we read her name in large letters on the after screen, *Barham*.

'A grubby looking party boarded the battleship, climbing aboard, remembering just in time to salute the quarterdeck as we stepped on it and fell in. Here we were reported to the Officer of the Watch as the "Fifth Battle Squadron draft"; he stood us at ease and said, "If any of you are chums get together; we only need five, the remainder will go to *Malaya*, *Valiant* or *Warspite*." After a big shuffling, four others and myself brought our kit on board and were taken charge of by Petty Officer Turpin who detailed some lads to help us with our bags and directed us to the boys' messdeck.

'We were an assorted bunch; Claud Westlake from near Liss in Hampshire, Eric Haynes from Kingsbridge Devon, "Brum" Sweet, Pat Kilby from Dublin and myself from Somerset. I was in Number 13 mess and the others were in different messes. The rest of the day we stowed our gear, managing to squeeze it all into a locker, except for the cap and ditty boxes which were stored in special racks in the mess. Issued with a free *Barham* cap ribbon we did our best to make a "tiddly" bow when tying it on.

'We enjoyed a very happy Christmas in *Barham*. Initially there had been some doubt as to whether we would be in harbour for the festive season, however, we were among the fortunate. Early in the morning garlands of evergreens appeared at the masthead and yardarms, while between decks we draped flags, loaned to us by the signal department. In accordance with custom, some of the boys borrowed petty officers' jumpers and assumed authority by ordering the PO's and leading hands to get on their knees to scrub and holystone odd inaccessible bits of the upper deck. Messes were decorated with Christmas cards and messages spelt out on the table with cigarettes. The boys eat goose and turkey for dinner, the carving being carried out by the divisional officers. The boys were permitted to smoke and the hands were also allowed to smoke on the messdeck. There was a church service before a messdeck inspection led by various bandsmen playing the 'Roast beef of old England' accompanied by the 'funny' party. Among the latter were Billy William's pirates equipped with Very pistols. Our Admiral, Hugh Evan-Thomas, and his staff came next, followed by a whole crowd of wardroom officers wishing everyone a "Happy Christmas". After dinner the ship quietened down, then gradually woke up at seven bells with the call "first dog watchmen to tea". For the rest of the day the lads made up sing-song groups and impromptu messdeck concerts. Some of the lads had a collection of Felix McGlennon's "Old Fashioned Songs", "Harry Lauder Songs" and "Ragtime Songs", so with a couple of mouth organs and somebody acting as drummer on the mess kettle and tea urn we made quite a racket. On the fo'c's'le men's messdeck I endured "The yellow idol" and "Devil may care" for the first time.

'At about 2200 I went for a stroll on deck for a bit of peace but then I heard music coming from a picket boat steaming down between the lines; it was a glee party singing a Christmas carol, and in spite of all the good wishes that we had received that day, which included a bumper mail from home, the carol party really stole the show.

'The first time we went to sea an old boy in our mess said to me, "I suppose we'll have to spread the sails again". "What's this, Nelson's Navy?" I asked, "You'll see," he said, and I did. Known as anti-range sails they were triangular pieces of black canvas set up between the funnels and aft ends of the superstructure, to break any good lines of our silhouette upon which the enemy could use his range finders. After a couple of hours came the pipe "Furl anti-range sails" and down they came, this being the only time that I set and furled sails in the Grand Fleet.

'Accompanying the squadron to sea was the four-funnelled cruiser *Blanche*, she burned coal and lolled along as requested on the horizon. We usually had four escorting destroyers, sometimes, when they came alongside in harbour we would hear members of the crew shouting up to us, "Anybody want to change ships?"

'At this time the ship's company of *Barham* went in three watches, red, white and blue instead of the usual port and starboard; and three parts of the ship fo'c's'le, topmen and quarter-deck instead of the old fo'c's'le fore-top, maintop and quarter-deck. I was down as a topman of the blue watch and came under the orders of the relevant petty officers. The topmen manned 'B' turret, right down through to the magazine and shell room. In harbour we fell in on deck at 0600; one watch worked the main derrick to hoist out the picket-boats, another watch scrubbed the upper deck and the watch below cleaned the battery deck down where the 6-inch guns were. Then came "Quarters, clean guns" and breakfast, after which came "Divisions" on deck and a march aft to prayers. Hymn cards were served out, then the band played the selected hymn and the chaplain said a few prayers including the one about "passing on the seas upon lawful occasions". Next we doubled round the upper deck to the tune of "The blue ridge mountains of Virginia" and "Pack up your troubles in your old kitbag" or some such lively ditty.

'We soon went down for turret drill and I found my place in 'B' handing room, next to the magazine. We did dummy runs of loading each time we closed up. The actual quarter cordite charges weighed 107 lb each and the usual loading was for three quarter charge, but the dummies were bumpy, ungainly things with copper nails at their ends — I know, for I soon ripped open my hand on the protruding nails. A few of the boys were sight-setters on the 6 inch and 15-inch guns, their position being right alongside the gun. One lad in 13 mess was 'cabinet-number' in "A" turret and received orders by voice pipe and phone. His turret officer was Lieutenant-Commander Carey, known to the lower deck as Bill. He was never known to get into a panic and he could work the main derrick with exactness and no bumps. One day at breakdown stations "A" turret received the message "The fore-top has fallen on to the roof of 'A' turret." This was passed to Bill who was reading *Punch* in his control position. His reply was, "All right, two hands go outside and throw the bloody thing off". After a pause the Gunnery Commander from the armoured tower asked what steps had been taken to deal with the breakdown and Bill answered personally, "I've sent two hands outside to deal with it". The Gunnery Commander queried, "Are you aware of the weight of the fore-top?" to which Bill replied, "All right, I'll send two more hands outside and if they can't do it I'll go out myself" and putting down the phone he carried on reading his magazine.

'Later, when I became a messenger, one evening I was sent into the officers' smoke room with a signal for a certain lieutenant. It was unusually quiet and deserted, except for Bill and a "Rocky" (RNR) lieutenant named Scales. They were both looking grimly satisfied. I enquired for the lieutenant and Bill said, "He's probably in his cabin patching himself up, he left here in a hurry with some other officers." Sure enough the lieutenant was in his cabin bathing an eye that was changing colour and I heard later that some of them had been taking the mickey out of Bill Carey and had gone too far. I was sorry to read a few years later that Lieutenant-Commander Carey was lost overboard off the coast of Spain while returning from a two year commission in a surveying ship.

'During "night defence" we sometimes manned the magazine and occasionally the chief gunner paid us surprise visits. The voice pipe number checked ammunition with the shell room below and the working chamber above and tested the safety and loading gear. In obedience to a distant voice pipe order he attempted to do many impossible things and seemed happy to answer "all correct" when he could not do them. In later years I was to find out the how, why and wherefore of those cryptic commands. The voice pipe number was a good talker and well versed in Navy lore so he rattled on to pass the time away — he couldn't leave his stand at the levers and voice pipe. He told us the story of "Bunga-Bunga", the hoax that had been played on the *Dreadnought* at Portland "way back" and could sing all the doleful verses of "When the flagship *Victoria* went down" commencing

He was a loving companion
He was a very good friend
In sunshine and in stormy weather
On Jack you could always depend . . . and so on

'After Christmas I got to know my way around the ship and soon settled down; they fed us well enough, nothing fancy but there was enough, now and then we had salt pork and pea soup but dinners were mostly beef roasted on top of the spuds, with peas and beans that had to be well soaked. Weekly there was a potmess stew in a big black pot, made by chipping all the meat from a piece of shin and getting it up to the galley for a good long simmer. At "stand-easy" the cook-of-the-mess went up and floated the doughboys in the pot and stirred in a couple of packets of EDS (Edwards dessicated soup). For tea time one could put down for a pot of jam against monthly pay day, which was five shillings.

'The chaplain, the Reverend Harcourt, had us all in his office and enquired of us if we had any particular problems that he might help us with and allowed us to bring along letters for censorship. His mission, he explained, was to be a friend to all and he had the finest ever specimen of a "parson's nose" that I've seen. Regulation church on Sunday mornings was a must for all boys; we had to look after the hymn books so it was more of a chore, but in the evenings there was a non-denominational service down in the chapel flat. A hymn or two on the harmonium and some homely words and above all, a smile and 'Good Night' from the speaker as we passed again to the clamour of the mess decks. His name, his rank, it matters not, in *Barham* he "went about, doing good".

'We boys were allowed time for training classes, seamanship that would pass us for able seaman; and gunnery from the diarist Petty Officer Gunnery Instructor Phillips. There was also a scheme for accelerated advancement to ordinary seaman at 17½, which four of us got stuck into and attended extra night classes. There was a general knowledge paper to be taken and we were told that the text book to swot up was the current *Pears Encyclopedia*. *Barham* had a ship's library which opened at Sunday lunch time so we went along there to browse. Among the books were Jules Verne's *From the earth to the moon*, poetry by Shakespeare,

Scott and Burns and the *1001 Gems*. Jerome K. Jerome contributed *Paul Kelver*, which we found disappointing as it was not a bit like *Three men in a boat*. In 1918 a bookstall appeared at the after end of the starboard battery and gave us a selection to choose from including books by Nat Gould and Edgar Wallace; a supply of newspapers was obtained whenever possible. The bookstall was managed by a chap called Cobbet; I think the idea of a bookstall was hatched by Commander MacKinnon and the Canteen Committee. The daring doings of 'Bashful Betsy', with the outsize bosom could be followed in *London Life*. The canteen sold *Fleet*, a monthly magazine that dealt with lower deck welfare. It accepted rhymes and lower deck ditties and at one time printed the 'Awful disclosures of an OD'. *Fleet* was edited by the celebrated Lionel Yexley. HMS *Tiger* also printed a magazine which circulated round the fleet and one edition contained a lengthy piece of rhyme that stuck in my mind. It dealt with a ship, the *Hoppit*, applying for paint so that she could be camouflaged and escape enemy torpedoes. After many signals and much delay the final verse said:

The paint is being (by Express)
Returned to the store of DOS
Who evidently did not know
The ship was sunk twelve months ago

'The canteen sold cheese in two pennyworths nicknamed Bunghole and Gunga-Din, for all its yellow side it was white, clean white, inside. Its weight was quarter-pound, but always had a 'jockey' or make weight on the top to tip the scales; there were HM *Ships only* cigarettes of all sorts including a 20 packet of Bond of Union, showing a picture of John Bull, Jock and Pat, these were popular give-aways ashore. During January and part of February, we in *Barham* occupied our thoughts with "going on the days" (long leave) and waited for the appearance of *Warspite*. Refitting at Rosyth she was due to relieve us at Scapa so that we could go into dock. We heard that she was coming, but then a delay after trials reminded old Jutland men that *Warspite* had taken some hammering at "Windy Corner" and was still a bit wobbly. So we waited, until 7 February when at last the signal came to sail and we headed south. *Warspite* passed us about halfway and wished us a happy leave. In darkness we passed the red lights of the Forth bridge and cleared lower deck to 'Out Ammunition'. There was much heavy work hauling the cordite cases, all full, out of the handing room doors, hand winch them up into the cooling space and round a few corners till we got a straight lift up (this was simplified during the refit when a removable plate gave direct access to the magazine — also more fearnought anti-flash curtains were fitted to the cordite doors.)

'All the ammunition was taken out during the forenoon and then we went into dock. At seven bells in the afternoon came the pipe "All men going on leave". We quickly mustered on the dockside. Master-at-arms John Derman stood on a bollard and served out the liberty tickets and railway warrants. We all wore HMS cap ribbons — at least until we were well down south when *Barham* began to appear again. Most of the lads sheered off on the London train at Crewe; we dropped about twenty at Bristol and when I alighted at Taunton there were only two left on the train. Coming back that way I nearly bumped into Lieutenant-Commander Boles at Taunton before I recognised him and saluted, to the evident delight of the ladies who were there to see him off.

'After leave we soon dropped into the old routine. The first order on getting back aboard was to get into a refitting rig, which consisted of a jacket and trousers of heavy canvas; which afterwards required a lot of scrubbing. The ammunition was taken on board, also coal for the galley and we chipped, scraped and then painted for about a month. I took a turn as call boy. Having been in a piping class in Impregnable I could pipe all right but wasn't much good at bawling out a long sentence such as "Away first and second picket boat, first and second cutters, first and second whalers, steam barge and launches, get your boats ready for coming in and both watches of the hands will be required in ten minutes time". Then I had a day as Captain Craig's messenger, relieving Boy Toms who had the job regularly; he always looked the part being neat and tidy in a tiddly suit, while I was still wearing my issue number ones. I spent the forenoon waiting outside the Captain's cabin, then after dinner I followed him down to *Gourko* which lay alongside, where he had his hair cut. I had a look in *Gourko's* shop which was well stocked with goods not obtainable in *Barham's* canteen. Her fore hold was fitted up as a theatre with stage and seats where the various concert parties usually managed a show during the few days that she lay along-side. SS *Borodino* also performed a similar service. *Barham's* ballad singer was Spike Denmark and his great piece was "When it's moonlight on that silvery Rio Grande".

There was topical parody — one taking off the soldiers' "Plum and Apple" that ran:

> Fifteen-inch control steaming round the flow
> Follow the director! Up and down we go
> For the T.S. wants more ranges
> and the turrets they won't bear
> and if we don't very soon get some leave
> we shall lose our hair

'One parody that was somewhat prophetic was taken from "In nineteen hundred and fifty" a song that we were singing about in 1912. The *Barham's* offering concluded with:

> The Navy by then will have made a great way in 1950
> Their lordships perhaps will have doubled our pay in 1950
> Model messes! Free clothing! and six meals a day
> and alongside the *Barham*, the *Gourko* will lay
> In nineteen hundred and fifty'

'My turn came to do a spell as a runner, that is a messenger for the signal distributing office, and for about six months I was kept very busy. Signals came to us from the signal bridge and the leading signalmen in the distributing office made carbon copies which the runners then circulated. There were three of us runners but Westlake, being a neat writer, copied out the 'fair' signal log so that left two runners to perform most of the running. One of the leading signalmen had been a dental mechanic in civil life and was given a transfer to continue his trade as the Royal Navy were short of dental folk. There was also a "dayman", a chap who repaired flags, ripping off breadths of bunting and running them in on a sewing machine. He boasted that he had castrated the Admiral on his promotion by removing the red balls from the rear-admiral's

flags to make him vice! Most urgent signals were announced down
the voice pipe so that we could stand by. A steaming signal came
down as "5th B.S. U.R. 22. Tack line numeral 2" which told us to
raise steam for twenty-two knots at two hours notice. The first
copy of the signal had to go in a hurry to the engineer commander
and be signed by him and then one in the engineer's office. Next
copy was for Captain (N) Adams. Then followed captain's flag
commander, flag lieutenant, secretary, commander, officer of the
day, officer of the watch. Commander (G) lieutenant-commander
(T), chief gunner and chief torpedo gunner, major of marines,
captain of marines, chaplain and mail office; sometimes even
more.

'There were naval air officers to be contacted about the Camel
that we carried on 'B' turret and usually a kite balloon being
brought to us by a 'K' lighter. Then, as often as not, another yell
down the voice pipe — "Revert to usual notice for steam" and we
would rush around to find the same people again in different
places, except for the decoders and Captain (N) who lived on the
bridge, next door to the chart house. Captain (N) used to get 'Q'
messages all numbered and signed for, they dealt with mines and
submarine sightings.

'Surprise signals came now and then in harbour. A passing submarine going out of the Forth sent a message to Lieutenant-
Commander Carey: "Sorry, am unable to accept your invitation
to dine". I delivered this signal and stood waiting for a reply. He
said: 'I don't know him! I haven't invited him! That is the second
time!" Then he relaxed and said: "When he comes in we'll tell
him to come whenever he can. I expect he'll be able to use a good
meal." As a runner one wore out the backs of the bottoms of
one's trousers by constantly going up and down the steel ladders.
I found that I could darn in a piece of material by inserting the
bits cut from under the collar of the issue serge jumper. Another
remedy was to ease your feet by wearing brown canvas shoes
after rubbing black boot polish into them. At inspection one could
slightly bend the knees exposing only the shiny black toe cap.
The reception among the officers was mixed. Some would nod
when they had seen the signal and some would say "carry on" and
others would give no indication that they had seen the signal and
left one in doubt as to whether they had got the message. So it

was left there until such a reply as "All right messenger, I don't want to read it all day" was received. I spent one whole forenoon searching for an RNAS observer who was bound to be in the ship somewhere. At 1230 I turned the signal, and the search, over to my relief came on again at 1600 and found the RNAS chap coming aboard over an hour later.

'One day we were out running torpedoes in the Flow, and one that we fired ran round our stern, narrowly missing the next ship and finished up on the rocks splashing and groaning and burning its light. The next astern sent us a signal — "From Torpedo Officer to Torpedo Officer *Barham* — do I hear that you have invented an amphibian torpedo" Old Piggy Heeling ran his eye round the office and selected me to deliver this to our lieutenant-commander (T) who was on the bridge. It was a somewhat dangerous mission as he was not usually sweet tempered. I climbed cautiously up and saw the lieutenant-commander's messenger, standing in the lee of the 6-inch control tower. Thrusting the folded signal into his hand I said, "Give him this and stand clear, let me get down first."

'Coming down that way one day in harbour I met the Admiral. He was bare headed in the doorway of his sea cabin, he said, "Fetch me a signal-pad, my son". I replied, "You can have this one, sir, it's got a dozen sheets left". He said, "Thank you, that will be enough" and smiled. I smiled back. In that moment I felt that we were all brothers in a big ship.

'Chief Yeoman Crompton was a great character for butting in with signals. I had a copy of one incoming to go to the Flag Lieutenant and found him conversing in a group with the Captain, the Admiral's secretary and the Flag Commander on the quarter-deck. The signal dealt with overcrowding on the last Dunfermline to Rosyth tram by drunken sailors; extra trams and a small patrol were suggested. I hovered on the outskirts waiting to deliver my chit when the chief came along, scanned it and took it from me. He went straight into the group and started, "I've seen this coming! Last Saturday a chap was trying to get his missus up the stairs of that tram while he had to catch hold of her arse with both hands and shove her up from below, it's a damn disgrace!"

'The Fifth Battle Squadron and battle-cruisers often spent

three or four days at sea together, at defence or action stations, as the occasion demanded. At night it was "darken ship" with a few dim lights in the superstructure and a bit of slow match burning in the recreation space where one could have a smoke. Back in harbour we oiled ship from *Montenol* or *Elderol* or one of the other of the toothpaste class of oiler. Not far from our billets lay *Lion*, *Tiger*, *Inflexible* and *Indomitable* shovelling in their coal from 'Duncan' colliers. In fact I came to use a coal shovel later on and always spared a thought for the old battle cruisers. Of all the music composed I would say that the sweetest tune to their ears was the Royal Marine band blaring out "The end of a perfect day" when the last hoist was dumped on board.

'During March and April we were occasionally at sea with the rest of the squadron. On 17 April Captain H.T. Buller joined the ship to relieve Captain Craig who left to command HMS *Renown*.

'A few of us boys took the accelerated advancement educational test in May, I passed with 80½%. There was a navigation paper on which I worked a run from Start Point to Lundy Island without finishing up on the rocks, also some mechanical problems that were right up my street, also a bit of mythology and some coaling station questions in the General Knowledge paper. We went up before the Captain to be noted as passed and as we came to our 17½ years were rated ordinary seaman.

'*Queen Elizabeth* joined with us for the Fifth Battle Squadron regatta in the summer of 1918. Boats crews had been away from *Barham* whenever they could be released from duties and the boys made up two cutters crews with a certain amount of rivalry. Most of the races would be for ten boats, then some with five, such as the signalmen's whaler, and the regatta finished with an all-comers' race; the course was crowded with boats as a ship could enter as many boats as possible, ranging from the skiff with three or four crew, to the launch with three on an oar "as far as you can get 'em in". Gambling was allowed on deck during the racing and a great deal of money was sent from one ship to another to back a "flash" cutter's crew or a "darkhorse" artisans' gig. Occasionally a boat would end a race with a Challenge, signified by the crew tossing their oars. Crown and anchor boards appeared on the fo'c's'le and for the first time I heard the patter "the more you put down the more you pick up". There was no tote running at this time but there were recognised bookies who would take bets.

'Our boys' crew were about halfway back among the results. *Queen Elizabeth* took top place when all the points were added up and I think *Warspite* came second. A few days later the Commander-in-Chief, Admiral Beatty, came on board *Barham* with his big cap atilt and six buttoned jacket; there was no mistaking him as he addressed us before presenting the regatta prizes, mostly to his own ship's company. There was no doubt about their crews — they looked good and it was generally assumed that the *Queen Elizabeth* skimmed the cream of sportsmen from all drafts that passed through her.

'On the afternoon of 9 July there were about four kite balloons, including ours, flying at a good height from big ships. A sudden thunderstorm came down upon us and all the balloons were struck by lightning. From the signal bridge came a hurried signal "Kite balloon on fire and descending". This message was given to me to take to the Commander; by the time I found him the basket and parachutes were salvaged and a hurriedly called "Watch for exercise" were tearing up yards of the balloon envelope. It was waterproof and one tailor later made up two mackintoshes to take home to his youngsters. The Commander read my message at last and said, "Hmmm, descending?"

'*Barham* received a great honour on 23 July when His Majesty King George V visited the ship during the afternoon while we were at Rosyth.

'On *Barham* in the summer evenings there was plenty of activity. Some of the youngsters would get the vaulting horse out and practise neck rolls. A north country physical training instructor took half a dozen of us on for wrestling and we performed half-nelsons and threw each other about on mats in one of the starboard 6-inch casemates. We attracted quite a bit of attention and a small gathering of fans named us the "Cumbersome and Westmoreland" school. On deck there were sand bags being thrown around. The canteen committee organised a whist tournament and the Commander's wife came aboard to present the prizes. The great navy game of huckers, that is ludo on a large scale, had not arrived in *Barham*; they were still performing 'priest

Sir Hugh Evan-Thomas leads three cheers for the C-in-C who came aboard *Barham* to present prizes for the regatta in July 1918

Barham with destroyer *Radstock* alongside

of the parish' and deriving much amusement from it. To be a good 'priest of the parish' player one had to have a good voice and not mind looking silly. Though the game still exists with some differing details the main theme as practised in *Barham* was this:

'About ten sat around cross-legged in a circle on deck and selected different names. The first is "Priest of the Parish" who provides and conducts the game, assisted by his second in command known as "My man John". The remainder are Red Cap, White Cap, Blue Cap, and so on, or else they use such navy nicknames as Cooky, Jimmy Bungs, Custard Lugs, Bunker Lid and Jago, Jack Sky, etc. A piece of rope or a leather belt is provided for punishment of offenders and, thereinafter named the stonniky.

'The priest orders "Name the caps" and then declares the court open with the following speech. "The court is open, no laughing, smoking, crabbing, joking without permission of the priest of the parish of this most noble and divine ceremony." Anyone offending these rules is declared out of office and is punished by a whack on the hand by the stonniky by all the court, each one saying, "And this is for the same". Commencing the dialogue, the priest then says, "The priest of the parish puts on his considering cap, some say this and some say that but I say 'Red Cap'." Red Cap then answers, and they go "Me, sir?" "Yes you, sir" "You lie, sir" "Who then, sir" — "Blue Cap" "What me, Sir" "Yes, you, sir" "Who then, sir?" among the various caps until some one, say Green Cap, is slack in answering or is scratching his ear and it's "Watch Green Cap", "Out of office Green Cap" by Man John. Then Man John holds up the stonniky saying, "Who demands this most valuable piece of money?" the answer by all being "I demand that most valuable piece of money". Man John says, "Green Cap, he being a very good flipper to the front did scratch his starboard lug during this noble and divine ceremony, for which I punish thee Green Cap". Punishment complete Man John declares, "In office Green Cap". The priest demands the stonniky "providing all dues and debts are duly paid" Man John saluting reports: "All dues and debts duly paid" and the game goes round again. Anyone can 'watch' the priest and Man John and can put him out of office appointing himself as the Priest and his substitute as the Present Man John, referring disdainfully usually to the late priest. A member can appeal to give extra punishment, and this can be refused — "Not granted, pass the stonniky". The priest and Man John are not "Flippers to the front" but must each be referred to as "a very good man in office" and must always be saluted when addressed. Some schools, as they were called, in-sisted that the priest had to be saluted with both hands and Man John with one and there may be other traditional routines, but that's how we played in *Barham* with Lofty Radford and Buster Sims as our tutors.

'As mentioned earlier, I had passed my educational test in May and now at 17½ I was rated ordinary seaman and joined the top-man's messdeck. It was 23 September 1918 when I went to num-ber 33 mess; it had about 20 able seamen and leading hands and four other ordinary seamen. We did most of the scrubbing, washing up and spud peeling, also lined up in the provision and canteen queues and fetched the bread. Our charge hand, Leading Seaman Wheeler was caterer for the mess and a topman, while we also carried Leading Seaman Druce, who was a quarterdeck man, and later left the ship to train for ship's corporal. Among the 'Hostilities Only' ratings was a chap from Bradford who had work-ed int'mills. I asked him about it. He said, "You know serge, we make that; you know khaki, we make that" and then the conversa-tion ended. Channel Islander "Froggie" Coolyard and a long service man from Weymouth, Tom King, always made a delicious rice pudding when they were cooks of the mess, plenty of it and good thick stuff. There was a barber on the topman's messdeck, he used hand clippers and borrowed a chair from the crushers' mess for any victim who was having short back and sides. A small queue waited their turn seated in the nearby iron wash deck locker. In the summer the locker contained an enamel bucket of 'goffers', an acidy sort of lemonade, selling at 1d per glass. The crushers' mess (Naval Police) was a horse box or curtained mess at the far end of the messdeck and through the forward door was "Joe England's caboosh". Joe was an old three badge petty officer diver who also made matelots suits and flannel dickies. He was also the custo-dian of draught boards, packs of cards and equipment that could be taken out on loan. Bezique was popular in *Barham*, more so than pontoon or crib. OD's usually blossomed out a bit after they left the supervision of the boys' messdeck. They quietly tried to smoke ship's leaf tobacco and modified their dress. The bow of their cap ribbon came round nearer the last letter of the ships name and sported extra swallow-tail ends. Jumper plunge could be dropped a couple of inches and that meant opening out the blue collars to suit, the black silk 'duff-bag' at the front likewise shrunk in size. If one fancied a 'bluff-bowed spread' to the shoulders a stitch or two could be put in the jumper and collar so that the silk showed more of itself and the knife-lanyard showed more on top of it. A friend of mine, a towney, came back from leave to show how his sister had fitted press studs to keep his collars down at the back. One windy Sunday morning, his being the only collar that stayed put, he was discovered and admonished; thereafter his collar had to blow up and down with the rest.

'Two other garments must be mentioned at this point, the first one might be called "Jack's Vedonis", being worn next to oneself. It was a kind of flannel foundation garment being of double thickness and about six inches deep and secured by six bits of white tape. There was a small money pocket stitched on and fastened by a metal button. Here the thrifty sailor carried his "last" ten-bob note — safe, but hard to get at. In emergencies ashore one borrowed a penny to get to the toilet to perform this intimate act. The other garment, blessed by endless generations of matelots, was known as the flannel dicky, that enabled one to present a clean front to the public and, incidentally, to the officer of the division, at all times. On entry big issue flannel shirts tended to lose colour after about a year of lower deck washing, during which the rinsing water was both meagre and murky, so the flannel dicky, a sort of 'top' or chest protection, came into being. It was fastened with tape and had an interchangeable back and front. Now if Joe England made the flannel dicky he could, and would, put the blue jean border on both sides of the garment, and this gave one four clean flannels to work on even if one wore only a football jersey underneath. The new seaman then turned his attention to his blue cap, removed the cane grommet from the crown and had it sewn round with a knife-edge finish. Before long leave he sent to Lewis's of Liverpool for a shore cap that had a wire grommet and a shiny silky interior arrangement that would hold his liberty ticket, pin-up girl and a packet of five Woodbines and then, with his blue handkerchief bundle, he was happy to step off on leave. His inverted creased bell-bottoms, 32 inches wide if he could get them, flapped around in the breeze so that he was an ornament in his home town as he rolled down the High Street. He had to wait a while for his overcoat, and permission to wear a white silk scarf with it, and pyjamas were only just making a coy debut among the Tiffies. At this time there were very few beards or sailors with glasses or who wore wristwatches. Two other well known topmen of the time were Stripey Barber and Buster Sims. The former sat on the bread barge of his mess in the evening sewing on the three Nelson tapes to collars that needed repair as usually after rifle drill one found that the backsight of the rifle had protruded slightly and caught the stitching coming down from the "slope". Buster Sims was a self-styled comic who with his pal Chowney occasionally gave their impression of a ship undocking in Devonport thus:

' "Let go number one hawser, Mr Polkinhorn."

' "Aye, Aye, Mr Jenkins" (Splash)

' "Let go number two hawser, Mr Polkinhorn"

' "Aye, Aye, Mr Jenkins" (Splash)

' "Let go number three hawser, Mr Polkinhorn"

' "Aye, Aye, Mr Jenkins" (Splash) and so on until Mr Jenkins had "gone for a smoke" or was "visiting the urinal". Polkinhorn and Jenkins were two shiphandlers well known in Devonport in the old days.

'There were one or two old lags on the messdeck also, one of them had been in chokey for 90 days' detention. He described one of their pastimes; "There's a big wall with two square holes in it about fifty yards apart. These holes are supposed to be furnace doors. You've got a big heap of bricks and stones on the ground in front of you and that's supposed to be coal – it's all more or less on the 'let's pretend' idea. When the petty officer blows his whistle you shovelled your bricks through the hole to a bloke on the other side. He shovels them into a barrow and wheels them up and tips them by the other hole. A chap then "feeds his furnace" with them and they come through the wall again to where there is another barrow and the barrow man wheels them back to you. No matter how fast you get rid of your bricks you always have plenty coming and it's the nearest I've ever been to perpetual motion." "How long do you do it?" I asked. "Till your shovel gets red hot and then you chuck them in with your hands," he said, "then for a change it's your turn to wheel the barrow."

'I was still working as a messenger in the autumn of 1918; we still went out on "spasms" and everyone was keyed up when I badly let the side down and could have been sent to chokey myself for negligence or worse! At this time *Barham* had only to let go a slip rope, cast off the telephone cable on the buoy and lead the squadron to sea at full speed. At about 1100 an important telegram was given to me for delivery to the decoding office, together with about a dozen ordinary routine signals. I put the telegram in my pocket for safety and there it stayed!

'At 1230 I went off duty until I came up to do the first dog. After 1800 I went down for a wash and, as I removed my jumper, the telegram fell out into the wash basin. If ever I felt the bottom dropping out of my world it was then. Leaving my soap and towel I dashed up the ladder and hurried aft, thinking to myself, "Supposing it was for us to go to sea and chase up Jerry, the fate of the nation could be on a scrap of paper in an ordinary seaman's jumper pocket." Past the quarterdeck-men's messes I rushed, past the Marines in their barracks, down to the after cross passage, up and along to the cabin flat where, breathless, I knocked at the decoding office door.

' "Telegram, sir."

' "Thank you. Carry on," said the decoding officer.

' 'It should have been delivered at eleven this morning, sir" I said and waited for the storm.

' "Where has it been?' he asked, looking up with a jerk. I told him.

' "Carry on," he said again turning quickly to his books. I went forward again to have my wash, and was about to start, when one of the ship's police came down with a corporal of marines.

' "Fall in aft at once outside the flag commander's cabin," ordered the corporal. They followed me along till we came to the staff cabin flat where they stuck me in a corner by myself and here I had time to think a bit as the minutes crept slowly by. Supposing it was something very important, what would become of me? I could have lost the war in an afternoon. I faced the firing squad in my imagination and it was not pleasant. The marine sentry on duty at the keyboard paced slowly to and fro with his creaky boots and wooden face, a bunch of keys jangling from a chain in his hand. Still I waited. Then Lieutenant Colville, the flag lieutenant, came out of the flag commander's cabin looking very harassed.

' "You are wanted in there," he said, and I braced myself, knocked, passed in and stood to attention. Commander Egerton was seated at his desk, absorbed in some papers. Above the desk there hung a motto which read "I shall pass this way but once", a picture group showing a woman and two children, and a small crucifix.

' "You may stand at ease", he said looking up. "How did it happen?"

'I gave my explanation. There was no excuse, I had simply forgotten the telegram in the hurly-burly of trying to find a dozen people to deliver their ordinary messages.

' "Fortunately for you, and fortunately for us all", said the flag commander, "the telegram was not of first importance. We had a repetition of it during the afternoon as we had sent no acknowledgement. But that is beside the point, and no doubt you realise what a serious offence you have committed however unintentional it may have been."

' "There is no doubt of that, sir," I answered.

' "You can carry on then," said he, not unkindly. Perhaps he knew his naval history well enough to remember that higher people than ordinary seamen had occasionally mislaid important messages.

'The flag lieutenant called me in next and he gave me a real dressing down. Being much younger than the Commander he appeared far more worried and upon him alone rested the responsibility for the making and distribution of all signals that came or went. After the initial outburst he dropped from anger to sorrow, as no doubt he could see that I was darned sorry that I'd let the section down. From him I went down the scale to the old signal bosun Mr Pitt; he painted a vivid word picture of the Admiral being court-martialled and himself shot at dawn for my benefit.

'I took it all in and returned to the signal office where old Heeling wagged his beard and loosed off at me with a general vocabulary for the final ten minutes that were left of my two hours off watch. When he had finished I felt small enough to crawl

out under the door. Next day a special messenger, Jock Chris-
stisson, was told off for telegrams and they were signed for and
checked at each office.

'Soon after that I got another blowing up, from the ship's
commander this time. I was sent to his cabin one morning at about
0700 to enquire the Dress of the Day. He was generally awake at
this time and regardless of the weather he usually said "fives"
and "threes" which meant that the seamen working on deck wore
white ducks while the special duty men wore blue serge. This
morning, however, Commander MacKinnon was slumped down in
his armchair asleep. Having addressed him twice with no effect
I went back to the office and told Heeling, "The Commander's
asleep and I can't wake him, though I've shouted in his earhole."

' "You'll have to get the dress of the day, we're waiting to signal
it to the squadron," growled Heeling. So off I went again, finding
the Commander snoring more loudly than ever. After addressing
him again three times I gently shook him by the shoulder. That
woke him up all right, and didn't he wake me up as well! When he
had finished I gathered that I had committed the grave offence of
"laying my hand upon an officer". He told me to "get out." which
I did, and then I had to knock and come in again to get the dress
of the day, which I had not had time to ask. It's a wonder that
they still kept me on as messenger for I was usually in any trouble
that came along.

'At this time the matelot's uniform began to look drab for the
issue collars washed out to a slate coloured grey, owing to inferior
dye. The cap ribbon, with its gold letters, was supplanted by one
with letters of yellow thread but this went dingy in a few weeks.

'We spent a few days at sea with the Fifth Battle Squadron
during August, and September was spent commuting between
Scapa Flow and Rosyth. We arrived in the Forth on 1 October
and to our sorrow we lost our Admiral, Hugh Evan-Thomas, when
he was relieved by Vice-Admiral A.C. Leveson. The new admiral
brought his own staff aboard and the officers gave *our* admiral
and his staff a good send-off; *Barham* was never the same without
him and his faithful airedale Jack.

'One evening as I sat in the signal office, somebody shouted
down, "Come up and have a look at this". We all went up on the
signal bridge, and away out in the entrance to the Firth of Forth

there floated something that looked like a big chunk of wood.

' "That's the new flying ship," said Yeoman Matthews, "she's due to arrive today."

' "What's she called?" asked one of the chaps.

' "*Argus*"

' "Well, it should be *Noah's Arkus* by the look of her," returned the other.

'It was much about this time that the big influenza epidemic started; it was found that the white suits were not very warm to work with on deck, so blue serge became the rig of the day in cold weather. Two ships of the squadron were down at one time and with every squadron in the fleet in about the same state, one wondered what would have happened if the Germans had started something. For weeks we drank quinine and carried our shipmates to the hospital ship *Berbice*.

'Curiosity prompted me to find out who or what Berbice was. It was given in my old dictionary as the name of a tribe that killed off their own folks when they considered them useless or too old to look after themselves. I don't think any of our chaps died — maybe *Berbice* didn't keep them long enough, but those of us who didn't catch it were relieved when all our old crew came back from convalescence. I often wondered who gave *Berbice* her name and I kept a look out for any fresh ship that came up just to see if there were any more as appropriately named. *Argus*, of the hundred eyes, was a good example. There was a cruiser called *Castor* up in the fleet and I expected to find a twin sister ship called *Pollux* around with her but I was disappointed.

'At the signal office they often twitted me about losing the telegram and Heeling now and then said, "Don't forget them" when giving me a pile of chits to deliver. One day there came the chance for me to get a dig back. A signalman, who was studying for leading rate, looked into the office and said, "Does anyone here know the Pilot Jack Table? Someone says I might get a question about it." There was not much response, so I said, "Let's see if a forgetful OD can help". I explained that merchant ships without wireless could report (e.g. have seen large German fleet proceeding south) by a four flag international hoist. To his query, I answered, "I've known it for years," as indeed I had for I saw it in an old signal manual that came my way when I was at school.

Had the international code and naval code been the same I should have been a signalman, but I kept calling the flag the Blue Peter and gave it up.

'Well, at last the Armistice came. There was a strong rumour of it a day or two before but on the day before the actual Armistice the bosun's mate came around to pipe "Belay the finish of hostilities!", to my mind a most peculiar message — as if one could do it by a whistle.

'On 11 November it was the real thing. I came up from the magazine, where we had been practising our weekly turret drill, to read that hostilities had definitely ceased. At this news the 'hostilities only' ratings began to pack their ditty boxes and throw their kit about with much generosity. The signal was made "Splice the mainbrace" — the most popular of all signals in the Navy — double tots of rum for all, or that is all those over twenty years of age who didn't have 'T' stamped on their card.

'There was a grand display on deck on the evening of Armistice day; everybody was up there singing, warmed by the extra rum that they had taken for supper. Searchlights from the whole fleet were sweeping the sky while rockets and Very lights were fired by some enterprising spirits on the bridge. Sirens, bugles and scratch jazz-bands added to the general din. I celebrated rather quietly with a large corn-cob pipe jammed full of leaf tobacco — my first real attempt. I had chosen my time well for everybody else looked a bit green in the glare of the lights. I heard that ashore the canteen was manned by bluejackets who rolled the beer barrels out onto the football field for a free for all!'

PART TWO

PEACE

THE YEARS BETWEEN
1919–September 1939

CHAPTER FOUR

Scuttled

On the first day of peace from the war that was supposed to end all wars the sailors were taken ashore to carry out the peacetime exercise of a route march. They wore gaiters and each carried a hazel stick about three feet long with a hard wood peg stuck into one end. The band weighed in with a march tune at intervals. Commander MacKinnon was with them at the start and at the finish but he disappeared somewhere along the route. A few miles walk along the country road did a power of good, especially with a bit of music. *Barham's* marine band did the crew well on board; at dinnertimes on deck there were march selections or waltzes and sometimes in the evening an hour's programme of dance music. When the string band played outside the wardroom for the officers' dinner sometimes sailors would creep along the aft deck and unobtrusively enjoy the benefit of their performances. At Sunday Divisions a great favourite was *Chu-Chin-Chow*, while the popular tune at the time of the Armistice was 'Me and my girl'.

On 21 November *Barham* went out to look for the German High Seas Fleet once more, and this time found it; it was the surrender of the High Seas Fleet. The Fifth Battle Squadron weighed anchor about 0200, carrying for the first time their red and green bow lights. As usual when going to meet the enemy, the ship went to action stations with turrets free and every one closed up at the guns and on the look out. John Bush was in the magazine sending up the cordite and of course saw nothing until about dinner time, when it was considered safe to let those below up on deck two at a time to see the fruits of their labour at last. John went up with a mate who accidentally kicked him on the jaw with his sea-boots as he climbed through the manhole above, he jokingly said that it didn't matter now, the war was over! They came up on the boat deck, witnessed the historic occasion, looking out on the port side and said, 'This is it.'

Yes, that was it all right. Those silhouettes they had been trained to distinguish at a glance now stood out with smoking funnels and the white flag flying. All of them, *Kaiser, Von der Tann, Markgraf, Bayern*; some of the crew borrowed the chaplain's glasses to try to count them but the lines faded away in the haze. A better view was obtained in the afternoon and several of the crew wondered why they hadn't come out to sea to have a go at the British fleet. They looked businesslike; they were long, low and blue grey, and despite their rusty sides they probably could have done the Navy considerable damage in a scrap.

To finish the event all ships steamed past the fleet flagship *Queen Elizabeth*, manning ship and cheering while the bands played the 'Conquering Hero'. It was an unforgettable sight, for the Forth teemed with craft of all nations and classes, including the American Squadron Flagship *New York* and *Admiral Aube*, an ancient representative of France.

During this ovation Admiral Beatty stood high on the bridge of *Queen Elizabeth*; he had seen the seasons through. It was a great pity that Admiral Hugh Evan-Thomas could not have spent another few weeks in the ship, to have enjoyed the scene with the crew; after all he had taken *Barham* through Jutland, the old Admiral was a good 'un, the crew thought.

In addition to the men o' war taking part in this grand march past were the tugs *King Orry*, *Volcano* and another. These ships provided a grandstand for Admiralty guests and officials who had no doubt helped to bring about the debacle that they had come to witness. It was nearly 1600 when the crew began to go up on deck for 'Sunset'. Usually they stayed below, but this sunset was different, for upon the notice board was a copy of the Commander-in-Chief's signal:

The German flag is to be hauled down at 15–57 (3–57 p.m.) today Thursday and is not to be hoisted again without permission.

Up on the signal bridge even Heeling looked happy. Already the blue and white 'Preparative' flag denoting five minutes to sunset was flying from all ships, while signalmen stood at each jackstaff and ensign staff were ready to haul down. Away in the background stood the framework of the Forth Bridge; between its spans the sun dipped, the waves splashed around Incholm and danced away to Braefoot pier. Men talked quietly, they were waiting for the curtain to fall.

'Ta-rah-rah. Ta-Ta-Ta-Taah!' from the bugles brought the crew to attention facing aft. Crisp and clear the long call of Sunset rang out, echoing as if a thousand ships were present, while slowly the flags of the Grand Fleet and the German Navy came down together. The watchers' thoughts went far away along the years to muster missing ships and missing shipmates to *Amphion*, *Vanguard* and the 'Q' boats; to the Cameroons, Zeebrugge and the Falklands. The bugles played 'Carry on' but first there came a long, long pause in which could be felt the efforts of four and a half years atoned for in one big sigh of relief — and thanks.

In the background a voice said quietly, 'Good night, King George' and it seemed just the right thing to say for the occasion. John Bush penned a few verses to record the scene, fresh in his mind, to capture for ever the scene of surrender.

Hindenburg, *Seydlitz* and *Von der Tann*
With *Moltke* and *Derfflinger* leading the van
Kaiserin, *Kaiser* and big *Bayern*
With *Karlsruhe* and *Frankfurt* all trailing astern
Here they come flying a big white flag
And after four year of it this is *Der Tag*.

Oh what did you lack, Von Reuter?
And why are you on your way
To lead your might with a flag of white
As they head for the Forth today?
What haven't you got, Von Reuter
That you're bringing the Kaiser's pride
To swing at an idle anchor
At the will of old Scotland's tide?

The last time that we met your ships
They dodged with a midnight twist
But today you have come with your squadrons dumb
In the chill of the morning mist.

Then what do you lack, Von Reuter,
And why are you sore dismayed?
Have you trained your haughty squadrons
Too long in the sheltering Jade?

We've loaded our guns and turrets,
They wait the firing bell,
Loose with a flag of truce
As scattered survivors tell.
Then what have you lacked, Von Reuter
And why has it got to be?
Have you tried to learn in the schoolroom
What other men learned at sea?

Here's *Barham* and battling Beatty,
They're meeting you once again,
And here is the *Lion* you sank with your mouth
She's leading the starboard train.
Oh what do you lack, Von Reuter,
What is it you have not got?
Have you treated your wardroom kindly
And suffered your men to rot?

Your ships were fashioned for fighting
Your guns are the pride of Krupp
Then where is the spirit of *Emden*
And why is your number up?
But sure is the sign, Von Reuter,
There's rust on your walls of grey
The canker has eaten the heart of your fleet
And so you have come today.

Passing to port are the stacks of Leith
Now they anchor off bare Inchkeith,
Grosser *Kurfurst* and *Derfflinger*
Markgraf, Karlsrühe and *Nurnberg*
Kronprinz, Brummer and *Kaiserin*
Regent Luitpold, Hindenberg.

Down come ensign and big white flag
On the sunset call at the end of *Der Tag*.

*

Soon the Grand Fleet slipped back towards the tranquil times of peace, scraping and burnishing the gun muzzles, removing the splinter mats from the vital supply pipes and from the upper bridges. Sailors beat their spears into pruning hooks and their North Sea underwear into brass-work rags; they talked about going ashore three nights out of four and of weekend leave from some ports. The very idea took some getting used to, for it seemed unreal.

John Bush was fortunate enough to be on ten days' leave at Christmas 1918. For this leave the railway companies gave their best assistance, providing the fleet with a hundred special trains from Rosyth, Port Edgar and Grangemouth. These were Grand Fleet trains and carried the crew all home with a minimum of changing and delay.

Just after midnight, after singing for hours, John Bush alighted at the nearest station, five miles from his home. He continues:

'In the clear moonlight I slung the blue bundle over my shoulder, lit the pipe which I had now mastered and tramped along the hard frosty road. Everything was still and peaceful, now and then an owl hooted but that was all. Overhead the Plough kept watch, the same Plough that I had looked up to through my small lookout at night defence stations. How far away those things seemed now as I turned by Two Elm corner on the last lap home. At length the four square tower of our old church stood out before me among the familiar poplars, pines and walnut trees. I had climbed them all not so long ago. Here indeed was peace.

'After leave we went straight up to Scapa to keep an eye on the German Fleet that had been sent there from Rosyth. We gave shore leave, I took the advantage to visit the town of Kirkwall, whose spire of St Magnus Cathedral had so long stood in the distance. Len Cooper and I landed one afternoon at Scapa pier, rambled round and partook of the best fried eggs and bacon that we had tasted for a long time. These were cooked to a turn by a girl named Jessie who impressed us so much that I began working

out my rail fare from Portsmouth so that we could spend my next
leave with bacon, eggs and Jessie! But Jessie was due to marry a
lighthouse keeper away on Longhope so I transferred my affect-
ions and appetite to regions further south.

'One night as we lay at Scapa, all quiet and peaceful, I was
called out of my hammock at 0100. "What's this in aid of?"
I asked Tich Goddard, another seaman who was sliding into his
pants.

' "Boarding party, I think. Jerry is kicking up a row," he
replied.

'Four of us lined up on the quarterdeck in the moonlight form-
ing an unimpressive boarding party. There was just one jack-
knife among us. Down in the drifter we went and were soon chug-
ging across the Flow to where the German Fleet were lying. Dark
hulls loomed up around as we came among them, they looked
enormous to us.

As we passed them our drifter's skipper hailed them through
his megaphone:

' "*Kaiser* ahoy!"

' "*Kronprinz Wilhelm*", came the first reply and Tich Goddard
said:

' "Here's little Willie, but where's the old man got to?"

'We got the *Kaiser* at length and drew alongside her. They took
our lines to secure us and our skipper shouted:

' "Case for hospital."

'We took him in gently enough in his bamboo stretcher though
Cook Bayliss, who had lost his dad on the Somme, was inclined
to be unsympathetic.

'Away down the lines we steamed again with everything still
and clear in the moonlight, it was an unforgettable trip among the
black hulls and dumb guns of the enemy. We climbed back aboard
Barham at 0330, so they gave us an extra hour in our hammocks;
it was not a comfortable hour though for I was shaken three times
by petty officers who didn't know I'd been out during the night.

'A few weeks after this the Germans must have been really
having some trouble for they kept firing Very lights through the
night. Next morning dismantling parties went to remove their
wireless installations. This took three or four days and once dis-
connected it was taken to a big shed at Lyness. The German sailors

were very short of soap so our lads exchanged tablets of it with them for badges, rings and cap ribbons.

'We were relieved and went to Rosyth for a spell to find that we could now go ashore in comfort and those who wished to could have a drink without restriction. Up to this time two beer tickets were issued to each man going ashore, which enabled him to purchase two pints at the canteen; the colour of the beer tickets was changed daily so that one couldn't save them up for a big splash next time.'

Early in 1919 there came an event which the Navy had long and patiently looked forward to — an investigation into the scale of pay and allowances. A body known as the Jerram Committee undertook this task and dragged the time-honoured skeleton from its dark cupboard. As far as one could see it had been brought to light only a few times since the day when Pepys gazed into the old oak chest at the Admiralty to find that: 'Home was the sailor, home from sea and there's nothing left in the till.'

Some members of the committee considered that the existing scales were adequate and that an able seaman with his board and lodging and one and tenpence a day was well enough off. Fortunately there were others with different ideas and all were granted a good rise. One of the crew from *Barham* came across an instance of the progress of sailors' wages in an old seamanship book about this time. The book, dated 1876, showed the able seaman's pay as 1/7d a day. In 1914 he received 1/8d, having advanced a penny in about forty years, or .02 pence per annum. The boy, first class, at 7d per day had not advanced at all. John Bush says:

Well do I remember the budgeting that went on among the married men when they received their monthly payment in 1917 to 1919. First they bought six pounds of soap and two pounds of leaf tobacco from the paymaster, this being duty free cost 1/6d a pound, then from the canteen they purchased a few pennyworth of Hudson's soap powder. At the bookstall they bought their stationery and paid the daily paper bill. At night they sent home by registered mail the largest postal order possible, leaving themselves a few bob to stick in their money belt to see them through. For supper they might lash

out on a bit of bacon and egg, but for the rest of the month
it was two pennyworth of cheese. There might be a mess bill
to pay but necessity kept this to a minimum while the money
that they made by washing clothes was kept for long leave and
maybe a pint or two between at the shore canteen.

During the time the Committee were in session discussion,
hope and doubt were lively among us thus: 'The Admirality
won't give us any more than a tanner and then they'll dock it
somewhere else to make up.'
'It isn't Admirality. It's Admiralty — I'll bet you.'
'All right, let's ask old Chopper Davis'.
'Chopper, how many I's in Admiralty?'
'Only one I, that's what they call the Nelson touch. They look
through the blind one when we want anything.'

The new rates showing a substantial increase were posted on the
notice boards one Saturday afternoon. At the time everybody was
asleep but never did a messdeck wake up so contented before or
since. Many of the able seamen rubbed their eyes, read the notice
again and thought they were still asleep as the jump up to four
bob a day was an unexpected shock. The only complaint came
from the 'Hostilities Only' ratings who, having borne the heat and
burden of the day, would soon be demobilised and not share in the
increases. At the same time a clothing allowance was introduced,
previously a man's 'free kit on entry' had to last him a long time.

In February 1919 *Barham* entered Cromarty Firth, saluted the upturned HMS *Natal* in passing and arrived at Invergordon for entry
into the floating dock. From here the 'Hostilities Only' men went
on fourteen days' leave, then returned to steam the ship to Portsmouth while the rest of the crew took 14 days, plus 28 days'
demobilising leave, so altogether they had six weeks' leave.

At this time John Baddeley, who had served on the ship
through her wartime life, was due to leave the Navy; for a short
time he considered joining the Royal Australian Navy, but was
scorned by his messmates. When he later suggested joining the
Royal Australian Air Force he says he was nearly slaughtered;
just imagine an ex-Senior Service man wanting to join the Air
Force! His pal, heavyweight boxer Buggs, had an ambition to be-

come a lion tamer!

On his return journey to rejoin *Barham*, now at Portsmouth, John Bush met up with Harry Rogers, who had made friends ashore in Swan Street Portsmouth; he says:

> They made us very welcome, after supper we kipped in their two fireside chairs and arrived back aboard *Barham* at 1000 next morning. We found the ship tied up at Farewell Jetty. A number of the 'Hostilities Only' sailors and pensioners had been demobbed and much about this time a considerable number of Chatham ratings came to the ship. This fresh intake injected quite a bit of new life into *Barham*, they brought with them their melodeons, which they played on deck in the evenings. They performed knees up in sea boots with a certain amount of grace. Included among the draft was a plumber appropriately named Leek. Another new rating practised playing the concertina in a box mess on the messdeck during the dog watches; he was not at all popular. From these new-comers, who said that Chatham intended to takeover the ship altogether, we learned or improved our knowledge of rhyming slang and backslang, and also the difference between Kentish Men and Men of Kent.

Admiral Evan-Thomas had long left *Barham*, as had Captain Craig; now she lost her Commander, MacKinnon, who had gone to John Brown's shipyard to stand by *Hood*. *Barham* looked different, the foretop mast had been set down and the main topmast set up; it gave her a sort of dashing battle-cruiser look. At the same time the sternwalk was replaced.

The Grand Fleet disbanded on 7 April and *Barham* was now flagship of the Second Battle Squadron Atlantic Fleet and lying in Portland harbour before taking the squadron to Cherbourg. On the morning she was to have been on the way out some trouble was encountered in unmooring. All the rest of the ships were 'ready to proceed' while the flagship's crew were juggling about with kinks in their cable. The blacksmith was ordered to knock the slip off some slack links that were to be veered out. There was a sudden surge of cable and a heavy 'ping' as the link parted; one half of the link went spinning high and outboard, the other half lobbed along the starboard paravane davit and hit Leading Seaman Druce a thump in the back, while the stud of the link came port side and hit a sailor lined up with the topmen, giving his wrist a wallop. *Barham* had to leave the anchor and six shackles of cable in the Portland mud; it was returned at Scapa some months later.

At Cherbourg the squadron were welcomed by the blowing of bugles, the waving of flags and the saluting of guns. *Barham* had a Sunday best march past on the quarterdeck to select a 'smart' party who were to go to Paris to represent the squadron. John Bush was not one of the party and he thought it rather hard that many of the old Jutland lads were not given preference; he recalls:

What I remember mostly about Cherbourg was the old wooden ship at the end of the pier, a band in the square playing '*Les voir passer*' — or 'See them pass by', and an incident that I hope helped to cement the *Entente Cordiale*. On the waterfront there stood a statue of Napoleon mounted on a horse, with his forefinger extended, as it was when he rode, before his army. A small stoker climbed the railings and sat astride the horse, behind the General. In one hand he displayed a Tricolor flag, in the other he carried a half bottle of cognac, well, a half-full half bottle.

Back in home waters again *Barham* prepared for the peace-day celebrations that included lighting up the fleet at Southend. Torpedomen worked on their special chore of making up illuminatory circuits that would light up the ships on the night. Lamps were rigged four feet apart for the ship's hull and superstructure, and three feet apart for masts and yards, while a special framework was set up in red and white for the admiral's flag. The switch on order was made by a shower of rockets from *Queen Elizabeth*. Aboard *Barham* the crew suffered because there was little light and ventilation below, as nearly all the juice was needed to keep the lights glowing. Along the waterline a bunch of Cockney torpedomen replaced the broken or dub bulbs and proclaimed that they were 'Volunteers! Volunteers! By the light of the silvery moon . . .'

Second and Third Battle Squadrons Atlantic Fleet illuminated at Southend peace celebrations June 1919.

A detachment for the peace march through London was hand picked, smartened up and drilled; it was a credit to the ship.

Barham went to Scapa again to watch over the German Fleet for a few weeks until relieved by HMS *Revenge*; then she returned to the Firth of Forth, arriving on a Saturday. John Bush remembers:

> The weather being fine and warm, the whole crowd of us were asleep on the fo'c's'le in the afternoon. I awoke to find Ern Cooper kicking me, asking:
>
> 'What do you think the Germans have done now?'
>
> 'Started another war?' said I.
>
> 'No, they've sunk all their ships themselves at twelve o'clock', replied Ern.
>
> 'Well, they should have hit the bottom by now', I told him.
>
> Then Jan Westcott awoke and we told him the news, to which he replied, 'That's done me a good turn anyhow. I've been 'armed drifter's crew' going round them, with a six pounder and a tin of corned beef, so many times that my head was beginning to get square with counting them.'

As I was travelling home by train shortly after this, two men in the compartment asked me what I meant by letting the German fleet scuttle itself. It took some time to convince them that I was miles away when it happened. Then another chap recalled the scare of a few months ago when it was said the Germans had burnt rings round their guns with acetylene to render them harmless or dangerous to anyone who fired them. This ring burning business mystified some of us but I've never heard the true story. There had been a lot in the papers about it, showing the rings both near the muzzles and further along the guns themselves.

'What good is a ship without the guns?' said one.

'Can't they put new guns in?' asked another.

'Not now, the darn lot have sunk,' replied the third, and so on.

They went on putting things right and I told them I'd try to be there the next time anything happened.

Scapa Flow looked like a lot of crazy clothes-posts; masts were sticking out of the water at all angles. Only *Hindenburg* had gone down gracefully with her upperworks still above water and the fleet used her as the starting point for boat races for a long time afterwards. *Baden*, one of the latest battleships, had been beached and provided an excellent museum piece for experts to examine in detail. They went through her with the proverbial small-toothed comb.

With the High Seas Fleet sunk in the waters of the Flow, let us now return to the British battleships, particularly *Barham*, that were now carrying out the peacetime procedure of visiting seaside resorts, much enjoyed by the sailors and the locals.

CHAPTER FIVE

Piping days of peace

Barham visited Bournemouth in the summer of 1919; the town advertised that they would give the 'Silent Service' a noisy welcome. The Hampshire town had its first Labour mayor that year. Sports were held at Merrick Park, attended by *Barham's* band. There were free rides on the Corporation trams for the crew.

Malaya, which had anchored at nearby Swanage, came to join *Barham* at Bournemouth as there were more facilities at the larger town. John Bush and his shipmate Harry Rogers had made friends with some cooks and housemaids in a big sea-front hotel, so they called to have tea with the 'downstairs' staff and in turn invited some of them to visit the ship the next day. Cosen's steamers kept loads of sightseers coming and going when the 'Optional' flag, red and yellow diagonal, was flying. After the ship left there were occasional letters on the notice board to seek people such as Seaman Jack Bender and Nobby Hall, pussers' names that some chaps had given to passing girl friends.

John Bush continues with the story:

'Penzance was the next stop and our musical rating went ashore in the evening with his concertina and joined up with the Salvation Army band playing on the sea front. There was a good bus service to Land's End which I visited and bought some lapis lazuli brooches to take home. We were restricted by bad weather at Aberystwyth, our next port of call; only one party got ashore and they had to come back to us by rail to Greenock! Here on the Clyde there was some industrial trouble and we were all organised into platoons for landing working parties. Brown gaiters were issued on loan and I used mine for cycling while on leave for a year or two until they were obsolete but still serviceable. Some parties landed and carried out dockers' duties such as unloading, until things returned to normal.

'Other places that *Barham* visited were Bangor, Kingstown, Arklow and Wicklow in Ireland. There was no leave ashore at Arklow, but at Wicklow I spent some time trying to read inscriptions on local monuments with a little help from a scholarly looking old chap who was surprised to find me so interested.

'From Kingstown, Harry Rogers and I went by tram to Dublin, getting off at the Nelson Pillar. What we knew as Sackville Street later became O'Connell Street. At this time it looked untidy and drab, mostly with the wreck of the old Post Office on the left going up towards Parnell's monument.

Harry and I had a walk around and were near to Nelson again waiting for a return tram when an old lady at a potato stall came at me shouting "Down wit yez, down wit yez" and banged away at my face with her nails and knuckles. I warded her off as gently as possible, but she kept screaming and scratching away and I moved off as quietly as I could for some onlookers were taking notice and the incidents that we had been warned against could have occurred. So Harry and I retreated while the old lady expended some of her spuds in our direction: one must give her credit — she was a good shot!

'At Bangor there was a more peaceful reception. Along the road to Donagadee at a roadside cottage an old lady, friendly this time, said, "Come inside and see my daughter and have a cup of tea, there are nice girls here as well as at Derry". Well, they made good tea and scones and as one daughter was married to a leading seaman from Dartmouth I suppose I was a likely candidate.

'I think it was about this time of the Sinn Fein troubles that I first heard of our ship's company called the Beery Barhams; there was certainly some loud, vulgar and prolonged singing in the returning liberty boats, a piece about little robin redbreast being especially popular.'

After a pleasant summer's visiting *Barham* returned to the Fleet base and at Scapa there was a naval pier that needed continual repair but here one could go up to the Flotta recreation centre, have tea and sit around for the dinner hour. At Rosyth one could get a mug of beer and a game of billiards, while at Invergordon one could pop into a shop and get a big bag of 'tea-breads' for a shilling or two. On Saturdays at Invergordon some of the crew used to hire bikes and cycle to Tain, this was far enough as the possibility of a breakdown had to be kept in mind.

Aboard *Barham* things were on the move. A new 'Jimmy the one' had arrived on board and he was at once nicknamed Aladdin, for during the messdeck rounds he carried a big torch with which he inspected the inside of tea urns. He instituted 'broadside messmen' instead of 'cooks of the mess', who were changed weekly and the messes were kept more organised by this method. Among the quarterly shift around John Bush joined Ginger Martin as petty officers' messmen, a semi-domestic position detached from the part of ship routine. The mess was composed of artisans, carpenter, plumber, armourers, blacksmith and painters who still wore the seaman's dress and badge with a hammer and axe, except that the armourers had a gun in addition. There was also 'Jimmy Bungs', a cooper doing extra time and one of a very few of his rating still in the service. The artisans were allowed to change their dress to jacket and trousers and peaked cap, nicknamed 'a cardboard foc's'le'. The armourers were allowed to become ordnance artificers providing they could first do a trade test which consisted of a forty hour job of filing, fitting and turning. It included a square threaded nut on a short bolt and a 'strap' fastened by a gib and a cotter. The candidates did without their tots of rum during the days that they worked on this.

The petty officers' mess had two ports, one of which was very handy for ditching the washing up water. It was a long way to bring it from the galley in the first place, for there was no hot ring-main in the ship. In the evenings the messmen did some fishing out of the port, 'jagging' they called it, with about a dozen hooks and some silver paper. This was very successful, so the young blacksmith became ambitious and made a crab net. It was too big for the port, so the messmen lowered it from the fo'c's'le and let it down on the bottom one night. The following morning the ship got under way for exercises, and had leadsmen in the chains. The port leadsman's line was fouled as the ship speeded up, and up came the net with a big crab in it, just as the blacksmith was coming off the fo'c's'le after securing the cable slips. At this point the officer of the watch became interested and the blacksmith, having claimed the crab, could hardly disclaim the net; he had five days' leave stopped and further porthole fishing was forbidden.

John Bush had some good luck one day when *Barham* was anchored in the Forth. He emptied the washing up water out of the scupper, as usual, and was surprised by a sudden chorus of shouting, for unknown to him, the side-party were outside in a copper punt touching up the waterline with 'long toms', long handled brushes. Misfortune had guided the garbage into their two pots of paint! Happily John had a jug of tea handy, and also some flakey jam roll, so peace was speedily restored. As all four of them talked about football and the trains from Pompey to 'the smoke' John suddenly caught sight of a wad of banknotes coming gently down stream; for an instant they looked to him like jelly fish hatching away, then he woke up. 'Look, quid notes!' he shouted and the seamen were quickly in action deftly manoeuvring their sculls and boathook while John indicated the position of some that were trying to get away. They secured the lot and shared them out, eight pounds each. For once Neptune had rewarded his worthy sons straight from his ample bosom! There were no ships ahead of *Barham* and the petty officers' mess was right for'ard under the bows of the ship. Away up stream lay the Forth Bridge and although one often heard of good luck pennies being thrown from passing trains, one could not credit natives with making such a high investment. The four benefactors met by chance in the Rosyth canteen some weeks later and drank the health, the very good health, of some person or persons unknown.

While John worked as a messman he also made some extra money doing washing for one or two of the artisans. He laundered their overalls and scrubbed their hammocks for one shilling each and occasionally picked and remade their horse-hair beds. After a couple of years' wear a pusser's bed got into about three lumps, two at one end and one at the top corner. The lumps were emptied out into a mess tub and then the bed tick was washed first, so that it could dry; all the bed was then picked and teased out. It was a long and sneezy job and nobody ever offered to help. After tea, the tick having dried, the horsehair was stuffed in again and the top sewn up. Finally the bed was stabbed in half a dozen places with canvas buttons and sailmaker's needle and twine. After supper — which made it look like a long job — the hammock was slung in the man's billet. He was told it was ready and charged five shillings for the chore.

When John Bush's term as a messman finished, another seaman with more culinary skill than he, he says, took over. He regaled the petty officers with rissoles, made with corned beef and spuds, fishcakes of tinned salmon and spuds, and a type of north country welsh rarebit, cheese and spuds.

It was about this time that ship's police changed their name to Regulating Petty Officers and the 'NP', known colloquially as 'nasty persons', letters were removed.

John Bush continues with the story, describing his last months aboard *Barham*, an account ashore and afloat of the first peace-time cruise of the battleship and his subsequent somewhat typical return to his home depot:

'After Christmas leave we started the New Year of 1920 with the spring cruise, which I am sure helped the general health of the Atlantic Fleet. We left the United Kingdom with a number of cases in their hammocks on board, but a week or two of sunshine and a few baskets of oranges soon put people back on their feet. *Barham's* first port of call was to Marin, the port for Pontevedra, which lay further up the gulf on the north-west coast of Spain. Vigo and Arosa Bay and Villigracia were all nearby. From Marin an ancient train and steam tram went up the road and up and down the hill to Pontevedra. The city crest showed two old ships going into the sunset and the date 1492. There was an old for-bidding fort with some sinister-looking garrison personnel. Two of us walked up the road and reached the town at about the same time as the train, and we didn't have to stop for wood and coal! We had a look at the fort and watched a march past with music. About fifty soldiers went by and round the corner in quick step, then my friend tossed a packet of Woodbines among the last two ranks, that at least put them out of step. Mimosa grew all along the road and also some red and white begonia-looking flowers that someone told us were the real orange flowers. All about the town were big enamelled advertisements for Singers Sewing Machines and we saw some in use, for all the women sat outside on the pavement to do their sewing. We went on to Gibraltar and sighted a full-rigged ship on the way; she had about four boats out, miles apart, and I heard that she was a whaler. A steam tender came into Gibraltar towing a big fish with its tail triced up to the mast, and one morning while we lay alongside the mole there was a similar big fish puffing and blowing around, looking for its way out to sea again.

'We came down past St Vincent and Cape Trafalgar during the dog watches and somebody quoted "Nobly, nobly Cape St Vincent" etc. Somebody else went down to fish out an old chart and we tried to work out just where Browning was at the time of writing. Our conclusion was that he was 'at sea'.

'I remember *Warspite* being with us at Gibraltar. An old school mate of mine, Ken Gare, was in her and together we climbed up the Rock, to the signal station. Next time we went round to Catalan Bay where some of *Barham's* crew brought back big lumps of stalactites from the caves. Next we went into the Mediterranean to meet the Mediterranean Fleet in Palma Bay and then went round to Pollensa Bay where, on a very stony football pitch, the usual Mediterranean v Atlantic football match was played. Two of us went off to look at a quaint windmill a mile away, but it was out of bounds. I went ashore at Palma and walked around inside the cathedral with a chap who had "read it up". It seemed that the building was still, after many years, being finished and we saw a few men chiselling away at the stonework; while so much remained to be done, what had been completed was beautiful.

'As we walked along the low stone pier back to catch the boat we overtook two little Scots stokers from *Barham*. They were discussing the merits of a Spanish picture that one of them had bought to take home. About two feet by three, framed, it represented an old Spanish Inn with a coach and horses, ladies on a balcony and guitars playing and dogs barking, all in gaudy green and red. We were a few paces ahead of the stokers when their discussion boiled over. There was a sudden yell and we saw one chap framed in the picture which the other had banged down on his head. The argument was still going on and the pier head patrol became interested and marched along to sort things out.

'We sailed over to Algiers. The rate of exchange was favourable to us and the lads recommended shopping in "a big sort of Gamages" called *Galeries Lafayette*. With suitcases of a handy size in stock matelots were beginning to look ahead to the time when the "blue bundle" would be no more. *Barham* gave a big ball while we were there; on deck the ship was parted off with canvas and flags from abaft the after funnel. There were long tables with exquisite crockery and cutlery, and big vases of scented stocks. We lowerdeck men saw nothing more than a furtive peep before the event began.

'Ashore most of us became involved in the Battle of Flowers. Hundreds of bunches were thrown and thrown back to the decorative floats crammed with local beauties. Later there was a kind of free for all, confetti battles, on one side of the main street. Most of the chaps came back aboard with the stuff packed down their jumpers and flannels. Many of them had lost their caps or cap ribbons.

'We met some British folk about as the ten day cruises were beginning to get organised by travel agencies at home. We talked to a party of holidaymaking school teachers. *Orvito* and *Orbita* were on this particular run.

'We were back for another week or so at Gibraltar, then it was time to start packing the bundle for leave. An expedition up Main Street for scent, silk and cigars was successful and soon we were homeward bound. From abreast of Lisbon the squadron ran into some dirty weather for a couple of days, one ship lost a cutter from its davits. We were all impressed with the performance of the boats, those sturdy destroyers escorting us chopping their way from Ushant to Scilly.

'It was about Easter when we arrived home and I remember the *Daily Mail* in a topical article on Easter leave concluding: "You will see them shortly with their smiling faces and their smart blue uniforms, adding a new note to the joyfulness of spring."

'That was to be my last leave from *Barham*. From Portsmouth we went north again and were in Cromarty Firth in May when I received a message to report to the captain's office; and in a day or two I left the ship for the Devonport Gunnery School. There were about a dozen in the draft, mostly going to become ordinance artificer's mates after training at Whale Island. Master-at-Arms Cooper gave me my sailing orders: "Kings Cross, by lorry with your kit to Waterloo, then you're on your own to 'Guzz', give them this when you get there" said he, handing me a "No

Tobacco" permit. We boarded the train at Invergordon at about midday and I looked out of the window all the way down until darkness then I slept until we were roused, up among the hustle of King's Cross. The Royal Navy lorry was waiting and we all piled our kit on it, that is, all except me! After a combined search of guards vans with no result the lorry and party went on their way while I made a statement at the luggage and lost property office, then went to Waterloo by tube. Here I presented my railway warrant and received another shock when I was told that I should have gone by another route. So up I went to see the superintendent of the line, to see what he could do; I climbed a couple of flights of stairs and entered an office where the superintendent sat with his typist. I showed him my timetable that the Jaunty had made and he said, "Your Jaunty, or whatever you call him, is wrong," This was rank heresy to me, I'd never heard anyone say this before and I didn't like it. After a little discussion I asked him, "Have I got to walk it to Devonport, if so I might as well start off now" and turned to go. I intended going to the old Union Jack Club, I had been advised by a Londoner that was the place to go if there was any trouble. Then the superintendent relented and wrote me out another warrant, so I smiled at the typist as I made my exit.

'I bought an ounce of baccy for my corn cob and boarded the train. We were a family party, two soldiers for Salisbury, two women with children and bags of sandwiches and myself. It was a happy journey with a forlorn ending, myself the last survivor alighting at Devonport on the old London and South Western Railway and asking the way to the depot. It contrasted sharply with my arrival at Portsmouth Town, for an overweight stoker petty officer with an armband indicating that he was on regulating duties broke off a conversation with two young ladies to say: "Dockyard Gates, then follow the wall round". After about half-an-hour's walk and more enquiries I came to a gateway, a clock tower and a white ensign. Something said to me "This is it", so I squared off my cap and rambled in.

'Immediately a regulating petty officer fixed me with his eye and said, "What are you?" I handed him my only credential, my permit for "No Tobacco". He said, "*Barham* doesn't belong here". I told him I was a Devonport rating and had come to my home depot to attend the gunnery school. "Where's your bag, where's your hammock?" he asked me, then, "When did you see it last?" "Invergordon when I put it on the train" I replied. He led me away to the guard room, saying in passing, "We've got a right one here."

'Next morning I arrived at the Gunnery Office to meet Chief Gunner's Mate 'Squeegee' Williams. Having lost my kit I couldn't spend the usual week in the clothing class. The old chief said, "Are you a seaman gunner, acting seaman gunner, recommended for a seaman gunner?" My reply to these questions were negative, upon which he made his own particular noise of disgust and disapproval. His eye wandered over a thin ringed gunner at the next table who said, "We've got to make a hundred and twenty of them in a hurry and get 'em out to sea again, put him down."

'So I was issued with a pair of gaiters and the old chief said, "Start hydraulics next Monday and get a *Vivid* cap ribbon." I remained *Barham* for another couple of days, and as the ship was a "Pomponian" I had a number of enquiries about her. My reply to them, and indeed to many others over the years, has never changed: "*Barham*? She was a good'un".'

CHAPTER SIX

Roaring Twenties

After the Grand Fleet disbanded Admiral of the Fleet Earl Beatty was appointed First Sea Lord with effect from 1 November, a position he held with distinction for nearly eight years. During this time there was, inevitably, a reduction in the strength of the Navy both in ships and men, but the same high standards were maintained.

One crew member who joined during this time of running down was Rodney Vernon Jones. With such a name the lad's career had been marked down for him at birth and he is one of three sets of brothers we will meet who served aboard *Barham*. This elder Jones served aboard *Barham* from January 1921 until June 1922; his brother Ian was aboard twenty years later. Rodney remembers that Vice-Admiral Sir William Nicholson flew his flag in her at the time, and in 1921 *Barham* was 'Cock of the Fleet'. On the Spring Cruise in the same year the battleship's football team beat Barcelona 3–1.

Bill Walters was another newcomer to *Barham* at this time; he joined in October 1921 as a signal boy, it was his first ship. The new boy was one of 69 members of the visual signalling department; as in earlier days he found that the 6-inch gun casemates were still being used by the 'firms' for tailoring, snobbing and barbering and during the night the same spaces were used as hammock billets. The commander at that time was Commander Burroughs who later retired as an Admiral, and from October 1922 Vice-Admiral Sinclair, known to all as 'Sandy', was Admiral of the Flagship.

Pets were still being carried on board and a goat, known as 'Bill' paraded at Divisions and at any special event, wearing a set of wartime medals and ribbons. His staple diet was paint from the anchor cables, and cigarettes! More animals were carried when cattle were embarked for Gibraltar, for the farm of the then

Governor, Lord Smith-Dorien. These beasts were secured in the Gunners' upper deck store, and as the ship received a bit of a dusting from the sea on the outward passage through the Bay of Biscay, the ensuing results and the reaction of the ship's company can well be left to the imagination.

An innovation was the holding of cinema shows on the upper deck, if the weather permitted. One of the interested spectators at the shows was Prince Charles of Belgium, serving as a midshipman in *Barham* at the time. John Bush mentioned earlier how there was not much light below decks when the ship was lit up; the same thing now occurred when the main derrick was being worked; this took all the power and there was none left for the messdecks. Boy Walters left as a fully trained signalman in January 1923. *Barham* spent 1923 at Invergordon, Rosyth, Spithead and Portland. On Remembrance Day an armed party landed for the ceremonial parade at Weymouth cemetery; and a two minute silence was observed on board. The whole of December and the beginning of 1924 was spent at Portsmouth, thus enabling both watches to enjoy Christmas or the New Year at home. Returning to Portland *Barham* found *Queen Elizabeth*, *Warspite* and *Malaya* already there, and *Revenge* in Weymouth Bay with the light cruisers.

In mid-January *Barham* left for Arosa Bay and on the second day out a heavy sea carried away the starboard cutter and later the jackstaff. A large quantity of water was being shipped on the fo'c's'le and getting below. As the captain turned the ship to lee to avoid the heavy sea, the port cutter was lost. The hands were employed drying out below.

Exercises from Arosa Bay included throw-off shoots at *Malaya* and *Warspite*, before the squadron eventually tied up at Gibraltar. Most of February was spent at the Rock before *Barham* proceeded to Malta at the end of the month. She then went back to Pollensa Bay, Majorca, where was more target shooting with the other battleships, then the fleet regatta; to Gibraltar and back to Portsmouth; up to Invergordon, the Moray Firth, Dunrobin, Scapa, Oban, Lamlash, Campbeltown. At the end of June she went down to the south-west, anchoring in nine fathoms off the pier at Teignmouth, a pleasant South Devon resort. The ship was open to visitors for a few days and a sailing tournament was held with

prizes presented by the local yacht Club. *Barham* went back to
Weymouth before returning to the red cliffs of Devon, anchoring
8½ cables off Torquay, where she spread the awning, and hands
were piped to bathe. Altogether an enjoyable twelve days were
spent at the fashionable resort. A Fleet Regatta was held and in a
race for the Redman Cup *Barham* was just pipped by *Warspite*.

The fleet was all assembled at Spithead on 26 July when King
George V reviewed it, sailing down the lines in the royal yacht
Victoria and Albert. After the review and 21 gun salute *Barham*
tied up at Portsmouth with the cruisers *Coventry* and *Curacao*
securing alongside.

In 1924 the Queen Elizabeth class was allocated to the Mediterranean Fleet, and in September *Barham* proceeded to her new
station as flagship of Rear-Admiral Sir William Fisher. Later she
successively flew the flags of Rear-Admiral C.M. Staveley and
Vice-Admiral Sir Michael Hodges.

In early September *Barham* was at sea, back to Gibraltar and in
mid-October to Malta, steaming, in order, *Iron Duke*, *Barham*,
Valiant, *Malaya*, spread at 2½ cables.

In a short refit at the end of 1924 and the beginning of 1925,
the searchlight and control positions were removed from the
mainmast and two 4 inch high angle guns were fitted.

Christmas was spent at Malta, January and February at Draga-
meshi Bay and Zaverda Bay, before *Barham* returned to Malta.
The central Mediterranean island must have been a ship lover's
dream in those days; in a four-week period from mid-February
the ship's log lists the following individual ships on the move; the
list excluded ships permanently at Malta, and flotillas: USS
Pittsburg and HM ships *Vampire*, *Vivacious*, *Whitshed*, *Weymouth*,
Chrysanthemum, *Queen Elizabeth*, *Marlborough*, *Dragon*, *Danae*,
Dauntless, *Wolsey*, *Broke*, *Emperor of India*, *Hermes* and *Mont-
rose*.

Barham went on to Majorca for a week, where the fleet carried
out a searchlight display and exercises before returning to Malta.
She variously anchored between 3 and 3A and 12 and 12A buoys.
While on a practice shoot at a range of 13,500 yards a shell hit
Chrysanthemum, the target towing ship. The sloop immediately
slipped her target and made for Malta with *Barham* following
astern.

Barham with *Valiant* and *Eagle* at Rapallo — summer 1925

Trophies won by *Barham* 1925–26 — including 'Cock of the Fleet'

In early June *Barham* was at sea again, this time with *Valiant*; to Palma, Valencia, Pollensa Bay, Rapallo, Corsica to Sardinia with a return to Malta at the end of July. A few days' leave ashore was given before *Barham* sailed to Corfu for the two days battleships' regatta, then to Argostoli with *Emperor of India* and on to Mudros, Thaso, Malta and Gibraltar. From Gibraltar she went back to Portsmouth for a short refit. Ammunition was unloaded and *Barham* entered dry dock on 2 October, the hands aboard were employed scraping the ships bottom. A second pair of 4 inch high angle guns were fitted.

Barham recommissioned with ratings from the Royal Naval Barracks and Royal Marine Barracks for further service as flagship of Rear-Admiral of the Mediterranean Battle Squadron and sailed for the Grand Harbour in Malta.

In June of 1926 *Barham* was again in dock, moved by tugs to No 4 dock where her awning was spread as protection against the blazing sun. The ship's bottom was scrubbed. Then she sailed from Malta to Argostoli and on up to Split. There is a strange log entry in mid-July: there are many entries of gear and tackle being lost overboard at sea, and cables and fittings lost in harbour, but while at Split 33½ lbs of beef was lost overboard!

The fleet regatta was held at Volo in September, with *Barham* returning to Malta at the end of October for a refit that lasted until the end of the year.

Barham sailed for Alexandria in January 1927, later returning and on to Gibraltar, up to Barcelona at the end of March, anchoring in 17 fathoms in the Bay, with overnight leave ashore but boys only until 1900. Then it was back to Malta in April and on to Alexandria at the end of May.

On 2 June the first of three deaths in as many months happened aboard the ship. An officer's cook died of ptomaine poisoning. He was buried ashore the next day, the timing caused some inconvenience aboard as the ship was dressed overall for the Sovereigns' Birthday. For an hour in the late afternoon the ship undressed and half masted colours while the funeral was in progress. The hard-worked signalmen then rehoisted colours.

Barham proceeded to Malta and Navarin where the second death occurred; an able seaman was found to have hanged himself during the dreaded middle watch. After Navarin, the flag was

Aircraft from HMS *Eagle* photographed from *Barham*, attacking the Med'
Fleet 1927

Barham in Malta 1927

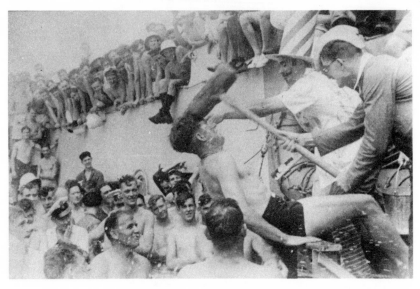

'Crossing the line' ceremony

shown at Skiathos, Suda Bay and Argostoli. In mid-August a petty
officer died aboard of haemoptysis and pulmonary tuberculosis.
After the funeral *Barham* returned to Malta, firing ten torpedoes
from the starboard tubes on a practice shoot; from Malta to Italy,
Naples and Genoa with leave ashore; then the Italian Riviera at
Rapallo, French Riviera at Villefranche and open to visitors.
In the middle of October she was in Aranci Bay, then she returned
to Malta.

In December 1927 *Barham* and *Ramillies* left Malta for a
cruise, to the unusual destination of the West Coast of Africa.
By this time Sir John Kelly was Admiral of the flagship and his
brother, Sir Howard, Commander-in-Chief of the Mediterranean
Fleet, boarded *Barham* and addressed the ship's company before
she left on her voyage. Both ships spent two days at Gibraltar
embarking provisions and torpedoes for magnetic pistol trials.
Range finders and 6 inch gun sights were also tested.

Four days out from the Rock the ships passed through a heavy
bank of fog, at the same time there was a quite noticeable smell
of seaweed and when the fog lifted a shoal of dead fish were
observed. While at sea the ships exercised their range-finding,
took turns for full calibre throw off shoots at each other and

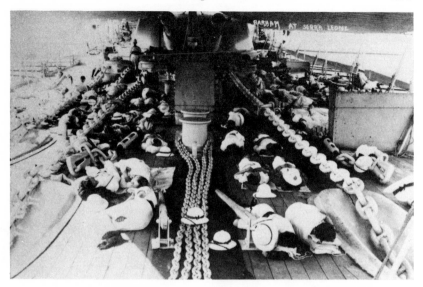

Marines and sailors sleeping on the upper deck at Sierra Leone

carried out experiments with the magnetic pistol.

Early one morning the ship's siren had to be sounded when she ran into a tornado, there was an east-south-east force 5 wind with heavy rain. On 10 January 1928 *Barham* anchored at Sekondi and the following day was open to visitors. The following week *Barham* arrived at Accra and then went on to Freetown where she dropped anchor. Here the hands embarked a hundred 9.2 inch shells which were no longer of any use, for dumping at sea. On 21 January *Barham* sailed from the capital of Sierra Leone en route to St Vincent in the Cape Verde Isles. Early the following morning the engineer commander reported to the captain that a strange noise had developed aft on the starboard side. Following investigation the noise appeared to be in the way of the starboard outer propeller. At midday the starboard engines were put to slow, stop, half astern and half ahead to observe the noise under various conditions. The noise disappeared when engines were going astern and when working up ahead but reappeared when steady speed was resumed. As there was no vibration it was decided to continue at normal speed; a careful watch was kept and fortunately 24 hours later it had disappeared altogether.

On arrival at the island a salute was fired to the Portuguese flag; after two days *Barham* left for Gibraltar. En route a heavy storm caused the ship to reduce speed, the jackstaff was again carried away and 'A' turret blast screens were torn. The following day Teneriffe was sighted and three days later she made her way through that narrow configuration of water that separates Africa and Europe and anchored at Gibraltar in time to grant leave to the starboard watch in the evening. The hands ashore lost no time in loading up with goods from the duty free port, as two days later *Barham* left the Rock, and on the early afternoon of 8 February 1928 secured alongside the South Railway jetty at Portsmouth where after de-ammunitioning, she proceeded into the dockyard to refit.

Barham spent five months refitting before proceeding out to Spithead for a short trial prior to the voyage back to the Mediterranean: her appearance changed when a new fore top with high angle control, the 15 inch director platform below, and a main topgallant were fitted.

When all the minor defects had been smoothed over *Barham* finally left for Gibraltar on Sunday 29 July, arriving early the following Wednesday morning to find the top of the Rock enveloped by the Levanter cloud. *Barham* stayed in the western Mediterranean for most of August before proceeding to Malta. After a week in Grand Harbour *Barham* sailed for Italy, staying ten days at Brioni during which a 15-gun salute was fired when, Italian Rear-Admiral Pola visited the ship for luncheon. During this time the signalmen were kept busy, dressing the ship overall, in honour of the birthday of the Crown Prince of Italy. From Brioni, she went on to Port Lido, then with *Resolution* to Spalato, and after nine days on to Imbros. En route the battleships took turns at a 15 inch throw-off firing at each other off Cape Matapan, a precursor of things to come!

At Imbros the destroyer HMS *Vivacious* took all those crew members that were interested on a visit to Gallipoli. From Imbros *Barham* went on to Spezia but during the voyage a serious accident occurred in which a rating was killed during instruction with a Lewis gun, as the result of which another rating was put under close arrest; the unfortunate victim was buried at sea the next day. *Barham* exercised with *Resolution* and *Vivacious* before returning to Malta at the end of October. Here the quarterdeck awning was spread before a launch was sent ashore with a rating sentenced to detention quarters by a Court Martial.

It was about this time that Bill Adamson, who subsequently went on to serve twenty-two years in the Royal Navy, joined *Barham*. His story is a commentary on that era: every Englishman is born with a touch of sea-salt in his blood but often it takes a national emergency or a personal problem to bring it to the surface and prompt him to volunteer for the Senior Service. Bill Adamson recalls:

It started in the twenties during the depression and subsequent unemployment. I felt I had to do something other than walk about with hands in my pockets so I decided to join the Royal Navy, travelling to Portsmouth to do so.

The period of training was uneventful except for the instructor finding it hopeless trying to teach me sea-shanties! In 1928 I was glad to join my first ship, *Barham*, currently the second flag in the Mediterranean. Trying not to sound too big-headed, I was sent there primarily as one of the football team as any man who had that little bit extra as regards sport of any kind was invariably sent to a flagship. This was because any ship showing outstanding abilities in the sports department earmarked the admiral, captain and commander for promotion! Needless to say, our team being selected from the Royal Naval Barracks at Portsmouth, the Royal Marine Barracks at Eastney and from the gunnery school at Whale Island, won everything that came along, including the Cassar Cup, Second Battle Squadron Cup, Battleship league and eventually the King's Cup. Naturally, all these wins reflected on the top brass and promotion duly followed and deservedly so as Sir John Kelly, our Admiral at the time, and our skipper Captain 'Yank' Somerville ['Yank' for flannel] were chips off the old block and fine officers. Lieutenant-Commander O'Leary, our sports officer, was promoted commander.

I recollect an incident that occurred about three months after commissioning when we were at Malta and I was detailed to help the shipwrights remove the aircraft runway from the 15-inch barrels of 'B' turret. I was standing on 'A' turret when the huge angle pieces plus the hoops binding them to the guns, swivelled around the barrels and caught me across the back of the neck, pressing my head into the turret. I was taken to the Sick Bay, but was about again in a couple of weeks. It wasn't until many years later that I realised that I had been making history because the removal of the runway was a transitional move from the old Navy to the new. Also, I think I must have been the only man in the world to have an aircraft runway fall on him!

Before the aircraft could be launched the turret had to be turned 42 degrees to starboard.

Barham was still in Malta for the Christmas of 1928 and one afternoon the Vice-Admiral gave a children's party on board. He is remembered well by Bill Adamson:

Sir John Kelly had a special chum aboard *Barham*, Tom Cornwall, the ship's plumber, who had at one time been a Royal Marine fighting alongside Sir John at Gallipoli. They called each other by their Christian names, and also other names – mostly nautical, when Tom refused to do a job in the dog-watches! Invariably it was some little private job that Sir John wanted doing and the conversation would go something like this.

'Sorry, John, I'll do it tomorrow'

'But I want it done now'

'Well, you can't have it.'

Eventually Sir John would give in and invite 'Plumby' aft to his cabin for a drink.

Sir John came down from the bridge one day during 'stand-easy', headed for the fo'c'sle, and on the way he asked if I had the 'makings' on me. I handed him my pouch and cigarette papers and he rolled his 'tickler', said thank you and carried on. He certainly knew how to influence the lower deck, a wonderful man and character, except maybe, to his brother, who was the Commander-in-Chief while Sir John was second in command.

One evening, as we were at the buoys in the Grand Harbour, Sir John was pacing up and down the quarterdeck when the Officer of the Watch approached, saluted him and said that the

Commander-in-Chief was arriving; Sir John asked him which side and receiving the reply 'Starboard, Sir' said 'Well, when Sir Howard comes aboard, tell him I'm ashore', and as the Commander-in-Chief climbed the starboard ladder, Sir John was disappearing down the port one!

The reference Bill Adamson made to Sir John's 'tickler' perhaps should be explained. One of the Royal Navy's perks is the monthly allowance of duty free tobacco. This comes in one of two forms, for pipe or cigarette smoking; the latter was issued in tins similar to that which contained issue jam made by the Grimsby firm, Tickler. Hence, a home-made roll up cigarette became known as a 'tickler'.

Perhaps also it is appropriate here to paint a short picture of Malta seeing that *Barham* spent so much time at the central Mediterranean island. To a matelot looking at Malta for the first time the spectacle is disappointing as this island steeped in history resembles a stone-quarry, with no visible greenery. He knows it must be better than it looks, for all the 'stripeys' talked of it with affection.

Malta's climate is good, if sometimes very enervating in the summer when the hot, damp sirocco blows over from the Sahara desert. In the twenties and indeed later in the thirties, Malta was a very lively place, particularly when the fleet was present. The social life (which for the officers included dinners, dances, tennis, cocktail parties, daylight and moonlight bathing picnics, race meetings, amateur theatricals, operas, golf, polo, racquets, sailing and cinema shows) reached, at times, a high tempo.

Barham entered Grand Harbour escorted by two tugs which nudged her to one of the vacant buoys down the centre, often there were as many as eight British men o'war anchored in the harbour. When libertymen were piped ashore they were taken to the customs steps; here they paid their coppers to catch the rickety Barracca lift up to the main road. It was close to here that centuries ago the Turks erected their batteries during the siege. Ashore the island provided all the amenities already mentioned, plus others for the ratings. Floriana, Sliema and St Julian comprise the suburbs of Valletta, the capital. The steep, narrow streets all had their fascination, their houses with overhanging verandahs and long festoons of drying laundry, their inhabitants talking on the doorsteps.

The main shopping streets Strada Reale, Strada Mercanti and Strada Stretta, affectionately known to generations of matelots as 'The Gut' were teeming with people. Among the taboos the crew of *Barham* had been warned about was home-made ice-cream. Once ashore they could see why, goats' milk was the norm and the animals were actually milked on the doorstep.

Taking a bus from the capital one was soon in the country where fields were no larger than an average back garden with each one walled and terraced to suit the contours. Little aqueducts carried water to the fields where the rich soil and frugality of the natives enabled them to be self-supporting. Out on the low hill in the centre of the island one could feel the full force of the prevailing north-east winds known locally as the Gregales.

Returning to Valletta and the fleshpots, Jack could hire a *karrozzin* to further explore the narrow streets. These horse-drawn taxis are common in continental coastal towns but those in Malta with their gay canopies are much more colourful and cheaper, so Jack was driven around with a feeling of opulence; soon he became used to the aroma associated with the island and the ringing of the church bells which the central Mediterranean island had in common with Gibraltar.

In mid-January 1929 *Barham* left Malta for Alexandria with *Resolution*; en route they carried out war routine, zig-zagging at speed and working parts of the ship in gas masks. Later there was a full power steam trial and the mean speed recorded by the Dutchman's log was 23.23 knots. On arrival at Alexandria *Barham* secured to a mooring buoy and saluted Egypt with a 21 gun salute. At the beginning of February *Barham* was back at Malta secured to 7 and 7A buoys in Grand Harbour, but not before the Admiral had inspected the ship's company at action stations. In the middle of the month *Valiant* left Malta, returning to Portsmouth for a large refit while the crew of *Barham* lined the rails and cheered her sister ship. The rest of the month was taken up with intensive exercises. She went to sea with *Queen Elizabeth* and *Resolution* for sleeve target practice, divisional torpedo firing at destroyer target line, 6-inch firing, and 15-inch gun firing at a target towed by *Chrysanthemum*.

Back to Bill Adamson:

As regards visits to foreign ports, well, we went everywhere, all the Riviera-Adriatic-Greek Islands, that included Imbros, Skiathos and Mudros, and to North Africa, and to the ship's company the very memorable twice yearly visit to Villefranche, Cannes and Nice.

In retrospect the good times are remembered, the hard work during exercises is relegated to the back of the mind. If it was not exercises with the Mediterranean and Atlantic Fleets, it was with the Red and Blue Fleets; and so it was in mid-March when the latter, designated parts of the Mediterranean Fleet sailed for the lovely Pollensa Bay off Majorca. Two Blue torpedo planes attacked, *Barham* swung to starboard, resumed course, then later swung to starboard again to avoid a torpedo bomber attack; then she darkened ship and formed single line ahead with Red Fleet and engaged the Blue aircraft carrier. Fire was then opened with star shell on a Blue destroyer on the starboard bow before the exercises were completed and the ships anchored in 4 fathoms off the northern coast of the Balearic Islands. While at anchor sailing races were held between the ships and HMS *Ceres* arrived with the First Sea Lord who later came on board *Barham* for a short visit. After more exercises between the fleets *Barham* secured alongside No 2 shed on the south mole at Gibraltar. It was near here, at Rosia Bay, that Nelson's fleet put in after the Battle of Trafalgar to bury their dead. Nearly a century later sappers blasted thousands of tons from the rock face at Gibraltar to build the harbour.

At the end of March the Commander-in-Chief came abroad to present the Football Cup to *Barham* and Bill Adamson received another medal.

A few days later *Barham* landed a field gun crew, two seaman companies and a Royal Marine detachment for review on the North Front. The following morning a sailing race for the Iron Duke trophy took place. At this time there were battleships in abundance at Gibraltar. There was *Nelson* of the Atlantic Fleet, which together with her sister ship *Rodney* were the newest battleships in the Navy, less than two years old; there was *Ramillies* and *Barham*'s sister ship *Malaya*.

From Gibraltar *Barham* went to Golfe Juan carrying out submarine exercises with *L21*, and *L18*, zig-zagging at eleven knots. Later there was an aircraft attack and five torpedoes hit *Barham*. From Golfe Juan she went on to Villefranche; at both ports the ship was open to visitors and thousands of the local inhabitants poured on board. Then she returned to Malta where 53 tons of coal was taken on for the galley.

At the end of June *Barham* proceeded to Patro, to Basiliki Bay, to Dragamensti Bay to Skiathos with *Warspite*, to Thaso with *Queen Elizabeth*, *Royal Oak*, *Royal Sovereign* and *Resolution*. The ship was open to visitors and sunbathing and picnic parties were taken ashore. Bill Adamson remembers one of those picnic parties at Imbros:

> It is unforgettable, our commander at that time was a monied man and he decided to give the ship's company a picnic there. We were divided into two watches and went ashore with all the food, drinks and fruit being paid for by the commander. As it was a deserted beach, most lads were running around in their birthday suits, when someone had the bright idea of poking a stick into a hole in the sand. In no time at all we were dashing madly into the water for the air became thick with thousands of very large wasps. One can imagine what it was like with about 500 naked bodies trying to dodge them, plus the air being blue with what we were calling the culprit! Of course, it ruined the picnic because the wasps, after chasing us, then settled on all our eats, so all we could do was to move along the beach, go for an undisturbed bathe, and also go hungry!

From Thaso *Barham* went to Nauplia and on to Argostoli; in mid-August the sailing regatta, took place and then she returned to Malta.

Barham had on board a mascot Bonzo, belonging to Sir John Kelly. He was a very friendly bulldog and insisted on leading out the football team, Bill Adamson recalls:

> He was dressed in *Barham*'s colours and had a kick about with us. He was on the books as an able seaman but one day he blotted his copy-book by pushing the ship's cat overboard

whilst in Grand Harbour and he also bit the bugler. He was put under stoppage of leave, but whilst we were in the dockyard he disappeared. Three days later he turned up again; we had our suspicions as to where he had been, but couldn't prove it; at the top of the 'Gut' was a pub kept by a Yorkshireman named Wally Britten. Now Wally had three bulldogs, all bitches, and we think he had Bonzo kidnapped so that he could prove his manhood!

Whilst Bonzo was aboard *Barham* he had the habit of picking up a spitkid, a large type of spittoon about two feet in diameter, and throwing it over his head. These trays were always Durescoed with a whitewash type substance and our doctors had a full time job keeping Bonzo's mouth in good condition. Unfortunately, when Bonzo was eventually transferred with the Flag to another battleship, they didn't know about this habit, or the necessary attention required, because *Barham* received a signal a few months later saying that Bonzo had died of blood poisoning.

One thing Sir John didn't care for was our being called the 'Beery *Barham*', so our skipper asked the wits of the lower deck to think of something else. Two of them, Nutty Schofield and his chum Bateman made a banner depicting some matelots leaning on a bar counter and the heading was 'The Bar-Jacks'. Now this was a play on 'Yank' Somerville's first ship, *Ajax*, and *Barham*, and was greatly appreciated by both the Captain and Sir John who said that the banner should always be taken on to the football field before every match; of course Bonzo would lead the way, and Nutty would literally drop a small anchor when they arrived. Great Sport.

The ship's company, looking forward to summer leave in Malta, were to be disappointed for a couple of days after arriving back in Grand Harbour *Barham* was ordered to Palestine where the Arabs and Jews were at loggerheads. When they arrived off Haifa early in the morning of 27 August, a fire was observed ashore, so the battleship anchored; later when more fires were seen two seaman platoons and a machine gun section were sent ashore under Captain W.L. Jackson who took over duties of Officer Commanding Troops, Haifa area. The seamen took over running the

railways, which then ran as armoured trains! Bill Adamson remembers:

> We took over the railway running between Haifa and Jerusalem.
> Some of the crew had to 'man' the desert villages, two to each
> village, and they assured us afterwards that they had the time
> of their lives, being treated like kings. The rest of us were on the
> railway, staying at the Franciscan Fathers' Hostel in Jerusalem,
> and the Haifa station on alternate nights. The leader or manager
> of this hostel was a Father Hunt, another Yorkshireman. Our
> searchlights kept their beams trained on the hills all through the
> hours of darkness, otherwise the Arabs would have been down
> on the town. When we withdrew the two men who had been
> in one of the villages came back, each on a donkey with an
> Arab leading on another donkey trailing a fourth donkey laden
> with hundreds of tablets of scented soap; the lower deck was
> smelling very sweet for months afterwards.

By the beginning of September the trouble had quietened down
and visitors were allowed on board. An RFA tanker came alongside and replenished *Barham*. By the middle of the month *Barham*
left for Larnaka where leave ashore was given from the Cypriot
port. After a week *Barham* proceeded to Port Said.

Being crowded, smelly, expensive and cosmopolitan this was
really no sort of place for a visiting tourist, but Port Said was
one place at which the crew were always pleased to arrive. The
lads hurried ashore to see if the poor donkey was still alive after
all his exertions with young ladies not normally expected of a
quadruped. Most of the dark-skinned population appeared to
survive by bilking the visitors or trying to sell them photographs
that wouldn't pass muster in decent society or volunteering to
escort them to establishments of doubtful reputation. Small boys
equipped with their boxes, brushes, polish and rags pestered the
sailors for ackers to shine their shoes. Others, as a sideline, posed
the question, obviously handed down through the years: 'You
like to meet my sister, Jack? She just like Queen Victoria, all
pink inside.' For those with decorated bodies here was another
opportunity to have a tattoo scratched on any part of their torso
that was still bare. After ten days at the Egyptian port *Barham*
finally arrived back at Malta for the final six weeks of the com-

mission. It was during this time that Bill Adamson remembers:

A Maltese shoemaker and two Maltese policemen came aboard looking for a 'Derek Topping'. On *Barham* we had a main derrick on the boat deck for hoisting the boats in and out, one of the orders was 'Derrick topping', hence the false name this chap had given; he'd had a pair of shoes made but hadn't paid for them. A similar occurrence happened earlier when we were in Port Said. Some of the chaps had tiddly suits made, but when it came to paying, the men were missing, and the businessmen just couldn't find them. Anyway, our lads thought that they had got away with it as we were leaving for Alexandria. What a surprise they had when we tied up in Alexandria, the businessmen were there waiting, they had crossed the desert and come around by the coast road. Our chaps paid up.

Our signal bridge was at the base of the mainmast, separated from the bridge proper by the boat deck. Our signal bosun was a right tough character by the name of Mr Smith. One forenoon there was a terrific roar from him 'waking up' the whole ship's company who were going about their work very placidly, it being a lovely sunny morning. Mr Smith was shouting to the young signalman on the captain's bridge, 'Hey you, I don't know your name, but get up and clear that halyard or I'll break your bloody neck.' The poor young bunting tosser went up like a monkey.

One evening, liberty men were coming aboard, catching the *dghaisas* down by 'The First and Last' in Grand Harbour when one chap, Leading Seaman Mitchell, who was a bit the worse for drink said, 'Anyone seen my brother?' — who was a stoker on *Barham*. Someone said, 'Yes, he's just swum off to the ship'. Now this was said as a joke, but the killick took it seriously, saying, 'Right, if he can swim aboard, so can I' and with that he dived over the low wall at the edge of the water, but being fuddled he failed to see a flat barge alongside, so he landed on his face. He didn't hurt his face very much as he already had a broken nose, but he spat out half a dozen teeth.

It was on 18 November that *Barham* finally left Malta for Gibraltar and home. Oliver Gordon served in *Barham* as the Squadron Navigating Officer; he says he always felt a thrill, in the piping

days of peace when on board a ship leaving the Grand Harbour
at the end of a commission to return to England. He writes:

Imagine a perfect day, with the sun shining in an almost cloudless sky. In the Grand Harbour the water is calm, and its surface
is deep blue. The *dghaisa*, that fast and handy two-prowed
Maltese boat, scurries to and fro. Your battleship is sailing for
England to pay off and re-commission after two years' service
on the Station. Everyone seems to know it. As the time of
sailing draws near crowds gather on the Barracca and other
vantage points on the Valletta side. Smaller crowds gather on
the promontories which jut out from the other side of the harbour.

'On board your ship there is much activity: furling awnings,
hoisting boats and the myriad other duties that must be done
before the Captain receives the report, "Ship ready for sea, sir.'

'A wisp of steam may be seen pirouetting from the top of
a waste steam pipe; a siren is tested. Your ship has been given a
special coat of paint for the occasion to ensure that she looks
her best on arrival at her Home Port.

'It is now ten minutes before she is due to slip from her
moorings. Bugles are sounding on board other ships of the
Fleet. You recognise the notes of the "Guard call", followed
immediately by the "Band call"; you hear the bugle "Clear
lower deck". The companies of other ships are massing on
their forecastles; soon their Royal Marine Guards and Bands
will be marching aft to take up positions on the quarter-deck,
to the tune of that famous old Royal Marine Regimental march,
"A Life on the Ocean Wave".

'A guard is paraded at Fort St Angelo; the crowds on both
sides of the harbour have increased; specks of colour show that
some friends and well-wishers are already at the end of the
northern breakwater. Two paddle-tugs with black hulls, red
boot-topping; brown upperworks, and yellow funnels, are
slowly nosing their way out of Dockyard Creek. In such good
weather it is a thousand to one that their services will not be
required, but they are always there in case of need.

'On board your ship officers and men are at "Stations for
leaving harbour": in other words they are fallen in by Divi-

sions on the upper deck and fo'c's'le. They are in two ranks facing outboard. Your ship's Guard and Band too are paraded on the quarter-deck. All duty men are at their stations. The Captain is on his way forward to the bridge. He has already received the report from the Engineer Officer that main engines are ready; it will very shortly be reported to him that the ship is ready for sea.

'It is now a minute to the ordered time of sailing. Up goes a flag signal at the yard-arm. Its purport is interrogatory — "Request permission to proceed in accordance with previous orders?" The Chief Yeoman of Signals stands near the Captain on the bridge, his telescope fixed on the signal mast ashore. There goes the affirmative flag "at the dip" to acknowledge your request; five seconds later this flag is hoisted "close up", thus informing you that the Commander-in-Chief has approved your sailing. Down come the signals, both ashore and afloat. The order is given to "slip" from the mooring buoys forward and aft. These orders are passed by telephone to the fo'c's'le and quarter-deck.

'Soon the ship is free and working engines ahead and astern to point her bow clear of the buoy ahead. Once clear, the engines are put to "half speed ahead" and slowly the great ship starts to gather headway. Another signal is hoisted at the signal station ashore. What is it? The Chief Yeoman of Signals reports to the Captain: "From the Commander-in-Chief, sir. Goodbye, good luck and *bon voyage*." A suitable reply is sent.

'Now the ship is about to pass the fleet flagship, wearing the Flag of the Commander-in-Chief. Your massed buglers sound the "Alert". Officers and men are called to attention; the Royal Marine Guard comes to the "present"; the Band plays the first few bars of "Rule Britannia". Acknowledgement is duly made on board the fleet flagship and, finally, in your ship the bugle call "Carry on" is sounded, when all divisions are stood at ease.

'What do we hear now? The flagship is calling for three cheers for our ship. We have always been "chummy ships" with the flagship, and both ships are Pompey-manned. I expect they feel a bit envious but they certainly give three hearty cheers, which we return with equal, if not greater, vigour. We are on the crest of a wave, so to speak; we have enjoyed our two years

on the station, but we long to see our own folks at home, and
for weeks we have talked of, and looked forward to, this day.

'We have passed the flagship and have exchanged the custom-
ary ceremonial and courtesies with more ships. Much handkerchief and hat-waving can be seen ashore. Our band strikes up
'Auld Lang Syne".

'On such occasions that tune always brings a lump into my
throat. The melody seems to echo and re-echo from the rocks
and white walls on both sides of the harbour. Our signal staff
is kept busy reading and replying to farewell signals from many
ships. We pass more ships, with a repetition of the previous
ceremonial and cheers.

'Now we get some breeze as we approach the harbour
entrance and our long "paying off" pendant floats gaily out
astern, with the silver-painted balloon on the end lifting several
feet clear of the water.

'The band is playing agian; this time the tune is "The Girl
I Left Behind Me".

'Hullo! Who are those on the end of the southern breakwater arm? A Regimental Band! Now isn't that a kindly
thought on the part of the 2nd Battalion of the Blankshires,
with whom we have always had a good entente. Yes, a pretty
compliment. They are playing "Will Ye No' Come Back Again".

'We pass a signal of pleasure and gratitude to their CO. Most
of our lady friends are near the lighthouse on the outer end of
the northern breakwater. The ship passes very close to the
breakwater and we can have a good look to see which among
among them have honoured us with their presence. There is
much waving and they give a gentle cheer.

'The ship is almost clear of the harbour entrance when the
Band starts its final effort, "Rolling Home to Merrie England",
another tune which always gives me a mild thrill when played
on such an occasion as this. It seems such an appropriate air
as we feel the first slight movement of the ship to a ground
swell of the entrance, and how the Band lets it go!

'We take a last look at the harbour and the ships before they
are shut to view as the ship turns northward. The buglers sound
the "Disperse", followed by "Stand Easy". Pipes and cigarettes
are lit and all eyes are turned shorewards to the white buildings of

Valletta and Sliema, their whiteness accentuated by the sun upon them. Slowly our eyes follow the coastline of Malta and away in the distance Gozo, the northern island of the Maltese group, comes into sight.

'The memory of the last hour or so will remain with us. Our pleasure at the thought that we are off at last, and will soon be home, is tinged with just a touch of sadness. For some of us, the older ones, there is the possibility that we may never see Malta again.'

On 28 November *Barham* docked at Portsmouth; so as the roaring twenties ended she was snug at her home base with the majority of the crew enjoying Christmas in the bosom of their families.

Bill Adamson was one of the returning crew; he recalls: 'I was much richer in experience and was able to boast half-a-dozen or so football medals.'

In the middle of the year 1930 *Barham* and *Malaya*, with *Barham* flying the flag, left Scapa Flow for a short courtesy visit to Norway. While on passage opportunity was taken to carry out trials on *Malaya*'s direction finding set during the two days at sea.

The division entered the Grip Holen before arriving at the final destination of Trondheim. The 21-gun salute from the ships was immediately returned from Fort Kristiansten situated just above the town.

The day after arrival official calls were made and returned and indeed the next few days were spent on excursions and parties for the officers, both on board and ashore. The Commander was very active on 10 June when shortly before noon information was received that a daughter had been born to the Crown Prince and Princess of Norway the previous day and that a 21 gun salute would be fired by the fort at noon. *Barham* was prepared; she and *Malaya* immediately dressed ship with masthead flags, turned out their Marines and the band and the gunnery officers were able to fire a similar salute on time with the four 3lb Hotchkiss ceremonial saluting guns.

The chief centre of interest at Trondheim was an exhibition which formed part of the festival being held over a four month period to commemorate the 900th Anniversary of the advent of

Christianity to Norway. There was free admission to ratings, as indeed there was at the cinemas. One evening the bands were landed and gave a two hour performance in the exhibition grounds. This attracted much local interest and large crowds. The locals also turned out to watch boat races, football matches, tug-of-war and other sports between ships' sides and local teams arranged in conjunction with the Vice-Consul; the results were usually in favour of the visitors.

One or other of the battleships was open to visitors throughout and one Sunday over 4,000 interested Norwegians came aboard *Barham*. When the ships left, the locals reported that the ratings' behaviour had been exemplary throughout the very successful visit. The Rear-Admiral reported:

> Our reception at Trondheim was extremely hospitable, great friendliness was evinced for the British on every hand with the exception, naturally of the Communist element. A sample of leaflets distributed on shore to the men is attached, also the Communist newspaper *My Tid*.

There were manoeuvres on the return voyage, turning circle trials were carried out independently to ascertain the drift angle.

Barham returned to the Home Fleet Command on 20 June when she dropped anchor off Scarborough, much to the delight of holidaymakers and the local boatmen. From Yorkshire she went down to Kent. *Barham* visited Deal while *Malaya* anchored a few miles along the coast at Margate. At Deal *Barham* was open to visitors and among the guests welcomed aboard was the commander of the local Royal Marines depot.

Early in July *Barham* proceeded round the Channel coast to Eastbourne and on the evening of arrival burned her searchlights for a display. From Eastbourne to Falmouth where the Fifth Destroyer Flotilla joined company. Next she went on to Seaton where some RNVR ratings joined for training. Trials were held off Dartmouth before *Barham* returned to Portsmouth just as *Victoria and Albert*, flying the Royal Standard, left for Cowes.

Barham streamed her paying off pendant at Portsmouth in November 1930.

CHAPTER SEVEN

Change of appearance, and role

Barham was in the hands of the dockyard superintendent at Portsmouth and the refit began in January 1931. Now lifeless, she would be moved by tugs over the next three years to different berths, under the big crane and in and out of dry dock. The steady clumping of the dockyard maties' boots on the quarterdeck quickly smirched the holystoned teak that bosuns had spent long hours keeping clean. The refit was more extensive than the other Queen Elizabeth class ships received; as the last to be taken in hand she benefited, because at this time the Treasury were not quite so parsimonious as they had been previously.

Flashing blue lights lit up the dark winter days on the lifeless hulk, acetylene burners cut away steel sections due to be replaced or modified, the blacksmiths' eyes being protected by face shields. The biggest improvement was the addition of extra deck protection and bulge modifications. Gradually, as weeks rolled into months and season followed season, progress was made and *Barham* began to look more like her sisters when her two funnels were trunked into one. The funnels were trunked to stop an unexpected back-draught which would possibly force funnel gases into the modified bridgework.

Clanging and hissing sounds emerged from below, occasionally being drowned by the deafening sound of riveting hammers as the new outline of *Barham* began to take shape. A tripod mast replaced the pole mainmast to carry the extra weight of the HA director; in the future this distinctive feature always positively identified *Barham* from her sisters.

The aircraft platforms, previously on 'B' and 'X' turrets from which Bill Adamson was hospitalised earlier, were replaced by a McTaggart catapult sited on 'X' turret; at the same time a large crane was fitted on the port side to handle the new Fairey IIIF seaplane. A HACS Mark 1 director was fitted on both the foretop and mainmast. Bridgework was remodelled, the lower bridge platform was extended aft to provide a new flag deck. The compass platform was raised and fitted with a roof and the torpedo control position on the charthouse completely remodelled and enclosed. A DF coil was fitted at the rear of the foretop with the office below on the after end of the 15-inch director platform. The 6-inch gun bays were enclosed to form individual casemates and the ammunition supply improved. Two Mark VI multiple pom-pom mountings were fitted on newly constructed platforms abreast of the base of the searchlight towers on the funnel, directors for these were fitted each side of the foretop. Two quadruple 0.5 inch machine-gun mountings were fitted abreast the control tower. Additional armour was fitted over the magazines and the after superstructure remodelled slightly.

The torpedo range-finder and the submerged torpedo tubes were removed and the latter compartments were sub-divided and converted into store rooms. Provision was made for stowage of aviation spirit on the fo'c's'le. With the welding completed, hundreds of yards of wiring relaid, and all except the most trivial tasks finished, the painters moved in to cover the new work with red lead before the final coats of battleship grey were applied.

The three years work spent on the refit cost almost £425,000.

While *Barham* was still in dockyard hands, Max Horton was appointed to the ship and eventually flew his flag as Rear-Admiral of the Second Battle Squadron, and as such was also second in command of the Home Fleet.

For Max Horton, an ex-submariner who was later to achieve fame as Commander-in-Chief of the Western Approaches whose hunting groups played such a decisive role in the Battle of the Atlantic, this was his first flag appointment. He was promoted rear-admiral after serving as captain aboard *Resolution* for two years. It is surprising for two battleships, not of the same class, to be as closely linked as were *Barham* and *Resolution*; throughout their careers, both before and after this time, there was a close bond between their crews afloat and shore. Captain J. Scott was appointed as flag captain to Max Horton and both appointments dated from the end of 1933; *Barham* completed to full complement in January 1934.

By the time Signalman John Wynne joined *Barham* from *Malaya* in May, all traces of the ship's being under refit had been removed. The brightwork was shining again and the deck was once more white from the holystoning.

John Wynne remembers:

Max was inclined at times to interfere with the handling of the ship and did not always see eye to eye with the Captain. He was very strict on time keeping and it was heaven help anyone late back from leave.

On 28 September *Barham* 'with all despatch' registered 22.2 knots on the measured mile, a good speed for a veteran battleship now twenty years old. John Wynne continues:

Barham was a very good sporting ship and when we went on the winter cruise to Scottish waters, the big fleet regatta was held. A tote was run on the ship so it was very competitive indeed. One of the jobs I had to do, along with other signalmen, was to time rival crews out practising at dawn, similar to the touts on Epsom Downs. We kept our boats shielded by a canvas screen, so rival ships' signalmen looking through those big ships' telescopes could not see what we were doing to our boats in the way of rubbing them down and putting on a secret buffers' potions to make them go faster through the water.

One of my favourite sports was running. I managed to make the ship's company cross-country team. In the Arbuthnot Trophy race on 29 October run at Rosyth for the Home Fleet, *Barham* came third; there were 150 runners and we held 28 places including a 6th, 10th and myself 14th. Our paymaster captain was very keen on cross-country so whilst in training we had very nice perks by having special food and plenty of make and mends.

The Second Battle Squadron at the time consisted of *Barham* as flagship, *Warspite*, *Malaya* and *Valiant*; they looked quite an impressive sight with *Nelson* and *Rodney* leading the line. At that period of time most ships had a mouth organ band, *Barham*'s was excellent, in fact they gave a performance at the Palace Theatre, Plymouth, all dressed up in special jackets. We

Barham 'shipping it green' in the Atlantic January 1935

Oiling destroyer *Escapade* 1935

had quite a few ship's concerts which enabled the officers and ratings to show off their talent. In the Home Fleet regatta *Barham* won the 'Cock of the Fleet', so a huge effigy of this was made and mounted on the for'ard 15-inch gun turret, to show off as we returned to Plymouth after the end of the cruise.

John Wynne says that the winter cruise was spent working very hard; however, the next cruise had its compensations in that it was to the West Indies. Crossing the Atlantic in January 1935 *Barham* ran into heavy weather, soon shipping it green with waves crashing over the bow and spume being sent over 'A' and 'B' 15-inch turrets. When the weather moderated, opportunity was taken to refuel the escorting destroyers; this was one evolution that was not practised sufficiently in peacetime and an area in which the British paid a heavy price in the Second World War. The Kriegsmarine with their purpose-built replenishment ships and the Americans with their fleet train were much more prepared.

John Wynne continues with another anecdote of his admiral:

Max really had cat's eyes. I remember on the spring cruise to

the West Indies we were doing night exercises and were expect-
ing an attack by 'enemy' destroyers, it was a pitch black night
and I was on watch on the admiral's bridge. Max shouted up to
the compass platform to the Chief Yeoman to see if he could
see anything, he said 'No', so he asked the leading signalman on
the admiral's bridge if he could; he also answered in the negative, the same answer came from the flag lieutenant and myself,
so he told the searchlight crew to open shutter on the starboard
beam which they did, lo and behold there was a nice 'enemy'
destroyer lit up, which none of us had been able to see.

This episode amused me in a way, because when the destroyer
scored a hit on us with 'torpedoes' the leading signalman said
not to worry, the big blisters we had on the side of the ship
just blew off and we would carry on unscathed — unfortunately
in the event his logic was to be proved tragically wrong.

Despite the heavy seas and continual exercising the actual cruise
had its lighter side and this was the trip beloved of all the rum-
bosuns aboard Beery *Barham*. Perhaps this is the time to mention
the old custom now that there is no daily issue of rum and the
money saved thereby is used for sailors' amenities. In the days of
Barham and before when Britannia ruled the waves every sailor
aged twenty or over was entitled to a rum ration. Until he reached
that age his ships' card was stamped 'UA' for under-age. If a sailor
did not wish to take his rum, for any reason, but a cash allowance
instead, his card was stamped 'T', for Temperance. The third class,
and in the huge majority, were those with their card stamped 'G',
for Grog. Chief and petty officers alone were issued with neat
rum, while the ratings were issued with 'Two and one' which was
a mixture of two parts of water to one of rum. This distinction
was made by Admiral Grogram Vernon, hence 'Grog'. The idea
behind it was that the ordinary sailor would not be able to store
up his diluted rum for a celebration or some such event, thereby
being incapable of standing his watch — it was thought that the
chief and petty officers were more responsible. The issue was
made at lunchtime and there were many who were facetious
enough to suggest that the timing was such that when a matelot
had drunk his near half-pint of diluted rum, in his slightly
inebriated state the forthcoming meal would taste acceptable how-

Flying off aircraft for HA gunners to practise early 1935

ever badly prepared or cooked it may have been!

The rum ration was also used as a way of repaying a favour. For a small service performed the donor was invited to 'come round for sippers' which meant exactly that. For a large favour one was invited to 'come round for gulpers' which was double the sippers or even more. Ratings and even chiefs and petty officers would walk nearly the length of the ship to accept these invitations, not necessarily because they wanted the rum, but because it was the accepted method of payment for a favour and not to 'come round' might have offended.

Over the years those that were so inclined became addicted to rum and it was natural that this was accepted as the spirit Jack would drink ashore, in fact it still remains the usual spirit drink of *Barham* survivors. Hence the cruise to the West Indies became the highlight for the rum bosuns, where the connoisseurs would be able to sample ashore the many variations of their favourite tipple relatively cheaply and where the ratings would be able to taste the real stuff, uncontaminated by water.

At the beginning of February 1935 *Barham* anchored off Barbados. Here the aircraft was flown off for the HA gunners to get in some practice. Ashore the ratings went for picnics and visits to the sugar plantations, being photographed with the local natives. The dusky girls ashore, with skin shades varying from ebony and apricot to albino with ginger hair, came from all over the island to meet the fleet, much to the joy of the sailors. The bartenders laid in extra stocks, took on more staff and in some cases even had their pianos tuned. What better for a matelot ashore than a pint in his hand, a pretty girl on his arm and his colleagues around him joining in a good old sing-song, often played by a member of the ship's company?

Barham went north from the Windward Islands, up to the Leeward Islands and Dominica where the pom-pom gun practised firing at a balloon; south again to St Vincent, back to Barbados, then north again to St Kitts, with a night shadowing exercise on the way.

At St Kitt's *Barham* landed a howitzer and a detachment, while aboard a boxing ring was rigged for a tournament. There was a black side when Captain Scott had to admonish an officer for carelessness and negligent performance of duty when carrying out the pom-pom test. His admiral would not condone any inefficiency. At the end of the month *Barham* steamed from St Kitts to the Azores and on to Gibraltar before returning to Spithead for the Jubilee Review. John Wynne says:

> The winter cruise was spent working very hard, but our summer cruises were very enjoyable showing the flag around holiday resorts in England. The spring cruise meant a change to warmer climes and gave us the opportunity of meeting old ships from the Mediterranean when the combined fleets met at Gibraltar, and what an impressive sight they looked. The time I spent in *Barham*, fifteen months in all to the end of August 1935, was a very happy time and passed all too quickly.

As a Home Fleet ship *Barham* anchored at Devonport. Here the commission ended and the battleship discharged her crew to their home depot, as under a re-distribution of battleships the Queen Elizabeth class were again allocated to the Mediterranean station. The reason for this allocation was probably the information that Benito Mussolini intended expanding his foothold in Africa and that his forces were massing in Eritrea ready for an attack on Abyssinia. So serious was the threat, which could also have involved the entrance to the Suez Canal, that units of the Royal Navy from all over the globe were ordered to the Eastern Mediterranean.

The drafting officer was hard pressed to find enough ratings to crew all the ships, and Portsmouth depot was selected to man *Barham*.

When the time came for Max Horton to haul down his flag he recorded, 'I have been happy in this ship, because she is efficient.' There really could have been no finer praise from such a hard task-master. Max Horton left the efficient *Barham* to fly his flag in *London* as Admiral Commanding the First Cruiser Squadron in the Mediterranean; as it happened, he was to be in close contact with *Barham* for the next twelve months.

Sid Haines, a stoker, was one of the new men selected to crew *Barham*; he remembers:

> The ship's company of the 1935 commission consisted of the

Portsmouth Division and as *Barham* was at Devonport and we were at Portsmouth the new crew boarded the battleship *Royal Sovereign* and sailed her round to Devonport, tied up alongside *Barham*, and to facilitate the exchange gang planks were put across to each ship. On commissioning, the ship sailed to Scotland for her endurance trials on the measured mile and a working up period, returning to Weymouth Bay for a short while before going on to Portsmouth for 48 hours in preparation for sailing to the Mediterranean.

Before *Barham* proceeded to the Mediterranean the signal staff of the Commanders-in-Chief had been busy at their transmitters and receivers. A provisional programme had been arranged for *Barham*, but before it had been fully promulgated it was cancelled. At the end of August the Director of Plans, Tom Phillips, who was later to lose his life a few days after *Barham* herself was sunk, as admiral in charge of *Prince of Wales* and *Repulse* off Malaya, signalled:

If *Barham* worked up at Gibraltar she would be there unaccompanied by any small craft, during what might be a critical period and the Commander-in-Chief Mediterranean would only have three battleships. At a later period *Barham* might not be able to join him without having an escort. Propose that *Barham* proceeds to Eastern Mediterranean and works up with such facilities as can be provided by the Fleet.

A further signal said:

Barham has completed to a maximum stowage of 1259 rounds of 4 in high explosive ammunition for HA firings, that is 59 rounds above the total output and reserve provided for the ship. This has only been possible by borrowing from *Queen Elizabeth*'s outfit. Fifty per cent of each ship's reserve is already in Malta. Commander-in-Chief Mediterranean has been informed of compliance with his instructions to the ship, except supply of 15 in. HE shell which is all at Malta. It is for consideration whether the amount of 30 rounds per gun for high angle practice will meet requirements in view of the shortage of high explosive.

A signal back from the Commander-in-Chief Mediterranean agreed with the decision that 30 rounds for HA practice per gun should be sufficient. *Barham* was instructed not to use high explosive HA ammunition for practice firings due to shortages.

A message timed at midday on 1 September from the Commander-in-Chief Mediterranean to the Admiralty and repeated to *Barham*, among others, read:

> Request *Barham* may embark following ammunition in addition to war outfit. 15 in HE shell 60 rounds. 4 in. HA HE shells maximum stowage including ready use lockers. Six monthly practice allowance for low angle guns 30 rounds for 4 in. HA practice.
>
> *Barham* is to proceed to Alexandria calling at Gibraltar to embark mails and refuel and at Malta to disembark ratings, refuel and replace practice ammunition expended.
>
> On approach to and departure from Gibraltar and Malta sub-calibre, full calibre and high angle practice firings are to be carried out. Arrangements are being made direct between *Barham* and the Rear-Admirals at Gibraltar and Malta.
>
> Speed on passage to be not below 16 knots, weather permitting, and not more than 18 knots.

Barham left Portsmouth on 3 September 1935 under the command of Captain N.A. Woodhouse. Sid Haines continues:

> On reaching the Mediterranean we continued through from Gibraltar, Malta, Alexandria, on to Port Said and after going backward and forward between Port Said and Alexandria we managed to change the colour of the ship from the Home Fleet dark grey to the lighter grey of the Mediterranean Fleet.

Barham arrived at Alexandria toward the end of September. Here at various times there were as many as fifty warships under the command of Admiral Sir Dudley Pound, who as Commander-in-Chief Mediterranean was flying his flag in *Queen Elizabeth*.

Alexandria teemed with warlike activity; there were battleships, cruisers coming and going on their business, destroyers of the Mediterranean Fleet fussing in and out of harbour; aircraft-

Preparing shells for . . .

. . . full calibre shoot 1935

carriers and submarines, minesweepers and fast minelaying cruisers; more destroyers from the Home Fleet; depot and repair ships, anti-aircraft cruisers; transports, store-carriers, oilers and the usual Royal Fleet Auxiliaries. Transports were arriving with troops and detachments of the Royal Air Force, their aircraft were continually flying overhead. These aircraft and destroyers kept an anti-submarine watch outside the anchorage. New camps and anti-aircraft emplacements were constantly being erected along the narrow strip of land which separates the Mediterranean from Lake Mareotis, and around the mercantile harbour.

The population was a mixture of Egyptians, Greeks, Italians, Syrians, Turks, Armenians and Levantines of all sorts. Ashore the natives, male and female, hailed the Navy with open arms as a source of much gain and baksheesh. The vendors of 'curios' guaranteed their wares to have come straight from the tombs of the Pharaohs, although they were probably made by one of their family only weeks before. The fleet were kept occupied ashore with athletics, soccer, cross-country runs, and on one famous occasion a route-march for the crew of *Barham*. At sea there were rowing and sailing races. The officers and men aboard probably did not think that this new peacekeeping role would be employed in two more locations before a further twelve months had passed.

The expected blow came on 3 October when Italian forces crossed the border from Eritrea into Abyssinia. Despite the presence of Italian warships at Alexandria the Royal Navy were not called upon, although the Italian liner *Ausonia* caught fire right at the entrace to the harbour, probably to blockade the British and French warships; naval tugs towed her away from the entrance, inside the harbour and let her burn.

Barham left Alexandria for Port Said and spent Christmas 1935 at the Egyptian port and was still there at the end of January, when, in company with the rest of the fleet, she half-masted her colours following the death of King George V.

Barham left for Malta towards the end of February, stopping over at Alexandria to replenish en route. After a pleasant week at Malta *Barham* proceeded back to Alexandria and was still there in early May when the Emperor of Abyssinia and his family fled the capital three days before Italian troops occupied Addis Ababa.

At the end of April more trouble had flared up in Palestine, and with the threat to Suez receding the Royal Navy were again despatched to the troubled area. On *Barham* there was an appeal for anyone with railway experience to volunteer for service at Haifa. Despite the traditional reluctance to volunteer for anything in the forces, four ratings responded to the call and were sent off with full kit including rifle and bayonet. On arrival they, with others, were given the task of keeping the trains running between Haifa and Beirut. Later Petty Officer Stoker V. Shorter was decorated for his service in the zone. *Barham* left for Famagusta in Cyprus, spent the day there before proceeding back to the East Mediterranean coast where she had performed similar policing duty seven years earlier. The Arabs were against the immigrant Jews, who they said, were buying up the best land. The Arabs declared a general strike and this was followed by acts of terrorism. *Barham* arrived at Haifa early on 27 May. There was little opportunity for going ashore, although this was the one place the chaplain and several of the crew would have enjoyed in more settled times. Guns were in position to cover the harbour and on Mount Carmel, those that did manage to get ashore reported that the town had few attractions and that the beer was poor. Destroyers carried out sweeps to seaward while aircraft from the carriers patrolled overhead, but as the situation appeared under control *Barham* did not remain long in the area and returned to Alexandria after stopping off at Port Said for 36 hours.

One crisis was following another in the Mediterranean, for on 18 July war started in Spain. This uprising obviously involved the Mediterranean Fleet which had already been fully occupied for the past ten months. There was little in the nature of relaxation and the only relief they had enjoyed was during the brief stays at Malta for docking. With the Palestine troubles over, at least temporarily, the Mediterranean appeared quiet at the end of June and proceedings at Alexandria wound up with a most successful fleet regatta after which the visitors proceeded back to their rightful stations.

Both officers and men were looking forward to a spell of leave at Malta before the pleasant second summer cruise around the islands and the fleshpots of the Mediterranean. The bulk of the fleet were already on their way back to Malta when news of the uprising was received.

Leaving Malta with destroyers and cruisers, from *Barham*'s quarterdeck

Towing exercises. *Warspite* and *Imperial* with *Barham* in background.

Shells being fused at the time of Spanish Civil War

Near collision with *Nürnberg* at Tangier

A military revolt against the elected Popular Front Government began in Morocco and soon spread to army towns in the Peninsula. The revolt was led by General Francisco Franco, under whose direction the rebellion assumed the aspect of Civil War. Soon after the rebellion began Germany and Italy, with other foreign powers, started to intervene. Troops, munitions and aircraft were sent to help the rebel forces. The Loyalist forces were joined by an International Brigade which included Britons. Early in the campaign the Government moved to Valencia as the rebel army reached the outskirts of Madrid.

Barham was still at Alexandria, but immediately raised steam and proceeded to Malta. After three days, during which the air was thick with wireless messages from the Admiralty, *Barham* left for Gibraltar to be nearer the centre of things. At this time the British ships had a broad red, white and blue stripe painted across the whole of 'B' turret to help easy identification from the air. Just how necessary this precaution was, was realised when the German pocket battleship *Deutschland* was bombed in the area and put in to Gibraltar to bury her dead killed in the attack. The ship's company of *Barham* took part in the funeral parade.

Britain recognised neither side as being right; her policy was one of non-involvement. The role of the Navy was to protect Britain's merchant shipping and where possible protect the interest of British subjects, including their evacuation.

For the crew of *Barham* this was a busy time; they were on a war footing and shells were fused. For the telegraphists aboard the battleship, whose sensitive fingers tuned their sets, this was the real thing, a real war not a make-believe one between the Red and Blue Fleets. Messages coming over the ether were in earnest, misreadings could possibly be fatal for British subjects caught up in the conflict. Messages addressed to individual ships in the area were usually repeated to the Admiral aboard *Barham*, so that he had a complete picture of what was happening in that theatre of operations.

Barham was active round the Straits and sometimes spent a few days at Tangier, on the other side. On one of these occasions she was almost in collision with the German warship *Nürnberg*; only the latter's being powered with diesel engines saved the day; she answered the helm quickly. *Barham* was at anchor at the

time. It was fortunate the collision was averted or there may easily
have been another international incident. On board *Nürnberg* at
the time was an officer in training who was to play a decisive role
in *Barham*'s fate — the future Oberleutnant Hans Dietrich Freiherr
von Tiesenhausen.

A Spanish Loyalist destroyer was sunk on 29 September and
HMS *Hunter* was mined but managed to make port though well
down by the bow. *Barham* carried out her watching brief over the
Straits where the porpoises continued their leaping out of the
water totally unaware of the drama surrounding their domain. An
unusual role for a battleship occurred early in October when
Barham escorted the submarine *Snapper* through the Straits. At
the beginning of the month General Franco was declared by the
insurgents as 'Chief of the Spanish State'.

While Max Horton spent much of his time in *London* at
Barcelona, *Barham* was never far away from Gibraltar and toward
the end of October a general review of operations so far was issued
from the battleship:

The situation confronting the British fleet was urgent and in
some ways unique. In July there were large numbers of tourists of
British nationality both in Madrid and in the towns on the north-
east coast of Spain. It was immediately obvious that the nature of
the Civil War was such that not only the property, but lives of
foreigners would be in grave danger. Accordingly certain units of
the fleet were ordered to proceed at high speed to Barcelona,
Palma and Valencia so that they could evacuate all who were able
to leave at short notice. From mid-July to mid-October 31 ships of
the Royal Navy were employed in this task; between them they
dealt with 2,000 British refugees and another 4,000 of 55 various
other nationalities.

French, German, Italian and American warships looked after
their own nationals, and there was excellent co-operation between
the ships. But there were thousands of people belonging to
countries who either had no navy or who could not send ships
in time to deal with the emergency. These, on the recommenda-
tion of the local British Consul, the ships willingly evacuated, but
the situation with Spanish nationals was different. However
inclined commanding officers were to remove to a place of safety
people who were destitute and in danger, they could not act

until permission had been given by the Spanish authorities, unless to delay for this would certainly have been the equivalent of condemning them to death.

The organisation for evacuating refugees became consolidated after the first few days; the County class cruisers, with their big deck space, the destroyer repair ship *Woolwich* and the fleet repair ship *Resource*, with their working spaces, were used as depot ships. Refugees were collected from up and down the coast by destroyers, or arrived by train from the interior and spent the night on board one of the larger ships. Early next day they were embarked in one or more destroyers, who set off at high speed before daybreak in time to reach Marseilles before the Customs closed. But, at the beginning, on two occasions one of the larger ships had to make a trip in order to evacuate a greater number than the destroyers could deal with. *Devonshire* carried over 500 refugees to Marseilles through a heavy storm in the Gulf of Lyons and *Repulse* took as many from Palma when it seemed likely that the town was about to be attacked. When the organisation was working smoothly it was unnecessary for anyone to pass a night in the somewhat cramped space that a destroyer offered, and it was found that these little ships could take as many as 150 in fine weather during the daytime. As an example, one destroyer made five trips up and down the coast to collect refugees and six trips to Marseilles or Gibraltar, ferrying them from the depot ships to safety during August. There was not much deck space, but what there was kept them sheltered and fairly dry in a calm sea. The refugees, many of whom had lost everything, and some of them having seen friends killed or taken away to certain extinction, were only too grateful for the security which a British warship afforded to feel too deeply the discomfort which must ensue when a ship of that nature had to carry large numbers of passengers. Above all, the unfailing kindness and thoughtfulness of everyone on board went a great way to alleviate the hopelessness and despair of these unhappy people.

At Barcelona, Spain's largest port, a County class cruiser, *London*, was moored continuously at the Mole so that refugees, after they had passed the customs and the embarkation authorities, could walk straight on board. Formalities in connection with leaving the country were by no means simple and became more and more involved as time went on. In nearly every case the Government officials were friendly, although overworked and harassed, but groups of men representing the trade unions, the Communist and Anarchist parties, or merely the authority of a revolver or a sub-machine gun, made the task of embarkation a lengthy one. What few possessions the refugees had been able to bring with them were searched for hidden money, of which a very limited amount was allowed to be taken out of the country. Any excess was immediately confiscated. Many had been able to escape with literally nothing except the clothes they wore. As the refugees arrived on board their passports were examined, they were given a ticket explaining to them where their accommodation could be found, such baggage as they had was labelled and put in charge of the baggage officer, and guides showed them where they were to eat and sleep. Normally, since they came on board in the evening and left at 0500 the next morning, they were given two meals, with lunch on the destroyer during the passage to Marseilles. At Valencia, the depot ship could not moor alongside and refugees had to be transferred in boats from the shore or from the collecting destroyers. When there was a swell on this was by no means an easy task, especially as there were among them many elderly people and invalids who had to be hoisted on board in a cradle.

The disorganisation of normal life on board was complete. The recreation spaces and half the mess deck accommodation, bathrooms, canteen, and nearly all the officers' cabins, were given up continuously to the use of the refugees. Both the officers and men willingly extended the hospitality of their messes far beyond that which they were called upon to do and went out of their way at all times to make the lot of those unhappy people easier. They themselves saw something of the horrors of the internal war. They watched the bombing of Malaga, they saw the barricades, the burnt churches, the disorganisation of all ordinary life, the indiscriminate looting and destruction inseparable from the uncontrolled ferocity of civil conflict, the prison ships in the harbour at Barcelona, the barracks overlooking the town; they saw heavily laden cars driven up the hill every evening and heard the shots that followed the trial of the victims. It did not seem much to them to give up their long expected leave or to share what they could of their comforts on board with people who were indeed escaping from the jaws of death. The discomfort and strain were very real. With the exception of *London* at Barcelona, mooring alongside was impossible, and the ships were exposed to the heavy swell of the western Mediterranean. For this reason refuelling had on occasions to be done at sea, an operation of great difficulty in anything other than a flat calm. They were constantly in danger from bombs, bombardments and snipers' stray bullets, always at a moment's notice to shift billets in order to safeguard the ship from being in a possible line of fire. Recreation and leave ashore were out of the question. The crew of some ships were on board in these conditions for five weeks at a time.

In most cases the Navy's dealings with Spanish officials were limited to obtaining permission for refugees to leave and seeing them through the customs; where many refugees arrived by train, there was always a liaison officer living ashore and meeting the train which arrived twice daily with an average of about thirty refugees, dealing with their luggage and arranging for their transport over the four miles between the railway station and the seaport. This would have been an impossible task but for the sympathy and goodwill of the two Civil Governors who followed each other in rapid succession; mention must also be made of Joe, the chauffeur of the car placed at the disposal of the commanding officer, a small but immensely strong man dressed in the inevitable blue overalls with red arm band and large revolver, of which he was inordinately proud. He was absolutely fearless and regarded his job as one of high honour and on being held up by armed militiamen at one of the many barricades he would fly into a passion of righteous indignation with the unfortunate guard who ventured to hold up a British naval officer. He was once entertained on board by the petty officers' mess and proved immensely popular, but the joy of his life was when he was allowed on one occasion to drive the ship's fast motor boat. The first Civil Governor was last seen early one morning boarding a commandeered train, his retreat being covered by armed gunmen, but even then he found time to bid farewell to the officers with whom he had had such friendly dealings. His successor was a man of very different character, an ex-army colonel, who quickly achieved order out of the chaos which had existed in the Governor's office.

His chief claim to fame is that when lunching on board he carefully inspected the guard of honour — Royal Marines at their
best — and politely remarked that they were quite as smart as his
own troops ashore, armed gangs of civilians!

But although relations with the authorities in the big towns
were uniformly good, the destroyers, as they went up and down
the coast to collect refugees from the smaller towns and villages,
sometimes found difficulty in getting permission to remove even
those of British nationality. Usually polite insistence was enough,
but on one occasion it took two bottles of whisky to persuade the
President of the local Anarchist Association to let them go, on
another something not unlike a threat of force.

No praise could be too high for the sterling work done by the
British consuls. In every case the commanding officers of the
British ships emphasized the untiring way in which they were
helped in their task, a task which, without this help, could never
have been accomplished. These men stuck to their posts in
conditions which, never easy, became increasingly difficult and
dangerous as, in many towns, the established authority of the
Government came more and more under the influence of armed
gangs. But their great knowledge of local conditions, their tact
and good humour in dealing with Spanish officials, the prestige
which, as British consuls, they universally carried with them
enabled the Navy to carry out its task of almost incredible com-
plexity.

The evacuation by *Repulse* of over 500 refugees mentioned
earlier was unique in that it was the only instance on the coast
where people were removed from insurgent territory. Palma had
been bombed each evening for a week and on 29 July the British,
French and German consuls agreed that next day all refugees
should be embarked at once; they arranged that their own nationals should come at certain fixed times, and on the next day
the embarkation began according to plan at 1000; by 1700 over
500 were on board and the ship sailed for Marseilles.

Just before weighing anchor Palma was subjected to the worst
air raid she had yet experienced as though to emphasize the
security of the battle cruiser. In a ship the size of *Repulse* it was
possible to accommodate all refugees in the captain's and officers'
cabins, the wardroom, the gunroom, the chapel, the schoolroom

and the flats adjoining them. The weather was bad all through the night but the refugees did not undergo undue discomfort. Their baggage was limited to three suitcases apiece and for the most part they stuck loyally to the limitation, though some of the suitcases were of exceptional size and one man was surprised and grieved to hear that he could not bring his car on board. There were twelve dogs which came as passengers and which were kept in one of the aeroplane hangers under the charge of a somewhat bewildered able seaman. They did not sleep so well as their owners and as a result few people amidships had a quiet night. Next morning the weather had improved sufficiently to allow passengers to come up on deck and with the aid of breakfast and the gramophone the unpleasantness of a rough night in a battle-cruiser was soon forgotten and Marseilles was safely reached in the early afternoon.

A ship that worked on her own was the hospital ship *Maine*. She was sent from Malta to Valencia early in August and because of the facilities provided by her hospital wards and many cabins she was admirably fitted both for receiving refugees and for transporting them herself. She made three return trips from Valencia to Marseilles and on each occasion carried several hundred refugees of all nationalities. Most of them had come down from Madrid and the refugees included many children for whose benefit a number of cots and tin baths and large quantities of sweets and toys had been taken on board before leaving Malta. The use of a hospital ship in this connection aroused much interest among her enforced passengers and one lady asked how many ships there were in the Red Cross Line. The passage from Valencia took four days including a call at Barcelona, so that there was more time for the passengers to settle down that in the rather hurried trips by destroyer. A regular routine of meals was drawn up, as far as possible friends and families were accommodated together, a quantity of cigarettes was made from Service tobacco and distributed as fairly as possible among those who had no money, and in the evenings there were entertainments of various sorts in which there were usually found refugees who combined with the ship's company in a weird and wonderful display of talent.

A great deal of valuable assistance was given both in *Maine* and in other ships by refugees who willingly acted as interpreters, notably two brothers of Dutch nationality, who, in addition, not only collected a sum of £17 for the Red Cross Society but also drew up a manifesto expressing their thanks to His Majesty's Government and to all officers, nurses and men on the ship, which was signed by every refugee on board.

Refugees were of every race and every age, from a nun of ninety six to a baby of fifteen days, and their characters, their personal experiences, the way in which they accepted their trouble, presented an extraordinary diversity, often pathetic, yet even in these circumstances often humorous. Probably the most pitiful refugees were the nuns, several hundred of whom were removed in Britsh ships from Valencia, Barcelona and Malaga. These poor ladies, some of them old, many of them infirm, turned out of their country merely for the reason that they were nuns, bore their lot with a fortitude that amazed and humbled all who saw them; and yet there were cases when it was only with great difficulty that the naval authorities managed to embark these helpless refugees when the fury of the undisciplined armed bands attempted to prevent their leaving, even after official permission had been given. During their stay in depot ships and their passage in destroyers they seemed to go out of their way to cause as little trouble as possible and to give what help they could to those who were as unfortunate as themselves. Their thanks as they left the ships was invariably sincere, coupled with promises to pray for the officers and men of the British Navy. The only thing that worried them was that they had nothing else that they could give to those who, it seemed to them, had preserved their lives. The diversity of refugees was amazing, there was the owner of a travelling circus who was heartbroken at not being allowed to bring his favourite camel on board a destroyer, there was the refugee who came on board drunk, there was the lady who, possibly with a recollection of the words of Pope Gregory, exclaimed as she left the destroyer, 'These man are not sailors, they are angels'.

Stories about children could be multiplied indefinitely. The sailor has always had a love for children, probably because he has to spend so much time away from his own, and many a seasick mother was amazed and gratified at the way in which these amateur nurses looked after her child. Extraordinary roundabouts were rigged up with the help of a capstan, capstan-bars and hammocks; the shipwrights, who could always make anything at a moment's notice, grew exceedingly expert in the manufacture of cots. It was a usual sight to see a small group of men and children earnestly playing trains under a turret or practising the art of house-building with the aid of wooden bricks from the carpenter's shop. In the bigger ships when there was enough space a separate room was set aside for mothers with babies, and on one occasion when a petty officer was in charge of this room he was much troubled by the refusal of the inmates to keep quiet when the time came for 'lights out'. Acting as a dictator he thrust various babies into various beds and went out. It said much for the authority of the Navy that the night was passed in perfect peace and quiet although in several cases the mother had the wrong baby. Nor were the officers inferior nurses to the men. There was a small boy in one cruiser who was initiated into the mysteries of poker-dice by the wardroom and, to everyone's delight, won hands down. And there was the officer who volunteered to carry a baby down a particularly steep ladder, the parents, knowing no English, being already at the bottom. As he descended the child screamed loudly and its 'nurse' was heard to threaten, 'If you don't stop that bloody noise I'll wring your bloody neck!' The child, appreciating the situation, like little Jacob, with a discretion beyond its years, was immediately frozen into a horrified silence and on his arrival at the bottom of the ladder the officer was thanked profusely by the baby's mother on his charming and soothing way with children!

One destroyer, having to spend a day at Ibiza before proceeding to Valencia with a full load of refugees on board, and little room for them to move about, found that life became trying when herds of children were continuously rushing about playing games, or just rushing about. More refugees were expected at any moment and tea had to be prepared for nearly 150 people. Something had to be done to relieve the harassed parents many of whom had lost home, money, belongings or even husbands. Someone had a brilliant idea. Why not a sailing picnic? The local authorities gave permission to land on a secluded sandy beach; the whaler and the motor boat, loaded to the gunwhale with shouting children of all ages, sizes and shapes, provisioned with biscuits, sandwiches, condensed milk and lemonade, left the ship and disembarked, being counted as they did so since the authorities insisted that all who landed should be taken off again. When the time came to embark once more heads had to be counted three times. First there were two too few and then one too many, but the latter turned out to be a local lad who had gatecrashed on what seemed to him to be a most delightful party.

One extremely small passenger will carry with him a reminder of this experience the whole of his life. He was taken from Barcelona to Marseilles on a destroyer at the age of fifteen days and was christened Douglas, in memory of the ship which brought him and his mother to safety.

One ship carried at the same time a complete troupe of dancing girls and an enormous American all-in wrestler, who seemed almost ashamed of having to flee from a revolution but who said on his arrival on board, 'Say, you can't wrestle with bullets'. Nearly all refugees tried to make as little trouble as possible, and for this reason the very few who complained of the food, the accommodation or the motion of the ship, stood out rather clearly in everyone's memory. There were one or two demands for 'first class accommodation'. There was a gentleman of a certain nationality who, on being invited to have a wash asked if it was compulsory and, when he was assured that it was not, declined the invitation with relief. And there was the pilot of an aeroplane which he had delivered in the early days of the civil war who found that the prospect of the fighting line was rather more than he had bargained for so he flew his aeroplane to the coast and crashed a few miles from one of the ports where a British warship was waiting. A breathless and rather frightened man, he arrived at the British Consulate, and he was brought on board next day. Within a short time an Anarchist execution squad was known to be asking awkward questions about him.

Many of the refugees arrived on board only a few hours after having seen their husbands shot or led away for summary trial. What reception they expected it is impossible to say, but the kindness and sympathy which they received from all on board did something to relieve the shock and strain of the terrible days through which they had passed.

Although there were few actual exciting incidents which affected the ships of the Fleet mention must be made of the rescue of *Gibel Zerjon*, the small Bland steamer which plied between Gibraltar and North Africa. One Sunday afternoon *Repulse* was at Gibraltar, where she had gone for a few days' rest after her work at Palma and Valencia. There were few quieter or more peaceful places than in a warship on a Sunday afternoon and *Repulse* was giving an excellent example of living up to Service tradition. Those who were not ashore were asleep and the scene was one of blissful peace. In a moment everything was changed. Funnels belched smoke, awnings were furled, with Blue Peters flying at each masthead and the siren blaring continuously. With the co-operation of the Second Battalion Gordon Highlanders, who lent private cars, lorries and despatch riders, the libertymen were brought back to the ship and in an incredibly short space of time *Repulse* was proceeding at full speed towards Melilla. *Gibel Zerjon* had been held up by a Spanish cruiser, forbidden to enter Melilla and ordered to return to Gibraltar. The destroyer *Codrington*, who was on patrol, had also been ordered to go to the assistance of the steamer. Two hours later *Repulse* came up with the steamer, the destroyer and the Spanish cruiser. When the situation was explained to the captain of the latter, who had no right to stop a British ship outside territorial waters, all was well and the incident closed.

Barham left Gibraltar and the area of the Spanish war at the beginning of the first dog watch on 28 October, for Malta. En route the ship's aircraft crashed. Opportunity was taken during the trip to carry out full calibre 15-inch and 6-inch shoots; the gunners were pleased to fire off some rounds after standing by for so long in the war zone. *Barham* tied up to the buoys in the centre of Grand Harbour on the last day of October and the crew enjoyed a well earned rest until a week before Christmas.

The festive season was spent at Palma, and indeed *Barham* remained there until returning to Malta in the middle of January. The next move was for the combined fleet exercises in the South Atlantic in March, with Gibraltar the base. *Barham* had to disengage on the last day due to a stoker requiring an emergency operation for appendicitis, and so arrived back at the Rock before the main fleets, much to the joy of the crew. After dispersal of the fleets *Barham* made for the French and Italian Riviera, cruising back to Malta in April.

Empire flying-boat brings mail for *Barham*'s postman to sort out

Barham at Malta, early 1938

We must now backtrack a little to follow events at home. As already mentioned, HM King George V had died in January 1936 and been succeeded by the Prince of Wales, who became King Edward VIII. In December 1936 the King decided to abdicate because of opposition to his intended marriage to a divorced American lady. The ex-king decided first to go to Zurich and on 12 December, Sir William Fisher, now Commander-in-Chief at Portsmouth, saw him off on the first leg of his journey. The destroyer HMS *Fury* had been made available to the former monarch and it slid quietly away, unescorted, out of harbour at 0200 into the cold waters of the Solent, en route for France.

Edward was succeeded by his brother who was crowned as HM King George VI in Westminster Abbey on 12 May 1937. The Coronation Fleet Review was to follow so *Barham* received orders to sail for Spithead, left Malta, spent 24 hours in Gibraltar and arrived at Spithead at 1600 the day after the Coronation. At the Review *Barham* was host ship to a Russian warship and the steam picket boat was one of three guard boats to protect the royal yacht *Victoria and Albert* from the small boat sightseers.

Barham put into Portsmouth for four days before again taking up station in Spanish waters. During this time she went to Barcelona to pick up refugees, which included the British consul and his family. The summer cruise was to the Greek Islands and at Mudros in September *Barham* won the Fleet Regatta, before returning to Malta.

The Spanish Civil War had now lasted a year and there were no signs of an immediate end. A new development had occurred, in that merchant ships were being torpedoed without warning, including British vessels. At a conference in Nyon the British and French decided to route Mediterranean traffic and protect it from the sea and air, attacking any submerged submarine sighted. Admiral Cunningham boarded *Barham* at Malta and sailed to Oran to meet his opposite number in the French Navy, to arrange to implement the agreement; the conference was held aboard. The Admiral returned to Malta by destroyer while *Barham* sailed for Gibraltar.

As a result of the conference destroyers of the Home Fleet and aircraft of Coastal Command were ordered to carry out patrols. The aircraft were based at Arzeu, near Oran, and it was here that

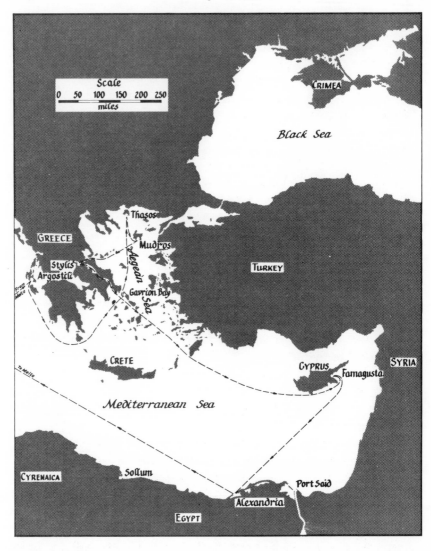

Eastern Mediterranean showing part of *Barham*'s autumn cruise 1937 and places of interest

Barham arrived next for a forty-eight hour stopover on 21 September before resuming the Spanish patrol, alternately putting in at Gibraltar and Tangier, before returning to Malta in early October.

There was practice with the 15-inch gun on the occasion of a visit from the Right Hon Duff Cooper who at the time was First Lord of the Admiralty.

The rest of 1937 was seen out with visits to Alexandria, Bizerta and a pleasant interlude at the Greek Islands, Corfu, Santa Quaranta and Astokos before returning for Christmas and the New Year at Malta.

In January *Barham* sailed to Famagusta, Alexandria and Dragames before on 10 February at 0930 she left Malta for home. She had an overnight stop at Gibraltar before ending the 1935-38 commission at Portsmouth on 18 February.

The next commission, after a refit, which lasted until the commencement of World War II, was served in the same area; several of the crew volunteered to serve in the ship again.

CHAPTER EIGHT

Last peacetime commission

Modifications to *Barham* during 1938 included the single 4-inch guns being replaced by twin 4-inch HA mountings, the torpedo control position removed from its position on the charthouse and replaced by a defence position and the ageing Fairey floatplane replaced by a more modern one, a Swordfish, from the same stable.

One of the fitters drafted aboard to maintain the Swordfish was Leading Aircraftman Ted Eustance. Airman Ted was posted as a member of the catapult flight for a thirty month commission with the Fleet Air Arm. It was a wet, dull day when he joined her in Portsmouth Dockyard. The battleship was in C Lock at the time undergoing her refit. As Ted climbed aboard up the steep gangway he was stunned by a big tea-chest swung clumsily round by a matelot as he tried to avoid the airman. Ted was wearing gumboots and was hard put to keep his balance on the greasy metal deck. He felt completely lost. There was a big conference in progress on the catapult turret and there were all kinds of dockyard engineers, ship's engineers, and gold braid awaiting the arrival of the Swordfish that the turret flight had already been preparing. To get to the catapult Ted had to climb over all kinds of lockers and up a metal ladder, then step across the wide gap between the outer guardshield of the 15-inch turret, up the ladder and on to the turret top. He just couldn't keep his feet on the wet, oily metal, and when the aircraft was lifted on to the catapult cradle they had to climb on to the mass of girders that formed the catapult and guide the floatplane on to the catapult's securing spools. Ted, in his gumboots, kept slipping and sliding awkwardly. If he should miss his footing he would fall forty feet to the quarter-deck.

This was to be his place of work every day for the next two and a half years. Everything was utterly strange and bewildering after

RAF life; the noise and clatter of drilling, welding and riveting on all sides, the tangle of cables and pipelines everywhere, the hundreds of stanchions, manholes, and steep, slippery metal hatches to negotiate, not to mention the strange names of authority — the Crusher, the Jaunty, the Buffer, Jimmy, bootnecks, Jack Dusty, Pusser, etcetera.

It was very bewildering to an RAF engine fitter, whose only nautical knowledge had been acquired on the Liverpool-New Brighton ferry. The pipes, too, were fantastic: Out pipes!, Clean out and stow away spit-kids!, Up spirits!, 'ands of the mess for spuds!, All the 'ands, 'eave-o, 'eave-o, 'eave-o; lash up and stow! Rise and shine, the mornin's fine, the sun's scorchin' yer bleedin' eyeballs! and the sight of the petty-officer of the watch coming through the messes shaking the hammocks of the still sleeping matelots, shouting at the same time, 'Hands off cocks, on socks!'

Still feeling lost on this their first day in the Royal Navy, Ted, the corporal rigger, the wireless and electrical mechanic, and the armourer wandered round this great fighting monster, blundering into forbidden quarters guarded by burnished marine guards, and bumping into awesome figures covered in gold braid who frowned at them in a way that made them tremble. They went on banging their heads and their shins on bulkheads and being shouted at by seamen petty officers until eventually they located their little store, which the sailors called a 'caboosh', shut the door and sank on to the bench to recover.

Such was a Royal Air Force man's first experience of the Navy. But gradually Ted grew used to it all. He found out that their seaplane cranedriver was an old friend from home, now a leading hand. He initiated Ted into Navy ways, although there were awkward moments like clambering along the boom and down into the crash boat, loaded with tools, which sorely tried him.

Ted was not the only new arrival on board for on 22 April 1938 Captain Algernon U. Willis DSO was appointed to *Barham*, in command. This vastly experienced officer was a clever and most able man who was later to receive a knighthood. Another 'newcomer' aboard was Leading Signalman Bill Walters, whom we met earlier joining as a boy in 1921. This time he served for nine months during the Munich crisis and says:

Barham sporting 'Cock of the Fleet' on B turret which is painted red, white and blue for easy identification from the air during the time of the Spanish War

Swordfish carrying out catapult trials off the Isle of Arran in the Clyde

Shipboard life was much the same but anti-aircraft guns and equipment had been added and the funnels trunked. We had a good ship's company, winning the 'Cock of the Fleet' for pulling regattas two years running and numerous other sporting trophies.

But now back to the Royal Air Force contingent aboard. The reason that the maintenance crew of the aircraft were mainly Royal Air Force was due to the fact that prior to 1938 the Fleet Air Arm maintenance of aircraft had been the responsibility of the RAF, and a 2½ year commission with the Fleet Air Arm was an alternative to 5 years at an overseas RAF station. Ted Eustance, after his early days with the ship in Portsmouth, sailed with her for trials in the Clyde where aircraft catapult exercises were carried out. The exercises included firing the aircraft off the catapult and picking it out of the sea by crane. After static trials had proved successful they were carried out under way. This was achieved by steering several points to port, thus creating a smooth slick for the aircraft to land in, then it was taxied alongside and recovered by crane. This was a slightly hazardous operation in choppy seas as the observer, a telegraphist air gunner, had to balance on the cockpit coaming, legs astride the pilot, and open the flaps in the centre section of the top mainplane, pick up the lifting ring and connect it to the crane lifting hook which was swinging perilously near his head. Once engaged the crane driver operated a trip wire, known as a Thomson grab, which locked the lifting gear and raised the aircraft out of the water. To avoid damage, several seamen armed with fending poles kept it from swinging into the ship's side. It was then swung into position on 'X' 15-inch turret and locked on the catapult trolley.

The aircraft launching operation was rather Heath-Robinson. The turret was trained on to a bearing of 45 degrees; the catapult crew then wound by hand the launching trolley back to its position at the starting point, the extendable part of the catapult was then wound forward, so giving a catapult length for launching of about sixty feet. The firing of the aircraft trolley was accomplished by a cordite charge which activated the hydraulics; the procedure was briefly this: the pilot started the engine, the operator of the cordite charge grasped the firing cable, the officer in charge of launching raised his flag and the affirmative signal was given from the bridge. The pilot then opened the engine to full revs and when he was ready raised his hand. The officer in charge then dropped his flag, the cordite charge was fired and the trolley shot forward to the end of the catapult, releasing the aircraft at take off speed.

After a short period at Lamlash, during which time the ship's company kept alive the ship's nickname of 'Beery *Barham*' by drinking the local pub dry, the battleship sailed for Portland and after exercises returned to Portsmouth for storing ship, finally sailing for the Mediterranean in June. One of the drills carried out took place in the middle of the Bay of Biscay, which was as calm as the proverbial mill pond. 'Hands to bathe, the port side', was piped, the seaboat was launched and the lads dived in.

The commander, named Chapman, regarded the Fleet Air Arm as a 'necessary nuisance'. During 1938 the Mediterranean was crossed from west to east and back again from east to west. One of the tunes the Royal Marines band often played was 'Waltzing Matilda', probably because *Barham* carried an Australian padre, Reverend Mawson, at the time.

On 8 November the Captain, in consultation with the engineer, decided on a full speed trial, and despite her very foul bottom, *Barham* managed 21.6 knots. Throughout the year the Spanish war had still been raging.

At the time the Mediterranean Fleet comprised *Warspite*, *Barham*, *Malaya*, *Hood*, cruisers *Arethusa*, *Devonshire*, *Galatea*, *Shropshire* and *Sussex*, aircraft carrier *Glorious*, depot ship *Maidstone* and the hospital ship *Maine* together with H and I class destroyers. It was a great fleet, well drilled and impeccably turned out, the pride of the Navy in fact. When in 1939 the fleet sailed from Gibraltar to take part in what were to be the last pre-war spring exercises with the Home Fleet it must have been the most impressive display of British Naval power since Jutland as in addition to the aforementioned ships the Home Fleet brought out *Ark Royal*, *Nelson*, *Rodney*, *Renown*, *Ramillies* and several of the Royal Sovereign class ships, and the newly commissioned Tribal class destroyers.

After the exercises *Barham* cleaned up and the Fleets were dispersed for the spring cruise, her destination was the South of

'Mitzi' rejoining ship after overhaul at RAF Abokair

Oars furled at Alexandria

France. As *Barham* left Gibraltar, with her brasswork agleam and painted up, the weather deteriorated rapidly and she was soon in the middle of a Force 10 gale. She was escorting a force of S class submarines on the surface; they were forbidden to dive by the Nyon Agreement, and consequently speed was restricted. For two days or more the ships faced the gale in the Gulf of Lyons and many aboard recorded this as the worst weather they had ever experienced in the Mediterranean. Several units of the Fleet had to run for shelter and one cruiser had her main mast broken. The wind was so strong that it caused the propeller of the Swordfish to 'windmill'. Eventually *Barham* arrived at Villefranche, bearing all the scars of the gale; the crew were ordered to clean up the ship before doing anything else. A contemporary English newspaper report read:

> With several of her boats swept away and her deck gear badly damaged the British battleship *Barham* arrived at Villefranche-sur-Mer this evening after having fought one of the worst storms in the Mediterranean for many years. *Barham*, which was due two days ago, was ordered by radio to escort the submarines *Clyde*, *Shark*, *Salmon*, *Sealion*, *Thames* and *Severn*, which were on their way to Nice, and were unable to continue on the surface. Battling against huge seas, *Barham* stood by the six submerged submarines for 48 hours until the storm abated. The submarines have arrived undamaged, but *Barham* will have to undergo repairs.

Barham arrived at Naples and tied up alongside USS *Omaha*, also on a courtesy visit, on Maundy Thursday 1939; she was not to stay long as the following day Italy declared war on Albania. The crew manhandled the ship from the jetty and left very hurriedly in answer to an urgent signal from Admiral Sir Dudley Pound, the Commander-in-Chief of the Mediterranean, on board *Warspite*, to rendezvous off Malta. As she passed through the Straits of Messina one of the three-badgers who was painting the brass rails with grey paint remarked, 'When the Navy orders us to paint over the bright work we mean business!'

Eventually the tension eased slightly and *Barham* returned to Malta, which was in mourning as the Pope had died.

The Spanish War was resolved on 1 April in General Franco's favour. The summer cruise laid down by the Commander-in-Chief Mediterranean for *Barham* was: to leave Alexandria 23 June for Malta, arrive 26 June, leave 18 July for Famagusta and stay there from 20 to 25 July, then return to Alexandria. However Famagusta was later altered to read Corfu, possibly as a result of a request received from the British Minister in Athens which read:

> If it would not throw out your whole programme and if it is in other respects practicable might I suggest that on political grounds visit(s) should be made to Salonika by one or more of HM Ships. The population there are inclined to be alarmist and I feel that such a visit would have a steadying effect. Four Royal Air Force flying-boats have just paid a visit to Salonika which was remarkably successful. Local authorities complain that they have had no visits from capital ships for some time. If it is decided to make such a visit might I suggest that the bigger the ship or ships the better.

The Commander-in-Chief forwarded the request to the Admiralty, adding:

> I have not so far considered sending ships to visit Salonika on account of its distance from Alexandria, but should be willing to do so should such a visit be politically desirable, which may well be so. Same considerations may perhaps apply to visits by HM ships to Corfu. It is known that visits to Corfu would be welcomed by the Greek government.

On 5 July the Commander-in-Chief Mediterranean signalled:

> Following visits are intended
> (A) *Warspite* to Smyrna 2–6 August
> (B) *Shropshire* and Second Division to Salonika 1–6 August
> (C) *Barham* and 6 motor torpedo boats to Corfu 20–25 July
> Summer cruise order will be adjusted accordingly.

The following day a coded cable was despatched to the British Minister in Athens, which when decoded read:

(Far left) *Barham*
approaching Naples
(Below left) Tied up at the
buoys at Malta

Last days of peace.
(Left) A and B turrets
(Below) X and Y turrets
as *Barham* gleams in her
Mediterranean Fleet paint

Please make necessary notification to the Greek Government for a visit by HMS *Barham* and 6 MTB's to Corfu from 20–25 July and of Second Division of destroyers to Salonika from 1–6 August.

Corfu; on the way the submarine *Snapper* carried out a torpedo attack on the battleship and aircraft alarm exercises were carried out until dark. *Barham* arrived at Corfu on the morning of 20 July and later the Motor Torpedo Boats *01*, *02*, *05*, *06*, *18* and *19* arrived and secured alongside the battleship. The Greek destroyer *Leon* was in harbour and HM King George II of the Hellenes was in residence ashore.

On arrival *Barham* fired a salute of 21 guns; coincidentally the day was the unofficial birthday of the Greek King so the ships dressed overall. *Barham* treated the local population to a half-hour searchlight display when darkness fell. While at Corfu the Greek government gave permission for the Swordfish to be flown off *Barham* daily.

On Sunday the Greek King paid a visit to *Barham* and the occasion was marked by dressing the ship overall until sunset. The King watched the ship's company march past and after lunch transferred to MTB *01* and watched the other MTBs manoeuvring for about an hour. His Majesty expressed pleasure at what he had seen, saying he thought *Barham* was in particularly good condition and he was impressed by the appearance of the ship's company. He returned aboard again in the evening for dinner with the Vice-Admiral and this was followed by a cinema show. The Royal party did not depart until the early hours of Monday.

Three cricket matches were played at Corfu in conditions of intense heat. The officers played the Club Gymnastique and lost 51–91, while two ship's company games with the Byron Club resulted in a 93–76 win and a 78–112 loss. The weather was consistently hot with calms and light airs, temperatures in the nineties every day of the visit. This degree of heat appeared to be exceptional, and to have followed on an unusually hot north-east wind a few days before.

The visit to Corfu proved a pleasant one and the cordiality and kindness of the local people left nothing to be desired. It was evident that the Albanian crisis in April had caused considerable alarm, and added to the existing unpopularity of Italy on the island. The ship was not formally open to visitors but was actually visited by several parties, by prior arrangement.

At 0500 on Tuesday 25 July the MTB's sailed for Port Vathi and *Barham* proceeded two hours later. Topped up with fresh water, oil and provisions *Barham* sailed for Cyrpus, to Famagusta, carrying out a sub-calibre bombardment practice at a drifting target en route. Arriving at Famagusta forty chief and petty officers and forty other ratings were invited by the Mayor and British residents to a picnic at Salamis Bay and this was very much appreciated by the lucky eighty men.

After prayers on Sunday morning *Barham* joined with *Malaya* and carried out a bombardment practice. At dawn the next morning both ships carried out a 6-inch practice at Akamas range, *Barham* opening fire first at 0410 and *Malaya* some fifty minutes later. Spotting aircraft were catapulted off for this practice, while the destroyer *Gallant* provided flank marking. On completion of the firing the capital ships parted company with *Barham* and *Gallant* anchoring off Latzi. In the afternoon 200 invited guests visited *Barham*.

At dawn the following morning, 1 August, while war clouds were gathering over Europe *Barham* left for Alexandria. An unscreened attack by the submarine *Sealion* on *Barham* was carried out as the battleship approached the Egyptian port.

On 4 August the French sloop *D'Iberville* arrived in for docking and the usual official calls were made. This day was also Queen Elizabeth's birthday so both ships fired salutes. Three days later *Barham* was at sea for exercises, but on return there was an accident, described later, which meant that these were the very last peacetime exercises carried out, as in less than four weeks Britain and Germany would once again be at war.

PART THREE

HOSTILITIES AGAIN

September 1939–November 1941

CHAPTER NINE

Home, to disasters

When the British Prime Minister, Neville Chamberlain, made his historic declaration of war broadcast at 1100 on 3 September 1939, Sir Charles Forbes was Commander-in-Chief of the Home Fleet. Under his command were the battleships *Nelson*, *Rodney*, *Royal Oak*, *Royal Sovereign* and *Iron Duke*, the aircraft carrier *Ark Royal* and the attendant cruisers, destroyers, minesweepers and smaller craft; the Home Fleet base was at Scapa Flow in the Orkneys.

In the Mediterranean Admiral Sir Andrew Cunningham had *Warspite* as his flagship with her sister battleships *Barham* and *Malaya* as well as the aircraft carrier *Glorious* and many lesser ships of the fleet under his command.

The ships had not long received the 'Most Immediate' signal from the Admiralty reading 'Commence hostilities at once with Germany', before the Kriegsmarine showed its hand when Korvetten-Kapitän Fritz-Julius Lemp, commander of *U-30*, torpedoed and sank the liner *Athenia* carrying children to the safety of Canada. A fortnight later on 17 September Kapitän-Leutnant Schuhart, in command of *U-29*, sighted the aircraft carrier HMS *Courageous* by chance in the Western Approaches and hit her with two torpedoes. The carrier sank in 15 minutes with heavy loss of life.

Unbeknown to the Admiralty the German ships *Graf Spee* and *Deutschland*, known to the British as pocket-battleships, were already in the North Atlantic with their supply ships *Altmark* and *Westerwald* when war was declared. Early in October a German force led by the battle-cruiser *Gneisenau* put to sea towards Norway with the intention of attacking shipping and to try to draw the Home Fleet in the path of waiting U-boats; the sortie failed on both counts; the Germans returned to Kiel and the Home Fleet to Scapa Flow. If the plans to catch the Home Fleet at sea failed, another and altogether much bolder plan had been evolved by Admiral Karl Dönitz, the Commander-in-Chief of the U-boat arm. His plan was to put a U-boat inside Scapa Flow.

When *Royal Oak* dropped anchor, after the abortive search, it was the last time she would do so, for on 14 October Günter Prien in *U-47* conned his submarine into the sheltered anchorage and fired three torpedoes which sank the battleship and killed 833 members of her crew. This daring attack made headlines all over the world. The Admiralty decided the naval base was no longer safe and ordered Loch Ewe to be used as the temporary home for the Home Fleet. To emphasise their decision as being correct the Luftwaffe attacked and damaged HMS *Iron Duke* at Scapa three days later.

On 23 November the armed merchant cruiser *Rawalpindi* on the Northern Patrol reported an enemy battle-cruiser in sight and followed this up by reporting it as *Deutschland*; in fact it was *Scharnhorst*. *Deutschland* had already secretly returned unobserved to Germany and been renamed *Lützow*. *Scharnhorst* with her sister ship *Gneisenau* was patrolling the Iceland-Faeroes Channel with the intention of dislocating Allied shipping movements; the orders for the German ships were not to take on superior forces, but the unarmoured *Rawalpindi* certainly did not fall into this category and was soon sunk despite the heroic stand of Captain Kennedy and his crew.

At sea the battleship *Nelson*, flagship of the Home Fleet, instead of going to the Clyde as planned, on 3 December proceeded to cover the Northern Patrol, as in the early hours the Admiralty ordered the armed merchant cruisers of the patrol to a wireless fix on an enemy unit. However, the fuel of the flagship's covering destroyers was low, and with a gale coming up the Commander-in-Chief decided the force must put into Loch Ewe to refuel. A further message indicated that the enemy unit was probably only a U-boat and this meant that the armed merchant cruisers could safely resume their patrol lines while *Nelson* and her screen set course for Loch Ewe.

On 4 December, almost at the end of the morning watch, *Nelson* detonated a magnetic mine laid some days earlier by a U-boat, as the Kriegsmarine had correctly guessed that Loch Ewe would be used as a base for the Home Fleet. At the time

Nelson was making 13 knots with the depth of water 19 fathoms; the ship took a list of 3 degrees to starboard but continued to steer perfectly and eventually anchored at 1210. There were 73 men injured but fortunately there were no fatalities; the news was kept secret and five further mines were exploded in the area where the incident took place. It was not safe for *Nelson* to sail until 4 January and eventually she arrived at Portsmouth dockyard for repairs four days later.

With *Nelson* being out of action another warship was urgently required by the Home Fleet, *Warspite* was already on its way home from the Mediterranean and now *Barham* was called home from Alexandria. It must be remembered of course that at this time Italy had not entered the war; the heavy forces could be used to more effect in Home waters than showing the flag in the Mediterranean.

All this naval activity had taken place in the first four months of the war, a period that is referred to by historians as the 'phoney war'! We will now turn the clock back and join *Barham* on this first day of the war, with Ted Eustance.

A humorous incident occurred on that fateful Sunday morning. After Divisions we gathered round the tannoy to hear a broadcast of the Prime Minister's announcement. One old stoker had just come up from the engine room complete with sweat rag and was looking very glum and angry.

'Cheer up, Stokes!', said his mate, 'the war won't last long and we'll soon fix old Hitler.'

'What are you talking about', growled the old timer, 'I'm not worried about that, I've just been down to the Goffer Bar and they've run out of nutty.'

Barham and *Warspite* were soon back at Alexandria and the rest of the Mediterranean Fleet dispersed when it was realised that the Italians were not joining in at the moment. The aircraft on *Warspite* and *Barham* were fully extended as a daily reconnaissance was necessary and our aircraft on one occasion flew nine hours a day for a week.

The news of my first child's birth came a few weeks later; she was born in Malta on 11 September, but I didn't get the news for six weeks! We returned to Malta at the end of October and my daughter had the unique experience of a full Naval christening aboard a wartime battleship, I still have the Baptism certificate.

Sid Haines remembers the last few days of peace:

> Just before the war, while in Alexandria the ship was alongside oiling, the foot valve of the oil inlet to the fuel tank was not opened in 'A' boiler room, which was the boiler room under steam for auxiliary harbour purposes, and the boiler room became flooded with oil and caught fire. The fire lasted three days and the messdecks above the boiler room had to be evacuated because of the heat. This meant a return to Malta for repairs and, on returning to Alexandria the crew had just finished lunch on the Sunday and were lying on the upper deck for a siesta when a broadcast was made over the tannoy system informing us that as from 1100 BST we were at war with Germany.

Frank Loy, who had joined as a boy seaman, remembers:

> Constant exercises were carried out before war was declared and then after several rumour-ridden weeks swinging round a buoy in Alexandria, swimming, sun bathing and roistering ashore, *Barham* was given the green light and in company with destroyers recalled from the China Fleet sailed for Gibraltar.

Barham slipped from B2 berth at 0700 on Friday 1 December en route to Gibraltar, by-passing Malta. Speed was gradually worked up until 20 knots was reached and the battleship continued zig-zagging at this speed during the day. Two days later, after the ship's company had attended Divisions and prayers, the destroyers *Duncan* and *Duchess* from Malta relieved *Defender* and *Dainty*. In the afternoon the island of Pantellaria, later to become well-known as an Italian island fortress, was seen. Europa Point was sighted to starboard on the afternoon of 5 December and course altered for the battleship to pass through the northern entrance and take up number 48 berth at Gibraltar. There was a provision and a central store lorry alongside so during the dog-watches and the following morning the ship was ammunitioned and provisioned. There was a make and mend for the port watch during the afternoon, but all told this time was very hectic and the war complement of additional officers and men added extra messing problems.

As darkness fell *Barham* put to sea again; she had waited until this hour to avoid the prying eyes of Axis agents in nearby Algeciras. There was a nasty moment less than two hours out from Gibraltar; with the battleship making 17 knots course had to be altered when a fishing felucca was sighted immediately ahead.

Frank Loy remembers at this time:

> My first indelible impression of war came as we passed through the Straits of Gibraltar bound for the open Atlantic. From my action station in the 15-inch gun director in the foremast I looked down on the smooth black sea, and heard on the inter-phone system the orders 'With full charge, and armour piercing shell, load the cages'. The ship was in all respects ready for war. The latest buzz in the for'ard heads said Halifax Nova Scotia, the signal from the Admiralty, repeated Commander-in-Chief Home Fleet, said Greenock Scotland!

With land left far behind, the next morning *Barham* was shadowed by a friendly French flying-boat for two hours. Two days later a ¾ inch rocket line was lost overboard when charts were being transferred to *Duncan* while the ships were making 18 knots. During the afternoon of 11 December the destroyers *Exmouth* and *Eclipse* were sighted at a range of 15 miles and as they closed Captain Walker gave them instructions for screening; later in the day *Echo* joined the screen. By now the battleship was well on the way home steaming through the North Atlantic up the west coast of Ireland. In the first watch both Tory Island light and Inishtuhull light were observed as the ship made its way round the top of Ireland on its way to the Firth of Clyde. In the early morning Islay and Rathlin Island lights were sighted as the battleship and the screening destroyers moved nearer their destination. Then occurred one of those regrettable incidents that are always liable to happen in wartime when ships are steaming in close formation without lights.

An order was given to change course when at 0427 there was a jarring crash as *Barham* collided with the escorting destroyer *Duchess*. Immediately the engines of *Barham* were put astern. The watch below were shaken out of their hammocks and as they made their way topsides they saw the spectacle for themselves. *Duchess* was turned completely over and floated for a short time bottom up.

Frank Loy says:

There were terrible scenes as *Barham* lost way and rescue attempts were made. Seaboats were turned inboard, hampering life saving operations. Men screamed as they drowned in the cold waters, choked by spreading oil fuel. In these early days of the war no escape ports were provided in ship's sides and the capsized for'ard half of the destroyer presented stark horror as men screamed through the small scuttles as they passed astern to their deaths. *Barham* struck *Duchess* between the forward funnel and the galley flat. Depth charges, not set to 'Safe' exploded in the after part of *Duchess* adding to the night's carnage. A young midshipman and Leading Seaman Charlie Bishop both dived into the icy cold water to rescue several men; they were the heroes of the night. Other *Duchess* men survived by walking down their ship's side and stepping on to the side of *Barham* by the 6-inch starboard battery. It took until we reached Greenock to clean off the oil from the survivors whom we had plied with hot drinks liberally laced with rum.

Many on the battleship thought at first they had rammed a submarine when they saw the upturned hull of their escort. There were only 24 men saved from the crew of 146. It was twenty minutes after the collision that the depth charges exploded and *Duchess* finally sank. When the order to change course had been given it is believed that *Duchess* obeyed immediately instead of waiting for the executive signal and so cut across the bows of *Barham*. When nothing further could be done, *Barham*, now off the Mull of Kintyre, proceeded on course and less than seven hours later let go the starboard anchor in 8 fathoms off Greenock. An hour later an oiler secured alongside and at 1400 a Court of

HMS *Duchess*

Enquiry into the collision with *Duchess* was convened on board.

In the meantime Admiral Forbes had transferred his flag to *Warspite* two days after *Nelson* had been mined. On 12 December he sailed twelve of his destroyers to meet an incoming troop convoy containing 7,500 men of the First Canadian Division in five liners, including the four-funnelled *Aquitania*.

To the tired crew in *Barham*, one event was following another. In the forenoon of 13 December there was an emergency air alarm and in the late evening she weighed and proceeded on the flood tide following orders received from the Commander-in-Chief; four hours later she took station on *Warspite*. Reports indicated that a German force was at large in the North Sea. Receiving this information Sir Charles Forbes sailed with *Warspite*, *Hood* and six destroyers and it was this force that *Barham* joined. The Commander-in-Chief obviously thought that the German force was out after the troop convoy but in fact its intention was nothing more lethal than mine-laying.

When in the morning of 16 December it was seen that the convoy, already escorted by *Repulse* and *Resolution*, was in no danger, *Hood* hauled out to port to carry out a throw-off shoot at *Barham*. The next morning *Barham* anchored at Greenock and at 1140 cleared lower deck to cheer in the Canadian troop convoy. On the following day the hands painted ship and whatever thoughts they may have had about receiving a little home leave at last were soon dispelled as the Commander-in-Chief was informed that the Admiralty had received a warning that there might be an attempt by a number of enemy merchant ships to reach Germany. The armed merchant cruisers that had been withdrawn earlier were sent back to sea while *Barham* and *Repulse* were due to sail as distant cover.

During the afternoon of the 19th twelve midshipmen were discharged to *Hood* and *Warspite* just before *Barham* weighed and proceeded to sea. While at sea in the next few days emergency stations were exercised and the capital ships had to alter course while the destroyers investigated 'contacts'. The destroyers *Khartoum, Imogen, Isis, Icarus* and *Inglefield* left in turn to fuel.

Steaming through the fog banks of the Denmark Strait and further north into atrocious weather *Barham* and *Repulse* hunted in vain for the enemy. Four hours on watch and four hours off, day after day, lookouts and gun's crews froze, cursed and looked forward to a speedy return to the Clyde.

When on Sunday 24 December the ships were still well out to sea the *Barham*'s crew became resigned to spending another Christmas away from home; while serving in the Mediterranean they knew there was no chance and this was accepted, but when they returned to join the Home Fleet, 'Home for Christmas' was the optimistic talk on the messdeck. Christmas Day 1939 was just like any other day for the officers and men in *Barham*; for Frank Loy it provided no relief from the cold and boredom from his lofty perch in the 15-inch director. He gazed out at the icy seas and loudly bemoaned his fate. Ted Eustance 'enjoyed' his Christmas dinner at Action Stations!

Christmas was just another day for Fritz-Julius Lemp, his officers and men in *U-30*; for the crew of this infamous boat that remains in the memory as that which sank the undefended *Athenia*, was also at sea again and the ships' paths were soon to cross.

On Boxing Day the British Force altered course while a destroyer investigated yet another 'contact'; on the following day the force altered course three times for the same reason. While making its way back to the Clyde and steaming south the force encountered *Hood* with her escort making her way north to relieve them. The 15-inch armament of *Barham* and the guns on *Repulse* were exercised in control runs on the great battle cruiser. On *Barham* the director tower followed her and the four 15-inch turrets followed the director while practising ranging and fire control against *Hood* as she raced north into the gathering darkness.

In the early hours of the morning of 28 December *U-30* struck again. Korvetten-Kapitän Lemp observed the small 325 ton anti-submarine trawler *Barbara Robertson* 35 miles north-west of the Butt of Lewis. His Type VIIA boat carried only eleven torpedoes and he decided to keep these for bigger fish and so attacked and sank the trawler with his 3.5-inch gun. The sinking was not immediately known by the patrolling British ships.

The destroyer *Isis* was detached to search for a lifeboat that had been reported in position 58.47N 08.05W. The Commander-in-Chief Home Fleet sent a signal timed at 1055 reporting 15 men adrift in an open boat. This signal, the three alterations of course that previous day while destroyers investigated contacts, and yet again an alteration of course in mid-morning for another investigation, should have altered the force to the fact that a U-boat was in the vicinity.

After *Isis* detached, *Barham* and *Repulse* were covered by the four destroyers *Icarus*, *Imogin*, *Inglefield* and *Khartoum* of the Third Destroyer Flotilla under the command of Captain(D) in *Inglefield*. At 1410 with a light north-east wind blowing causing a slight swell, *Barham*, steaming at 19 knots commenced a new zig-zag, she was in station four cables astern of *Repulse* with the destroyers in screening positions. At 1441 the ships were near the end of a port leg of the zig-zag which had begun eight minutes earlier when there was an explosion as *Barham* was hit in position 58.34N 06.30W.

Frank Loy says the order 'Train fore and aft and secure' had just come through; he continues:

As I reached out of the tower to pull up the protecting shield an enormous roar rent the air, a huge volume of water, tinged with red and yellow flame rose out of the sea, climbed before my eyes above the 85 foot height of our tower and crashed onto the ship.

Fritz-Julius Lemp had again been on target with a torpedo from *U-30*, although this was not immediately apparent on the battleship. At the time of the explosion there was clearly doubt in the minds of most of the ship's company as to what had happened, and their attitude was one of surprise. The engines were stopped and put astern but the way was not completely taken off the ship. The ship's company were piped to 'Emergency Stations' as six blasts were sounded on the siren and two cones were hoisted base to base. Able-seaman John Wright below deck says:

> For a few agonising moments, the ship shuddered as if shaken by a giant hand, then seemed to leap from out of the sea as the full impact of the torpedo's explosives took effect. To most of us at stations below the waterline, every second seemed an eternity as we waited and wondered if our last moment had arrived. We were not long to be kept in suspense, as very soon afterwards a bugle's vibrant notes echoed through the ship's warning system.

Barham hoisted an incorrect signal that she had been hit on the starboard side, whilst listing to port, and, from the W/T signal made, there appears to have been some doubt in the Captain's mind whether it was a mine or torpedo. After the engines had been stopped and put astern it was not until fourteen minutes after the explosion that they were put to 'ahead' again.

John Wright continues:

> When the command was given for all ratings to fall in on the quarterdeck I cannot recall with any certainty if ever I moved so quickly before, or since that day, but at least I do know for sure it couldn't have taken me longer than 30 seconds flat before reaching the upper-deck. My normal time for this evolution was usually around the four minute mark, and I wasn't even in the first eight.
>
> When safely mustered on deck, the commanding officer addressed us, explaining briefly what had transpired and stating the measures to be taken in saving the ship. Whilst this address was going on, something of a stir was created amongst the orderly ranks of fallen in sailors, as the ship's engines which

had been stopped, suddenly sprang into life and a wild dash to
the guard-rails ensued, as some among us thought the ship was
about to give up the ghost. How were we to know that the
engine room staff, had either by order or design stayed put at
their stations.

This very unseamanlike action of ours in rushing the guard-
rail, brought forth its deserved reprimand, plus the stern warning that should anyone feel like going overboard, they would
almost certainly perish within a very few moments of immer-
sion in the icy sea. After this episode the only other ripple of
near panic to occur was in the personage of a certain rather
elderly three-striped seaman, who was to suddenly remember
that tucked away in his locker, lay the illegally bottled up tots
of rum he had been saving for a Hogmanay beano; it hardly
needs mentioning, he was among the first to return below, when
the hands fell out again. The first steps in getting the ship safely
home were now being put into operation; these consisted of
among other things, training all turreted main guns on to a
starboard bearing thus helping to counteract the pull of her
damaged port side. All bulkheads and watertight doors in the
vicinity of the severely flooded compartments were shored up,
and work commenced in pumping out the many hundred tons
of unfriendly sea water.

For a time, all went reasonably well, as the pumps held their
own, but later, so great became the pressure on the creaking
bulkheads, that yet another measure had to be brought into
being. This constituted the ship's company being divided into
two hourly watches, and formed into human chains, armed
with every vessel deemed suitable for baling that could be commandeered.

So tense did the ship's atmosphere become at times that
everyone not actually on duty kept as near to the upper-deck as
possible, the lower part of their chests adorned with Admiralty-
issue lifebelts, now grossly swollen walls of tortured rubber.

Sid Haines remembers:

At the time the torpedo struck I was in the engine room,
working on the oil and bilge pumps. All the lights went out and
the secondary oil lamps were also put out by the blast. The
torpedo had struck for'ard and the battleship had her nose well

into the water. At first the ship was stopped for what seemed to me to be ages and I felt as if I was alone down there on the pumps. I made my way to the engine room floor above and the rest of the engine room staff were there in a small group. The telegraph rang for slow speed ahead and then up to half speed to 18 knots. All the ventilating fans were put out of action and the telephone communication with the bridge, so an emergency portable set was rigged up and with it being so hot in the telephone cabinet, the engine room stoker took turns of one hour about to pass on the hourly revolutions and emergency messages.

Frank Loy says:

When we were torpedoed on the port side abreast 'A' turret four young seamen, amongst them my special friend Jock McGuire from Dundee, died instantly in the shell room. As the ship listed quickly to port 'A' shell and handing rooms and storerooms up to the main deck were flooded. As hands went to abandon ship stations the submarine escaped into the depths.

The trim in *Barham* was steadily regained as gigantic submersible pumps were put to work. Down by the bows with thousands of tons of sea water flooding the forward compartments the badly damaged ship held her own against the elements. When the ship's company were mustered by Divisions the four young seamen were found to be missing. At intervals of 15 minutes the ship's tannoy system crackled with the calls of Bosun's Mates requiring the missing men, giving their names, to report to the Master-at-Arms. Alas, they neither heard nor heeded the calls; their broken bodies were found later when the ship docked.

The destroyers on the screen at first continued with *Repulse*, but later *Imogen*, *Icarus* and *Khartoum* joined *Barham* and carried out a circular anti-submarine patrol round the ship. It was the captain of *Repulse* who ordered this move; he said later:

As the screening destroyers had taken no action, I at once ordered the three nearest to *Barham* to close her. It appeared that the screen had not observed the attack and it was probable that the submarine had fired from outside the screen. Allowing a six minute run of the torpedo and the time taken for the destroyer to turn and close, an interval of 15 to 20 minutes would have elapsed before the destroyer could reach the probable position of the submarine, assuming it had dived deep. I considered, therefore, that instant action was essential, every second counted, and that if the destroyers closed *Barham* at once they could best be instructed by *Barham* as to the direction and distance in which to hunt the submarine.

When *Barham* was hit, the damage control and repair parties proceeded to their stations at once. At 1455, when a rough estimate of the damage was available, reports showed that the engines and boilers were undamaged and the flooding appeared to be under control; *Barham* proceeded on course at ten knots. As the extent of the damage became clearer, speed was gradually increased, a speed on the engines of 16 knots was reached by 1520. This, allowing for zig-zagging, gave approximately 14 knots. It was found possible to maintain this speed except for periods when it was found necessary, temporarily, to reduce speed on the advice of the damage control officer and on account of a peculiar noise in the starboard low pressure turbine which occurred at times.

Despite everything morale was of a reasonably high order and the crew on board *Barham*, proud that their ship had been able to withstand a torpedo attack, worked with a will in an orderly fashion. Naturally the question of leave cropped up, the most debatable point being from which port it would be given. The Scots on board were even being rash enough to stake a cherished rum issue on the certainty, in their minds, of the ship putting in at a Clydeside dockyard.

At 1624, *Isis*, returning from her mercy mission, rejoined the screen. She was accompanied by the destroyer *Nubian*. *Barham* was ordered to act independently and *Nubian* was directed to screen *Barham*. It was nearly dark at 1700; darkness lasted until just after 1900, after which there ensued a very light night with a full moon. *Repulse* had been ordered to proceed independently at high speed and the 1st and 2nd anti-submarine forces at the Clyde were ordered to proceed to screen *Barham*. *Repulse* took

Isis and *Inglefield* with her owing to the probability of the presence of U-boats between the Hebrides and Northern Ireland.

Earlier the Commander-in-Chief of the Home Fleet sent a message to *Repulse* and *Barham* asking that further consideration be given to sending two destroyers back to hunt for the U-boat which had torpedoed the battleship, but the idea was discarded. At this time, 1725, it was not known for certain whether *Barham* could maintain her speed and it would have been dangerous to leave her with an inadequate escort, particularly so as *Khartoum* had no depth-charges left. There was also the time element; it was three hours from the time of the attack and the submarine could have made its escape in any direction.

Another signal from the Commander-in-Chief ordered the Flag Officer in Charge at Liverpool to prepare Gladstone Dock for *Barham*, the battleship being notified at the same time.

John Wright says: 'It came almost as great a shock to the Scotsmen as the explosion when the news that our destination was to be Liverpool, and thus bang went a few dozen tots, plus the Scots' hopes of a Ne'erday at home. Enough even to make a haggis weep!'

During the evening *Barham* altered course to avoid a minefield that had been reported by *Icarus*; later Bana Head light was reported on a bearing of 166 degrees, land was near. At 2325 the destroyers *Faulknor* and *Mashona* were sighted and were ordered to proceed in accordance with orders issued by the Commander-in-Chief.

Barham continued to hold her speed during the night and in the morning was met by *Kandahar* who joined the screen. There was an alarm midway through the afternoon watch when a destroyer reported that she was investigating a contact, and a minute later that she was 'in contact' on the port bow of *Barham* and a minute again later dropped two depth-charges. *Icarus* joined in the hunt but this was called off when contact was lost and both destroyers rejoined the screen and the circumstances were reported to the Commander-in-Chief. By now *Barham* was in the Irish Sea and twice had to alter course to avoid a trawler and shipping; Morecambe Bay light was sighted abeam at a distance of 2½ miles and an hour-and-a-half later the destroyers were ordered to cover *Barham* from seaward while the battleship stopped to embark a

pilot and secure tugs, for after seemingly endless hours of day and
night battling against a fate determined on overtaking her *Barham*
had reached the longed for safer waters of the Mersey.

Early in the morning of Saturday 30 December *Barham* entered
Gladstone Dock and shortly afterwards secured alongside the
north wall. It was a desperately tired but happy bunch of sailors
who greeted a silence left by the stopping of all engines as the
lame duck was taken in hand.

Early on New Year's Eve the hands were employed disembark-
ing ammunition into a waiting lighter. By 3 January the ship had
been sufficiently lightened to commence pumping out the dry-
dock, props were skilfully positioned and soon the ship was
resting on the bottom. Next day the bodies of the four men
killed by the torpedo hit were recovered from 'A' shell room;
the oldest of them was only twenty-two years of age. John Wright
says: 'That some had to die in the explosion was a tragedy which
affected us all deeply and took a very long time in getting over,
thankfully though, the number of casualties had been small.' The
funeral took place the next day with full military honours, the
Marine band and most of the ship's company attended the inter-
ment at Liverpool cemetery and on the ship the colours were
half-masted at the time.

The full extent of the damage could be seen now the ship was in
dry-dock; the torpedo struck the port side between 44 and 50
stations, at a depth of approximately 28 feet. The greatest angle
of heel experienced was seven degrees and this was corrected by
pumping over oil fuel. The estimated draught immediately after
the explosion was 40 feet 6 inches forward and 27 feet aft; this
was partly corrected by transference of oil fuel and on arrival
in Liverpool the draught was 39 feet forward and 29 feet 6 inches
aft; normal draught under the conditions would have been 31 feet.

How much heavier the casualties might have been was rather
discomfortingly revealed when an expert examination of the
damage showed that the area covered by the explosion had ter-
minated but a bare few inches away from the main forward magazines. At the time of the torpedoing the watertight door organisation was in the cruising state.

After the ship had been hit the lookouts in *Barham* were
questioned as to whether they had seen anything; their replies

were negative, but two leading aircraftmen looking out of a scuttle on the aircraft store on the port side of the deck saw a feather of spray as though something was cutting through the water about 1,200 yards away. It appeared for a second or two before disappearing, then both men saw it again bearing approximately Red 90 degrees and travelling at slight inclination towards the ship. Almost at once an explosion occurred and they saw no more.

Both these ratings were experienced in aircraft-carriers and other ships, and were quite definite that what they saw was the feather caused by a periscope and not the bubble track of a torpedo. The captain of *Barham* recorded the opinion that what they had seen was not, in his opinion, a periscope and so the evidence was disregarded. Ted Eustance disagrees with his captain about the periscope sightings. He was also in the store at the time and remembers that a current favourite record, 'Roll out the barrel', had just been put on the gramophone turntable when Yorkshireman Jimmy Whitelegg, from Elland, who was looking out of the scuttle said he could see a periscope. As Jimmy was known as a joker nobody took much notice, but another man looked out and said he could also see a periscope; then there was the explosion.

Repulse reported that a second torpedo exploded in *Barham*'s wake. If this was so the angle between the torpedo which hit *Barham* and the one which exploded in her wake would be approximately 12 degrees if fired from the position described by the two airmen.

It was considered unlikely that a salvo would have been dispersed to this extent at such a range, and that it is more probable that the submarine fired a dispersed salvo from a position outside the screen. What the airmen probably saw was the ripple of *Khartoum*'s wake, observed Captain Walker.

The captain of *Repulse* reported that no sign of a torpedo track was visible from his ship. About ten seconds before *Barham* was hit a lookout observed a disturbance in the water to the westward of *Barham* on a bearing of Green 140 from *Repulse*. A minute later the captain himself observed a disturbance in the water which was plainly visible close to the westward of *Barham*'s track and fine on the starboard quarter of *Repulse*. The disturbance appeared similar to the effect of a depth charge exploded at 100–150 feet. This may have been caused by a torpedo which had missed *Barham* and detonated at the end of its run or on crossing tracks.

The captain of *Repulse* considered it possible that the U-boat fired three torpedoes at maximum range from outside the screen and that one missed ahead of *Barham*. In *Repulse* a small underwater explosion was heard, shortly followed by a larger one similar to that of a pattern of depth charges. An Avro Anson on patrol which had been in the close vicinity passed over at 1500 on a southerly course and was ordered to search for a submarine to the eastward of *Barham*, but the pilot replied that he was out of fuel and returning to base.

At the time of the explosion the captain of *Inglefield* was in his sea cabin. The first he knew of the incident was a series of explosions following quickly one upon another. The sound was similar to that made by a destroyer dropping a pattern of depth-charges. The captain then immediately went to the bridge and observed that *Barham* had hauled out of line to port, reduced speed, and hoisted two cones point to point at the starboard yard arm.

Inglefield by this time was in the port bow position, *Repulse* and *Barham* had just altered to the mean course after completing the port leg of the zig-zag and they were therefore in line ahead. *Inglefield* immediately turned to starboard with the intention of carrying out a search and at the same time ordered *Khartoum* to take her position on the screen.

Khartoum, however, had also altered course and informed *Inglefield* that she had been ordered by *Repulse* to go to the assistance of *Barham*. The stationing signal was therefore negatived. At this point it became clear that *Repulse* was taking charge so *Inglefield* regained her position screening *Repulse*.

The commanding officer of *Imogen* was also in his sea cabin when the torpedo exploded; he likened the sound to that caused by a depth-charge. Arriving on the bridge he saw that *Barham* had not turned with *Repulse* and immediately altered course to close *Barham*. It was observed that *Barham* was flying the signal 'I have been struck by torpedo starboard side' it was seen that the battleship, however, was listing to port. As only one explosion had been heard it appeared that *Barham* was uncertain on which side she had been struck. *Icarus* was already sweeping to starboard while *Khartoum* was manoeuvring at high speed to port. *Imogen* reduced speed to 15 knots before crossing *Barham*'s bow and a sweep was carried out on her port side. No echoes were obtained and so no depth-charges were dropped.

The commanding officer of *Khartoum* was informed by his officer of the watch that there had been an explosion in *Barham* and he arrived on the bridge in time to see the column of water falling. This appeared to be on the starboard side, that is on the far side, and the captain understood the officer of the watch and the yeoman of signals, who actually witnessed the explosion, to confirm this. Further confirmation was provided by *Barham* hoisting two cones, base to base, on the starboard side although this signal is used in torpedo exercises. *Khartoum* held her course thinking that the boat would be required to screen *Repulse* while the other destroyers hunted, as it was known by the commanding officer of *Repulse* and by Captain (D) that all the depth charges on *Khartoum* had been expended. The order then arrived from *Repulse* to stand by *Barham* in case she required assistance. Being still under the impression that *Barham* had been hit on the starboard side *Khartoum* proceeded to carry out an anti-submarine sweep about one mile to starboard of that ship's original course. By reason however of *Barham*'s list to port, and despite the two cones still hoisted, the captain enquired again of his two bridge companions and was informed that the explosion had been on the port side. He accordingly passed under *Barham*'s stern to the port side, by which time *Imogen* had arrived and was sweeping there. *Khartoum* then took up the unoccupied position on *Barham*'s port bow.

Admiral Sir Charles Forbes, Commander-in-Chief of the Home Fleet, aboard HMS *Rodney* wrote:

This was not a creditable performance on the part of anyone concerned. It should have been apparent to all present that a U-boat was in the vicinity when *Isis* was sent off to pick up the 15 men in an open boat.

When *Barham* was struck by the torpedo none of the destroyers on the screen, except *Khartoum*, appeared to have 'noticed' it until their Commanding Officers, who felt the explosion, appeared on their bridges.

Barham hoisted an incorrect signal that she had been hit on the starboard side while listing to port and there appears to have been doubt in the captain's mind from the W/T signal made, whether it was a mine or torpedo. The engines of *Barham* were stopped and put astern and it was not until 14 minutes after the explosion that they were put to 'ahead' again.

No hunting of any description was carried out or ordered by any senior officer present or the captain of *Barham*. Instructions laid down in the Manual state that the first two anti-submarine vessels to close should be directed to search and hunt in the estimated position of the submarine.

The instruction referred to by Sir Charles Forbes was Article 205, paragraph 7 of Fleet Tactical Instructions. Another clause read; 'The function of the close screen is to counter-attack immediately any submarine which they themselves sight or detect, or which is indicated by an anti-submarine patrol aircraft.'

It appeared to the Director of Training and Staff Duties Division of the Admiralty that apart from the initial failure to observe the explosion, the responsibility for the absence of effective offensive action did not rest primarily with the destroyers. He thought that failure to counter-attack appeared to have arisen because of *Barham's* incorrect signal indicating that she had been hit on the starboard side. This was the reason *Inglefield* accordingly proceeded to search that side, as did *Icarus* after originally closing *Barham* and confusion was further increased by the battleship's apparent uncertainty about the cause of the explosion — in spite of the depth of water and the earlier submarine report.

The Director of Anti-submarine Warfare wrote later:

I am sure nobody imagines that four destroyers can give anything like 100% protection to two capital ships. The real protection is the moral effect of the destroyers being present, which in its turn is dependent on the hope that any U-boat commander will realise that, although he might succeed in torpedoing a ship, he would then be hunted relentlessly until destroyed. That this was not done on this occasion, is most regrettable.

The director then pointed out that the Senior Officer of Destroyers had only taken over his command six weeks previously. He also stated that it was not the general practice of destroyer officers to be hidebound by written instructions when such an emergency arose and thought that for success in future it would be better if the Senior Officer of Destroyers was given a free hand to act as he thought best.

After the attack the Rear-Admiral Destroyers felt it necessary to issue a temporary memorandum to Home Fleet destroyers on the anti-submarine protection of a disabled ship which said:

> The instructions issued in Fleet Tactical Instructions visualise an unscreened ship damaged or broken down possibly after an action, and indicate a method of protecting her from submarine attack while stopped or on subsequent passage at very low speeds. It seems necessary to emphasise that the best way of protecting a screened ship which is damaged by torpedo fire from a submarine is to counter attack at once with all screening forces. If it is in doubt which side the attack came from, screening forces, each their own side under their senior officers, are to search. If the side is known the senior officer of the screen is to organise a search by all destroyers on that side but destroyers should not wait for a signal but proceed at once to hunt. *That a ship screened by destroyers should be torpedoed is an insult to destroyer command* and destroyers are to see that any submarine which does attack under these conditions is sunk.

The Rear-Admiral referring to the attack and the wrong signal hoisted by *Barham* added, 'The destroyers were much too slow off the mark'.

The Director of Anti-submarine Warfare added a footnote: 'I fully sympathise with Rear-Admiral (D)'s dictum "that a ship screened by destroyers should be torpedoed is an insult to the destroyer command": and I am only surprised that he did not add "that destroyers should wait for orders before taking offensive action is an insult to the destroyer command".'

The attack was reported in the British press under the heading 'Battleship's escape: Now in harbour after U-boat attack'.

With so many warships at sea, providing targets for U-boats, our naval casualties have been remarkably few. Latest victim is a battleship, whose name has not been revealed in order to avoid giving information to the enemy. Hit by a U-boat's torpedo, the battleship was able to reach harbour under her own steam. She was not seriously damaged. Of her crew of about 1,100 only four ratings are reported 'missing, presumed killed', another was seriously injured. According to the German High Command the attack took place off the west coast of Scotland and the vessel is one of the Queen Elizabeth class. It was ascertained on enquiry that the battleship referred to in the Admiralty announcement was the same ship as that mentioned by the German High Command. There are five battleships of the Queen Elizabeth class, all of about 30,000 tons. They carry eight 15-inch guns, powerful secondary armament and aircraft, and steam at 24 to 25 knots. The ships *Queen Elizabeth*, *Warspite*, *Valiant*, *Barham* and *Malaya* were completed between January 1915 and February 1916. They are heavily protected against attack.

It is now time to return to Liverpool. When fully inspected it was seen that the bulge structure of *Barham* had been opened up over an area of 32 feet and forced inboard 6 feet. It was the extensive damage to the bulge that had caused the flooding although fortunately the armament and main machinery were not damaged except that the main for'ard turrets were out of action due to their magazines being flooded. A conference on the refitting programme was held on board. Condenser tubes were replaced as were the turbine blades. Extra armour plating was fitted with rivetting going on day and night so that there was not much sleep for the crew still aboard. While the refitting was in progress a workman from Cammel Laird was injured by a falling wooden batten. It was much about this time that two ratings returning rather inebriated from a run ashore fell from the side of the dock on to the concrete below and were killed. These two were also buried in Liverpool cemetery and it is often said that six men were killed as a result of the torpedoing, whereas it was four as stated, plus these two who died accidentally.

When the full extent of the damage was assessed, and an estimate given for the time needed for repairs, the ship's company were given long leave, in turns; it was their first taste of travelling in blacked-out wartime Britain.

Along with the mining of *Nelson*, the torpedoing of *Barham* was one of the best kept secrets of the war, and Ted Eustance found himself in trouble when he was at Lee-on-Solent immediately afterwards waiting for *Barham*'s seaplane 'Mitzi' to arrive, for imperilling security by asking after her whereabouts. The Swordfish floatplane K8363 finally left the ship for the Royal Naval Air Station on 21 January. Ted Eustance was not the only member of the ship's company to leave; Captain Walker left, as did 27 marines on draft. Two parties of boys joined from the Royal Naval Barracks at Portsmouth; when leave was granted these boys had to be back on board at 2115, whereas the men were granted all night leave. Sid Haines left the ship in April to take a Stoker Petty Officers' course at Portsmouth.

A party, consisting of Lieutenant-Commander Paine and Lieutenant Atkinson and 82 ratings, had earlier been sent to man the guns on the crippled *Iron Duke*. This party returned on 13 April and proceeded on eight days leave. A further contingent with Lieutenant-Commander C.R. Stratton-Brown and Lieutenant A.J. Cobham and 88 ratings, including Frank Loy, took their place, returning on 18 May.

Next day, 16 May, seven ratings were lent to the Tribal class destroyer *Maori* about to leave for the Norwegian campaign. One of these ratings, Cyril Lassiter, took leave of his twin brother, Signalman Norman, who remained in *Barham*. They had joined the battleship together in 1938. Unfortunately Cyril did not return to *Barham*, he was one of the fatal casualties in the destroyer. A contingent of marines from *Barham* were also sent to Norway.

While they were away some of the remaining hands chipped the ship's side, for she undocked on 19 April and berthed alongside the north wall. On 25 April the Foreign Secretary, Mr Anthony Eden, visited the ship during the morning. On May Day the hands were surprised to receive the order that dress of the day would be No 1's. Just after midday all was revealed, when they were mustered to a position on the jetty as Their Majesties the King and Queen visited the dockyard. Two weeks later the new Captain, Geoffrey Cooke, ordered lower deck to be cleared so that he could address them.

On 28 May there was an air raid alert at 0400, the 0.5 inch guns crews were closed up, while upper deck parties rigged hoses and emergency landing parties fell in with their equipment. After two hours the parties fell out. Later that day *Hood* entered Gladstone dock.

While repairs were taking place a new anti-dive bomber device was fitted on *Barham*'s 'B' turret; this fired small parachute mines into the air. Later, in action, they were found not to be successful as they tended to drift back on to the ship, consequently the device was removed at Port Said.

In June, after Dunkirk, with things looking very black indeed for England, contingency plans were made for *Barham* to carry the royal family to Canada should there be a German invasion. Fortunately the now nearly repaired battleship was not required for this purpose.

CHAPTER TEN

Fiasco off Dakar

A number of events occurred while *Barham* was at Liverpool. In the middle of February Captain Vian in HMS *Cossack* had released 299 prisoners from the German prison ship *Altmark* in a Norwegian fiord, and the phrase 'The Navy's here' slipped into the English language. On 9 April Germany had invaded Denmark and Norway; some men from *Barham* were transferred to ships going out to fight at Norway. On 2 May British troops withdrew from Norway and eight days later Belgium, Holland and Luxembourg were invaded; parachute troops landed near Rotterdam. On 11 May Winston Churchill was appointed Prime Minister in charge of a National Government; three days later the Dutch ceased fighting and two weeks later still the Belgian Army capitulated. By now the British Expeditionary Force had been driven back to the Channel coast but on 1 June the bulk of them had been safely landed back in Britain less their equipment, from Dunkirk. On 10 June, Benito Mussolini, the dictator of Italy eager for some spoils, declared war on Britain and France. The Battle of the Mediterranean started the next day when Italian planes bombed Malta; eleven days later Alexandria was bombed.

Meanwhile in France, the Germans captured Paris on 14 June and eight days later a French delegation agreed terms for an armistice. A French puppet government was set up at Vichy under Marshal Pétain, the hero of Verdun in the First World War.

General Charles de Gaulle, a little known French General, arrived in England in mid-June. This extremely tall man, who looked even taller wearing his pill-box hat, had only recently been promoted but had commanded the 4th Armoured Division in action at Abbeville. Prime Minister Winston Churchill was disappointed that not one well-known French politician had made his way to England to take command of those Frenchmen who wished to carry on the struggle against Hitler; at this time the French General was lacking experience as a politician, for it was only in later years he was thought of as a statesman. As nobody else crossed the Channel, General de Gaulle was recognised as the leader of the 'Free French' in the war against Germany, they did not recognise the armistice made by the Vichy Government.

In the hot summer of 1940, with Hermann Goering's Luftwaffe attacking shipping and airfields in the south-east and when Britain stood alone fighting the foe just 25 miles away on the other side of the Channel, plans of an offensive nature were being prepared. It was feared in London that the Axis might seize the important French naval base at Dakar in Senegal and thereby threaten the vital Atlantic shipping routes. Concern was also felt in the United States, for Dakar was the nearest point in Africa to the American continent.

Winston Churchill and his War Cabinet colleagues were keen that the African port should come under the banner of the 'Free French'. Plans were made for an Anglo-French force to sail for West Africa under the code name of Operation Menace. At the end of August a motley collection of warships and transports carrying British and Free French troops sailed from the Clyde, Scapa and Liverpool, all bound for West Africa. Admiral John Cunningham was selected to lead the naval force, General Irwin was to lead the British force, while General de Gaulle headed the Free French contingent. The intended date for the departure of the fleet had been 15 August but the forces were not ready at this time. This was the day when the Battle of Britain was at its highest and the Luftwaffe suffered heavy losses.

Barham, now ready for sea again, but not worked up, was selected to lead the naval ships of the operation; this was to be known as Force M. It was thought that the trip would serve the dual purpose of protecting the ships and give the crew the opportunity to work up at the same time. *Barham*, with an escort of four destroyers, left Scapa on 28 August for Gibraltar where it was to pick up the ships attached to it from Force H, based on the Rock. Among the ships was the battleship *Resolution*, eight 15-inch and twelve 6-inch guns, the famous aircraft carrier *Ark Royal* and 6 destroyers.

The convoy for Operation Menace left on the last day of August; finally assembled, it comprised six transport, including *Westernland*, *Ettrick* and *Karanja*, carrying some 2,700 French and 4,200 British troops, two Free French sloops, storeships, the cruisers *Devonshire* and *Fiji* with seven destroyers. Unfortunately *Fiji* was torpedoed, though not sunk on the first day out.

Barham arrived at Gibraltar with her escort on 2 September; ten eventful months had passed since she last left the shadow of the Rock on her way back to bolster up the Home Fleet. The *Duchess* had been rammed and *Barham* had been torpedoed, but the repairs in Gladstone Dock had once again put the grand old battleship back in action. Four days at Gibraltar were sufficient to refuel and replenish before *Barham* left the Straits sailing south again to visit another familiar port, Freetown. It will be remembered that *Barham* had swung round a buoy in the Bay there during a visit to the Sierra Leone capital on the West African cruise of 1928. None of the crew of that commission still remained on board but stories of the stifling heat below decks in that latitude had been passed on and were soon found to be true when the big ship arrived on 15 September.

In the meantime there had been another development four days earlier when a force of six Vichy French warships from Toulon sailed through the Straits of Gibraltar into the Atlantic before turning southwards to Casablanca. The Admiralty ordered *Renown* with an escorting force of destroyers to shadow the French warships but by the time the battle-cruiser raised steam and put to sea, over seven hours had elapsed and the French squadron had a big lead. The British had no objection to the French ships going to Casablanca but instructions were received that they were not to be allowed to enter Dakar, which was thought to be under German influence.

British aircraft, patrolling round the French force at a discreet distance, reported that the ships had reached the Moroccan port; but after refuelling, the French ships sailed again unseen during the night and steamed south to Dakar.

When an airborne reconnaissance revealed the ships were no longer at Casablanca *Renown* retraced her route the 150 miles back north to Gibraltar, for the destroyer escort to refuel, and to await further orders.

While the crew of *Barham* and the other heavy units were sweltering at Freetown the remainder of Force M was still at sea. The convoy was already 350 miles south of Dakar en route to Freetown when a few minutes after midnight on 14 September Admiral John Cunningham received a message from the Admiralty ordering him to use every available ship to prevent the French ships reaching Dakar.

The cruisers *Australia* and *Cumberland* which had recently joined the force from other commands, turned back together with *Devonshire*, *Ark Royal* and their escorts, with the intention of intercepting the French ships north of Dakar, but by the time they arrived, the French ships had already docked, at midday on 14 September.

Aircraft from *Ark Royal* confirmed the six Vichy French ships were at Dakar; there was nothing left but for Force M to once again proceed to Freetown to regroup, replenish and replan. When the ships steamed into the large bay at Freetown, surrounded by the lush green tropical hills, they were soon surrounded by the native boats plying their wares, just as if they had been peacetime cruise liners. The crews on the warships, and the troops of the convoy were still officially unaware of their ultimate destination; they were soon put in the picture by the natives for it was an open secret in Freetown that the expedition was bound for Dakar.

As the last ships entered Freetown, planners in London had already decided to cancel the operation, but when this was communicated to the men on the spot in West Africa they were strongly against this, and in the end the Prime Minister was swayed by their argument. In the afternoon of 18 September full authority for the launching of Operation Menace was received from London.

General de Gaulle was on board *Westernland*, a 16,000 ton Dutch liner with Free French troops; he was very anxious that the confrontation of Frenchmen by Frenchmen should succeed through threats of force rather than bloodshed. General Irwin, in command of the British military force, was aboard *Devonshire* with Admiral John Cunningham, and they, together with General de Gaulle, were nominated as joint leaders of the expedition.

The replanning had been agreed by all parties when news arrived that the Vichy French warship squadron had left Dakar on

19 September; although it was not clear at the time, they were bound for Libreville. *Australia* and *Cumberland* were already at sea and Admiral Cunningham notified General de Gaulle that he was going to sink the Vichy French force if they refused to do as they were ordered by the British. In the end this was not necessary, but their breakout caused *Barham* to be ordered to sea.

The battleship left harbour in mid-afternoon, quickly passed through the boom defences while the boilers were being flashed-up and an hour later the old battleship was steaming at 19 knots. Speed was later reduced when paravanes were streamed. Night action stations were secured during the last dog-watch. After an uneventful night *Barham* dropped anchor at Freetown at 0630 the next morning. Three hours later Major-General Irwin and his staff arrived on board and a further three hours later Vice-Admiral John Cunningham and his staff were piped aboard as the Admiral's flag was struck on the yardarm. All was ready for Operation Menace.

In mid-morning of Saturday 21 September *Barham* weighed anchor, passed through the boom defences, out past Sierra Leone lighthouse, on the way to Dakar. Even out at sea the heat was still oppressive. On board *Barham* the water from the cold taps came out hot. During the afternoon the 6-inch gun cruiser HMS *Dragon* joined from the South African Squadron and in the early hours of Sunday she was despatched to investigate when a ship was sighted; an hour later it was seen to be HMS *Cumberland*. Soon after dawn *Dragon* was again despatched to investigate another ship, this time a merchant one, but it was found to be the British ship *Thongate* about its lawful business. *Barham* was making 14 knots later in the morning when the destroyer HMS *Foresight* closed her port side and transferred despatches. During the night speed was increased by one knot and at 0600 on Monday the ships were closed up outside a foggy Dakar, waiting for the operation to begin.

With hindsight this would appear to have been a heaven-sent opportunity for the force to land and seize the town before the alarm could have been raised but there was never any chance of this happening as General de Gaulle rightly wanted a bloodless coup with no French lives lost. He was, however, to be disappointed; the inhabitants ashore did not know of him and had no desire to join his Free French forces. This fact soon became apparent to a small party of Frenchmen who had surreptitiously made their way ashore; unfortunately they were unable to communicate their findings back to the ships.

Six biplane Swordfish aircraft took off from the carrier *Ark Royal* and flew over the town through the fog dropping leaflets containing appeals to the forces and civilians of Dakar to join the Free French forces. The biplanes were fired on by the Vichy French battleship *Richelieu* and French fighters also attacked the planes. A Free French sloop approached the harbour and two motor boats were lowered and despatched ashore with letters for the military commanders. The letters were delivered but the motor boats were quickly sent on their way — the reply was unfavourable. By now the authorities ashore were fully alert to the strong force offshore which comprised *Barham, Resolution, Ark Royal, Devonshire, Cumberland* and ten destroyers. The *Westernland*, carrying General de Gaulle, was also in sight of *Barham*.

At 0950 a large French flying-boat was sighted on the starboard beam of *Barham* and a quarter of an hour later shore batteries opened fire on the destroyer HMS *Foresight*.

General de Gaulle had made three broadcasts to the French sailors ashore telling them of the powerful force outside the harbour and saying that there would be no trouble if his landing was unopposed — if it was he threatened that the large British force he had with him would intervene. General de Gaulle made his fourth and last broadcast after the shore batteries had opened fire. Admiral Cunningham sent a message ashore saying that he would be compelled to return fire if the shore batteries recommenced firing; he received a reply saying that unless he moved twenty miles from the port the firing would recommence.

Admiral Cunningham replied by bringing in his force to 4,000 yards. At 1058 a lookout on *Barham* sighted a French submarine on the surface on the port bow and fire was opened with the 6-inch guns. At much the same time *Foresight* was hit for'ard by the shore battery. At 1103 the submarine was hit twice by destroyers. At the same time *Barham* was ordered to open fire on the Cap Manuel batteries ashore, together with *Resolution*. Altogether more than 100 rounds of 15-inch calibre shells were fired from the battleships. A shell from ashore hit *Cumberland*, reducing her speed. Soon after this hit Admiral Cunningham ordered a cease fire and withdrew out of range.

The submarine that had been hit by *Barham*'s 6-inch guns was *Persée*; she was finished off by depth charges but most of her crew were saved by vessels from the shore.

Some of the battleship's 'overs' caused damage in the town and the Governor General ashore confirmed that any landing would be opposed: 'French blood had already begun to flow'.

At 1254 a destroyer obtained a submarine contact and *Barham* altered course away; 18 minutes later *Barham* observed a periscope 2,640 yards away and again altered course. At 1400 *Barham* set course to southward to make contact with *Westernland*. An alternative plan, to land a force at Rufisque, west of Dakar, was cancelled when aircraft reported the movement of two Vichy French cruisers toward Rufisque Bay and submarines were also believed to be in the vicinity. One of two destroyers escorting the cruisers was hit by a British shell and sank with heavy casualties. In the early evening a Blackburn Skua from *Ark Royal* made a forced landing on the port bow of *Barham* and the crew of two were rescued by the destroyer *Fortune*.

During the evening the joint commanders received a message from Winston Churchill telling them to continue with the operation. An ultimatum expiring at dawn on 24th was delivered just before midnight. In essence it said that as there was a danger of the port being handed over to the common enemy it was the duty of the Allies to prevent this eventuality and if permission to land was not received by 0600 the powerful forces at the Allies' command would open fire.

The French admiral commanding the port was most upset at the ultimatum; he had never considered it likely that the Germans would occupy the port; the very thought was repugnant to him, but he had no intention of bowing to de Gaulle's pressure.

Barham turned back toward Dakar before a reply was received from the ultimatum. When the reply did come, signalled from the battleship *Richelieu*, it announced that Dakar would be defended to the end.

At dawn Admiral Cunningham ordered an air strike from *Ark Royal*, the targets being *Richelieu*, the cruisers and the forts.

Heavy bombing was heard, on land, in the *Barham* at 0700 as the aircraft carried out their task. The French shore defenders fired on the aircraft and the ships. At much the same time the Vichy French submarine *Ajax* sighted *Barham* and *Resolution* and dived for an attack. Destroyers located the submarine on Asdic, so when she surfaced to make an attack she was forced below again by a rain of depth-charges. The attack so damaged the submarine that she was forced to the surface where her commander gave the order to scuttle. It was shortly before 0900 that *Barham* sighted the submarine flying a white flag, and the destroyer *Fortune* on the port bow; the destroyer took off the crew of *Ajax* before the submarine slowly sank to the bottom.

At 0935 *Barham* opened fire with its main armament against the fort on Cap Manuel, the six guns on Gorée Island and the battleship *Richelieu. Resolution, Australia* and *Devonshire* were also engaged firing at the port which was now covered with a smoke screen. At 1013 Admiral Cunningham ordered a cease-fire. The heel and trim of *Barham* was faulty due to damage to the starboard lower bulge. Two hours later *Barham* was bombed by two enemy aircraft which were fired on by the battleship's 4-inch guns.

On board *Barham* the crew were just able to snatch a corned beef sandwich before being engaged again from the shore at 1250. The ships steamed parallel to the coast and *Barham* opened fire on *Richelieu* with her main armament at 1307. At 1322 *Barham* was hit, probably by a 9.4-inch shell from Cap Manuel. The shell hit the fore superstructure and on the starboard bulge amidships but caused little damage and no fatalities. *Barham* ceased fire and retired southwards zig-zagging at 16 knots; two hours later action stations were secured and the ship reduced to fourth degree of readiness. Soon afterwards *Resolution* parted company. An hour later *Barham* joined company with the convoy that had anxiously been waiting for news of the events at Dakar. General de Gaulle arrived on board from *Westernland* and no sooner was he aboard when a Swordfish from *Ark Royal* force landed on the starboard side of the battleship. Both crew members were rescued.

Lieutenant A.J. Cobham, whom we met earlier, and was now turret officer of 'B' turret, speaking of the damage recalls:

The effect of the hit was to make a mess in the space through which the shell had passed and it killed one rat! Several of us were looking at the rather superficial damage, when we realised that had 'B' not been trained on the beam, the gunhouse would have taken a direct hit on the side.

Humidity conditions were quite appalling and I soon abandoned any idea of the crew wearing anti-flash gear. In fact we wore overalls and nothing underneath. In the magazines men were passing out, being dragged out into the handling room, having a bucket of water thrown over them and then going back in to have another bash. Between bombardment runs we withdrew to seaward and the gunhouse crews were allowed on top of the turrets. Completely disregarding the Captain, Admiral and General on the bridge above, we all stripped off our overalls and in our birthday suits faced the breeze holding the overalls over our heads to dry out. I should have said that first on stripping we would wring out the overalls, getting a good mugful out of each!

General de Gaulle was disappointed that the ship's guns had failed to neutralise the shore batteries. He was also disappointed to hear that the Vichy French battle-cruiser *Strasbourg* had sailed from Toulon. In the event he suggested that he should proceed to Bathurst, to give his confined troops a breather while further plans were made. He left *Barham* just as the dog-watches were changing and returned to *Westernland*.

After de Gaulle left, the British commanders decided to have another try the next day, notifying General de Gaulle and the War Cabinet of their intentions.

Barham joined the company of *Resolution*, *Australia* and *Devonshire* and all steamed at 12 knots through the night. At 0330 *Ark Royal* was sighted. Two hours later a reconnaissance aircraft flew off from the carrier together with anti-submarine and fighter patrols. The aircraft were attacked by French fighters.

When dawn broke it was a clear day; the fog and the smoke of battle had disappeared, the sun shone in the cloudless blue sky, affording maximum visibility. At 0710 *Barham* sighted land and was ready, all closed up, for the bombardment. Her target was the battleship *Richelieu*. Just before 0900 a spherical object was sighted on the starboard bow and fired on by the close range armament. Four minutes later *Barham* altered course to starboard as she was engaged by *Richelieu* and the shore batteries; a minute later still, torpedo tracks were sighted on the starboard quarter and *Resolution* was struck by a torpedo on the port side amidships, immediately taking on a list.

Everything was happening now, at 0904 *Barham* making 18 knots steadied on course and opened fire on *Richelieu* from 21,000 yards with her main armament. Two destroyers made a smoke screen to protect the listing battleship while *Foresight* attacked the submarine and at 0910 reported that she had sunk her; actually the submarine had made good its escape.

The British ships were unable to see their targets as the enemy again generated a smoke screen but *Barham* hit *Richelieu* and *Richelieu* hit *Barham* both with 15-inch guns; in both instances the damage was slight. *Barham* altered course to cover *Resolution* and ceased firing shortly afterwards at 0921. *Resolution* was still able to make 12 knots and *Barham* zig-zagged astern of her. By now the convoy was in sight and soon afterwards *Ark Royal* was seen. Action stations was sounded again at 1040 when two bombs were dropped on the convoy; fifteen minutes later another French aircraft dropped a bomb on the starboard beam of *Resolution*.

When *Resolution* had been torpedoed and was seen to be badly damaged Admiral Cunningham weighed up the situation and decided to withdraw — had he but known the French ashore were nearly out of ammunition and almost ready to surrender! In England the Chiefs of Staff agreed with his decision as there now appeared no chance of occupying Dakar.

In the early afternoon *Barham* spent an anxious seven minutes stopped while an engine defect was made good. Twelve hours later, in the early hours of 26 September, *Resolution* also stopped, her list was slightly reduced to 11 degrees and gradually the fires were being put out. *Barham* remained in the vicinity until 0535 when the ships proceeded at 5 knots but four hours later *Barham* was requested to take the stricken old battleship in tow. Both tow ropes were soon fixed and a cutter took pumping gear to *Resolution*. Just after 1100 *Resolution* took the strain of the cable; the peacetime practice of *Barham* taking a battleship in tow had not been wasted. Course was set and the battleships made 8 knots, later increased to 9½ knots. In the early evening a full calibre firing was carried out to clear the 15-inch and 6-inch guns. The two battleships continued together during the night, protected by their escorts; the only scare came when a small vessel was sighted; *Devonshire* investigated but everything was in order. In mid-morning the port tow parted and it took over two hours to pass and secure a new tow. The line held and the battleships were making 12 knots at midday.

The next morning, Saturday 28 September, *Ark Royal* and *Australia* parted company and the cruiser *Delhi* joined. During the afternoon *Resolution* was sufficiently repaired to make her own way and *Barham* hauled in both wires but continued in station astern of the damaged ship. Colours were later half-masted on the ships for thirty minutes when the funeral of a rating from *Resolution* took place.

At long last Freetown hove in sight at dawn on Sunday. The rest of the force had arrived two days earlier. *Barham* came in through the boom defence and anchored in 14 fathoms, in the early afternoon the Admiral's staff transferred to *Devonshire*. In mid-afternoon Major-General Irwin left *Barham* and at 1730 Admiral John Cunningham transferred his flag back to *Devonshire* while the general staff were transferred to quarters ashore. Leave was granted to the first part of the starboard watch for the afternoon.

Early the next morning a tropical downpour brought off-duty men on deck for an impromptu cool shower — much enjoyed by all and a make and mend was piped as per tropical instructions. The port watch were allowed ashore. At the change of dog watches a tornado warning was received and later anchor watch was set and steam raised for slow speed; fortunately the danger soon passed and the tornado warning was hauled down, the anchor watch fell out and the engine room reverted to 4 hours' notice for steam.

Barham stayed at Freetown for a week, just sufficient for the crew to relax after the tension of the previous month. The experience had been invaluable and the officers and men had shaken down into a well-knit fighting organisation, confident in each other's ability and confident of their ship's ability to withstand attack from other surface vessels. At Dakar there had been attacks from the French battleships, submarines and aircraft but *Barham* was virtually unharmed — nothing in fact that a few days in dry dock could not put right.

While in Freetown the sailors enjoyed the fleshpots ashore, just as their older colleagues had when *Barham* visited the West African port during the late twenties. There was no such thing as black and white women, they were all women! The bars and dance-halls were crowded with the perspiring matelots and marines bedecked in their white tropical rig. Swimming parties were organised and the week in harbour relaxed the nerves and enabled the crew to recharge their batteries for further assignments ahead. Gradually the force left Freetown and the stagnant heat. On 3 October General de Gaulle sailed with his armada to Duala; next day the Gibraltar-based Force H left with the British transport ships. *Resolution* remained at Freetown for temporary repairs, later returning briefly to the United Kingdom before crossing the Atlantic for a major refit at the Philadelphia yard.

The crew on board *Barham* knew their runs ashore were numbered when Force H sailed and so it turned out to be, for on Sunday 6 October the battleship raised steam and left Freetown for the very last time. *Barham* sailed at 1800 with the P and O ship *Ettrick* and the British Indian Steam Navigation Co *Karanja*, both now transports, and they were escorted by the destroyers *Escapade*, *Echo*, *Greyhound* and *Fortune*.

At a conference held on board *Barham* before sailing, the Master of *Ettrick* gave his maximum speed at 13¾ knots. In consequence the Commander-in-Chief South Atlantic was informed that the speed of advance of the convoy, allowing for zig-zagging, would be 12¾ knots and not 13½ as signalled in an earlier message. It was realised that the length of the route and the number of days it would take to reach Gibraltar would in all probability make it necessary for *Barham* to fuel the destroyers on passage when weather conditions were favourable. Because of the fuel question it was also appreciated that it would be impracticable for the destroyers to investigate or board merchant vessels met en route.

Barham, *Ettrick* and *Karanja* proceeded in single line ahead, ships three cables apart with the destroyers in a screening position by day and during moonlight. After moonset, one destroyer was stationed five cables astern until daylight.

Barham streamed paravanes on reaching the end of the swept channel; the port paravane samson post and derrick having been destroyed by a 9.4-inch shell at Dakar, the left gun of 'B' turret was used successfully, with the turret on the beam for streaming and recovering the paravane. On Monday *Barham* recovered paravanes during the first watch and later in the day, during the dog-watches, exercised three emergency turns. On the next day, owing to *Barham*'s consumption of fuel being greater than was anticipated, it was considered necessary to adjust the route and pass inside the Cape Verde Islands and course was altered to follow this new route at noon. It was anticipated that this increased consumption was due to the damage caused by an underwater hit on the second day at Dakar. It was also noted that the ship was carrying 4 degrees of port rudder.

On Thursday 10 October, with the weather conditions being favourable all four destroyers were oiled within a four hour period, *Echo* taking the most with over 71 tons while *Greyhound* only took 47 tons. In the afternoon of Friday an Admiralty message was received about the possibility of another French ship making for Dakar and shortly afterwards *Barham*, *Escapade*, *Echo* and *Fortune* altered course to the eastward, leaving *Greyhound* in charge of the convoy. During the evening there was a fatality on *Barham* when a Portsmouth Marine was killed by a shot from his own pistol.

By Saturday the scheme of search decided upon was to spread one destroyer 60 degrees on either bow at maximum visual signalling distance and retain one as anti-submarine screen. By this means a front of forty miles, twenty miles either side of the centre-line between Puerteventure Island and the mainland, was covered during the day; after sunset the moonlight was as bright and it was possible to continue this sweep until three-quarters of an hour before moonset at 0330. The wing destroyer towards the moon was clearly visible from *Barham* at eight miles, so it was certain that no ship could have slipped through the sweep during the dark hours; the night sweep covered at least 24 to probably 30 miles.

Gibraltar 1941.
(right) in . . .
. . . and (below) out of
No 1 dry dock

At moonset on Sunday the squadron was turned 180 degrees and speed reduced to 10 knots until 0630 when the old course was resumed and *Australia* joined. The cruiser was stationed at maximum visual signalling distance on the starboard beam with *Echo* being ordered to adjust her station to the maximum visual signalling distance on the starboard beam of *Australia*. Visibility was very good throughout the day until 1700 when there were occasional rainstorms. An hour later the ship search was abandoned in accordance with an Admiralty signal. Course was altered to 360 degrees to get well clear of the French Moroccan coast during the night.

In the early hours of Monday a defect to the forced lubrication system caused *Barham* to stop engines for 30 minutes, at the same time the opportunity was taken to transfer a sick rating from *Escapade* to the battleship for treatment.

Early on Tuesday *Barham* arrived at Gibraltar and before midday was secured in No 1 dry dock. Nine days of hard labour by the dockyard mateys, and two days by the hands painting the ship's bottom during which time there were air raid alerts, were enough to make *Barham* ready for sea again. While she was waiting for her next assignment, three Italian two-man 'human' torpedoes were launched from a parent submarine in Algeciras Bay on 30 October. Two immediately malfunctioned, but the third succeeded in navigating to within 75 yards of *Barham* before it became stuck on the bottom. The crew set the timer and attempted to escape but both were later picked up. The subsequent explosion was the first intimation the authorities had of the new weapon.

Later, after provisioning, oiling, ammunitioning and a short sea trial, *Barham* embarked her seaplane and a contingent of 600 troops, among them the 12th Field Regiment Royal Artillery for passage to Malta. These soldiers had boarded the French liner *Pasteur* at Cardiff for the outward journey to Gibraltar and once aboard the battleship were hidden below decks away from prying eyes. Their guns arrived at Malta later, in another ship. *Barham* sailed in company with *Ark Royal, Berwick, Glasgow* and *Sheffield* on 7 November, parting company two days later. After a short call at Malta for the disembarkation *Barham* continued on to Alexandria with *Malaya*. The battleships had not long arrived at the Egyptian port when there was an air raid alert. Two days later *Barham* was off again, this time to Crete, to Suda Bay, returning on 19 November. While oiling at Alexandria a cap was left off the oil gauge dipstick and a match caused a flashback which did considerable damage to a 6-inch turret compartment.

The rest of 1940 was spent at Alexandria. Christmas came and went; for all the crew it was the last they ever spent aboard the veteran battleship.

CHAPTER ELEVEN

Mediterranean attacks

At the beginning of 1941 all was looking well for the Royal Navy in the Mediterranean. The Army, too, had the Italians in full retreat in the Western desert and had occupied Crete. However, unbeknown to the Allies at the time, Hitler now took a personal hand in events, his first move being to fly in a striking force of his Luftwaffe to Sicily. The Navy, and its bases, were to be singled out for special attention.

The Commander-in-Chief Mediterranean, Admiral Sir A.B. Cunningham, with a touch of imagination, did not order *Barham* to sea until 2 January. New Year's Day is not a good day for activity anywhere after seeing in the New Year.

The stern anchor was weighed followed successively by the starboard and port anchors and at the beginning of the last dog watch course and speed were set for leaving harbour. Speed gradually increased to 15 knots as the night zig-zag commenced. *Barham* was in company with *Warspite*, *Valiant*, cruisers and destroyers, *Illustrious* joined later. The object of the battle fleet was to assist the land forces by shelling Bardia.

Fighters from *Illustrious* were overhead protecting the fleet as the three battleships launched their attack. The 15-inch guns on *Barham* opened fire to port at 0810 and ten minutes later the 6-inch guns followed suit. The fleet changed course at 0830, so then the starboard guns were brought to bear. A cease-fire was ordered just before 0900 when the target area had been saturated and thick clouds of smoke were seen ashore. At 19 knots the battle fleet made good its escape without any enemy opposition except for a few ineffective bursts from the coastal batteries ashore.

Barham returned to Alexandria early next morning and anchored. The ammunition lighter was quickly alongside and when the hands had finished ammunitioning, the oiler took its turn.

Next day the Army took Bardia, capturing 25,000 Italian garrison troops at the port, many of them shell-shocked.

While *Barham* had been at sea the drafting officer had been busy and in the next few days some ratings were discharged to *Jervis* and *Woolwich* and 12 Maltese ratings and 62 Royal Air Force men joined the ship for passage to Malta. Early in the morning of 11 January *Barham* slipped her buoy and left with HMS *Eagle*. Next day *Perth* and *Gloucester* were sighted and a short time afterwards *Barham* took station on *Warspite* and *Valiant*, later in the day anchoring in 11 fathoms at Suda Bay.

Illustrious had been severely damaged by air attacks two days earlier, being singled out for special attention despite being in company with *Warspite* and *Valiant*.

Barham was at sea again on patrol early the next day, the Swordfish was sent aloft to observe, for at no time was *Barham* ever fitted with radar. The objective was to strike at airfields in the Dodecanese with aircraft from *Eagle* but adverse weather caused a cancellation. Two days later the battleship was back in Suda Bay.

Barham left Crete the next morning and at sea tested the searchlight and practised with close range weapons and anti-aircraft trials. The African mainland was sighted early next day, *Barham* and *Eagle* changed stations and on arrival at Alexandria *Barham* reduced to six hours' notice for steam. The ship's company were given leave on alternate days until 2200. Two ratings were taken for detention ashore after warrants had been read. At this time there were many changes of staff; a new petty officer telegraphist and a NAAFI hand joined and ratings left for other ships or to join the pool. '

Another new arrival on board at this time was Telegraphist Ernie Rowles. Ernie volunteered for service in the Royal Navy on the outbreak of war, his brother Jack was already in the Navy and serving aboard *Barham*. On his home leave Jack used to bring presents home from the Mediterranean for his family in London, and tales of foreign parts left no doubts in Ernie's mind as to which arm of the service he would volunteer to serve. Ernie was a Chatham rating and by the beginning of 1941 was serving aboard *Warspite* in the Mediterranean. Hearing of this, Jack 'claimed' his brother. A transfer was arranged and a telegraphist from *Barham* took his place in *Warspite*. This move probably saved Ernie's life, for when *Warspite* was hit later the other telegraphist was killed.

Ernie was quick to notice the difference between the two sister ships as *Barham* had received no major refit in the six years prior to the outbreak of war. He found *Barham* was probably the only ship larger than a destroyer to retain canteen messing. The leading hand of the mess purchased food with a monthly allowance, the food was prepared on the messdeck by 'cooks of the mess', ordinary hands who took turns. After preparation the food was taken to the galley for cooking and collection for serving when ready. A cigarette and a cup of tea with evaporated milk usually sufficed for breakfast, although the stokers liked their bread and jam. Sometimes money was shared out between the Mess if there were any savings, but usually by the addition of a few coppers from each rating they lived well; that was more important than savings.

Ernie soon found that the ship was alive with cockroaches and weevils were often found in the ship's biscuits. He found that, as on *Warspite*, the messdecks were overcrowded by the full war complement and there was not enough room for all hammocks to be slung, so many slept on mess stools or stretcher beds. He found all bathing was done from buckets in bathroom flats with clothing being dried in steam lockers. Hammocks needed to be aired frequently, this was usually done by laying them out on deck.

Barham was at sea again shortly with *Eagle*, then back to Alexandria for evening leave ashore for the ratings. While at sea on 23 January *Barham*'s anti-aircraft gunners opened fire on two Italian Cant Z seaplanes and enjoyed the twelve minutes action although they made no claims. Air raid warnings were received aboard on two occasions while *Barham* was moored at Alexandria, it was at this time that Axis aircraft were dropping magnetic mines in the Suez Canal, which for a time cut the main artery for the Middle East forces round the Cape route.

Tobruk had been captured on 22 January, Derna eight days later and on 6 February Benghazi was captured by the Army of the Nile which progressed towards Tripoli. The War Cabinet's later decision to reinforce the Greek forces meant a postponement of the African progress and left inadequate forces to hold the newly captured territory.

German aircraft based in Sicily rendered Malta practically useless as a Naval base, there being too few fighters to protect the fleet. Consequently no large ship striking force could be based there, so the supplies and reinforcements to the Axis forces in North Africa could not be attacked with the results that supplies were built up and Rommel's Afrika Korps eventually advanced almost to the Egyptian frontier.

In the middle of February the Commander-in-Chief was requesting more aircraft to act as eyes of the fleet as the Luftwaffe, taking over from the Regia Aeronautica on the Sicilian airfields, had tilted the balance in favour of the Axis. In consequence *Barham* did not have a busy month.

At the beginning of March the first troop convoys arrived in Greece. Towards the end of the month the Italian Navy put to sea with a battleship, eight cruisers and thirteen destroyers in order to intercept these convoys. The Italians had been promised Luftwaffe support, which in the end was not forthcoming.

Through Ultra, the name given to information derived from the decoding of Enigma, the German cypher machine, Admiral Cunningham had received intelligence of the sortie; he ordered a troop convoy to reverse its course at nightfall; after having put in train a deception plan, whereby he was seen playing golf ashore during the afternoon, Cunningham stealthily returned to *Warspite* and put to sea after dark on 27 March with *Barham*, *Valiant* and *Formidable*, escorted by nine destroyers. Other light forces, under the command of Vice-Admiral Pridham-Wippell were ordered to join with the Commander-in-Chief from Crete the next day.

As no air support materialised the Italians turned back on 28 March. An early morning report from a *Formidable* aircraft gave news of four cruisers and destroyers and an hour later Pridham-Wippell reported three cruisers and destroyers to northward. The Vice-Admiral recognised the 8-inch cruisers, knew they could outrange his squadron so decided to try to draw them toward the Battle Fleet then steaming at 22 knots still some ninety miles distant.

At 1100 the Italian battleship *Vittorio Veneto* was identified after some earlier inconclusive firing. Accurate fire from her 15-inch guns caused the British cruisers to hurriedly withdraw under cover of a smoke screen; the Battle Fleet was still eighty miles short. Naturally Admiral Cunningham was following events closely and was fearful that the enemy might escape before he arrived. Consequently *Valiant*, currently the fastest of the three battleships, was ordered to proceed ahead at her best speed to support the cruisers. A striking force from *Formidable* attacked the Italians causing them to turn away, thereby giving the British battleships no opportunity of attacking during daylight. However, the aircraft had done well, hitting the battleship and slowing it down.

Another air strike again hit the battleship in mid-afternoon, further reducing its speed to eight knots, but this later increased to twelve. Aircraft from Crete joined in the attack and a hit was claimed on a cruiser. During the evening a third attack from carrier borne aircraft found the Italian ships protecting the damaged battleship, but hit the heavy cruiser, *Pola*.

At 2111 a radar report from Pridham-Wippell's force indicated a large enemy ship stopped five miles to port. An hour later *Valiant*, the only one of the British battleships fitted with radar, confirmed the radar plot at a range of six miles.

The battle fleet was deployed in line ahead; *Warspite*, *Valiant*, *Formidable* and *Barham*. The main armament was ready and trained on the correct bearing. At 2225 two large Italian cruisers with a smaller ship ahead of them were identified from *Warspite*. *Formidable* was ordered out of line as *Warspite* and *Valiant* opened fire at point-blank range. *Warspite*, with main and secondary armament set *Fiume* ablaze, *Valiant* was also pumping shells into the same target; later both switched to *Zara*, with *Valiant* doing most of the damage. *Barham* joined in after *Formidable* had moved out of line, her initial salvo shattered her own searchlights. The target was the smaller leading ship, later identified as the destroyer *Alfieri*; her broadside ripped the Italian apart from 3,100 yards. *Barham* then joined in against the stopped cruiser *Zara*, hitting her with five 15-inch broadsides and seven 6-inch salvos.

The whole action only lasted a few minutes. Three enemy destroyers did attempt a torpedo attack but were driven off, one being sunk later. At 2300 the Commander-in-Chief ordered all ships not engaged with the enemy to withdraw northward to be out of range of shore based aircraft by daylight.

During the night *Jervis* came upon the crippled *Pola* and torpedoed her. British destroyers rescued some 900 survivors and later an Italian rescue party collected another 160 men and a Greek force another 110 Italians. The fleet arrived back at Alexandria on the 30 March, experiencing air attacks en route. There was jubilation at Alexandria, for in the battle, now known as the Battle of Matapan, British losses were one aircraft and crew, against three Italian cruisers and two destroyers and casualties amounting to 2,400 officers and men.

While the sailors were enjoying what relaxation they could in port, with the Axis land forces not too far distant and their Air Forces overhead too frequently, decisions were being made about *Barham* thousands of miles away in London.

The Allied army were heroically holding out in Tobruk so the Axis forces were having to supply their forces through Tripoli some eight hundred miles from Alexandria. Admiral Cunningham was under pressure to bombard the port; he was against it because of the enemy's air superiority, and thought it was a legitimate air force target.

Further suggestions from London hinted that the port should be blocked and the old battleship *Centurion* was nominated as the blockship. Admiral Cunningham was not against the suggestion, but the ship could not be brought round the Cape in sufficient time.

Easter came and went with *Barham* firing off a round at an Italian three-engined Savoia-Machetti SM79 on Good Friday. A few days later a bombshell hit the desk of the Commander-in-Chief Mediterranean in the form of an Admiralty signal, the gist of which was that Tripoli harbour was to be bombarded and blocked, with the blockships being *Barham* and *Caledon*. The Admiral was appalled, as would have been the battleship's crew, past and present, had they known of the plan. The signal concluded:

The use of *Barham* for this purpose will no doubt fill you with the deepest regret, but it is considered far preferable to sacrifice one ship entirely with the chance of achieving something really worthwhile than to get several ships damaged in bombardment, the result of which might be most disappointing.

Winston Churchill, with memories of Zeebrugge still fresh in his mind said the order was to convince the gallant Cunningham of the almost desperate risks that should be run at this crisis. It was as well that Admiral Cunningham was made of stern stuff, for he vehemently protested against the suggestion that he should sacrifice a first-class battleship like *Barham* and immediately replied to this effect, with his usual respect.

> I have seen fit to query their Lordships' decision . . . and request that the matter be considered afresh. In the meantime *Barham* is fortunately due for docking and under this pretext will be de-stored and prepared. I would prefer to attack with the whole Battle Fleet and accept the risks rather than send *Barham* in unsupported . . . should one of the battleships be seriously damaged in these circumstances I should attempt to use her as a block-ship, removing her ship's company by light craft subsequently.

Fortunately the Admiralty concurred with the commander on the spot that after all perhaps a bombardment would be as well.

To further reinforce the opinion that the Commander-in-Chief was well and truly in charge of the Mediterranean situation, Captain Mack, in *Jervis*, leading a destroyer flotilla sank a complete convoy of five ships sailing on the supply route on 16 April; the Royal Navy lost the Tribal class destroyer *Mohawk* in the action.

Two days later Admiral Cunningham took his fleet to sea again, for a dual purpose. *Breconshire* was to take aviation fuel to Malta and refuel destroyers, four empty vessels were to be escorted back and the Fleet was to go on and bombard Tripoli.

On Friday 18 April *Barham* weighed anchor at 0530 and left harbour with *Warspite*, *Valiant*, *Formidable*, *Phoebe*, *Calcutta* and a destroyer escort. The carrier flew off her planes at 1040. There were constant air-raid warnings and the fleet continually had to zig-zag. Full action stations were manned for the hour at sunset. Next day the fleet anchored in Suda Bay to refuel, just after midday. The mountains inland gleamed brightly as the sun caught each ridge. Two hours later the fleet was at sea again, altering course for *Formidable* to fly off her aircraft. Early Sunday

Barham oiling at Suda Bay

afternoon three bombers were sighted out of range of the guns, and in the evening the fleet altered course while the destroyer *Havoc* dropped depth charges on a possible contact. After dark the fleet increased speed and steamed south ready to bombard Tripoli before dawn. On *Barham* hands were at first degree readiness at 0300.

The plan was for RAF Wellingtons and Fleet Air Arm Swordfish aircraft to bomb Tripoli before the battleships arrived. At sea the Fleet were able to identify their target in the darkness as the submarine *Truant*, stationed four miles offshore, flashed a light seawards to mark the spot. All was silent as *Warspite*, *Valiant*, *Barham* and *Gloucester* approached. The fleet opened fire on the harbour at 0500 and for twenty minutes there was no return fire from the enemy. Aircraft from *Formidable* dropped flares and spotted for the fleet but their task was made difficult by dust clouds rising from the carrier aircraft attacks. *Barham* ceased fire at 0522, altered course and reopened fire again for another fourteen minutes, ten minutes later. There were clouds of smoke and dust and a fire burning as the ships made off at high speed. *Formidable* and the escorting destroyers rejoined the battle fleet while the Malta-based destroyers accompanying the empty cargo ships to Alexandria and others which were present at the bombardment returned to the island.

It was later confirmed that a supply ship was sunk and a torpedo boat damaged in the bombardment. Enemy aircraft made a half-hearted attack with three Ju 88's, two of which were shot down by fighters from *Formidable*.

The Battle Fleet arrived back at Alexandria on the morning of 23 April, *Barham* anchored in ten fathoms just after midday and a make and mend was declared for the afternoon. The following day the ammunition lighter came alongside and the ratings were kept busy but the port watch had a run ashore from 1630–2200. There was no shore leave for anybody next day which was spent provisioning ship. Oil was taken in over the weekend and the starboard watch enjoyed over ten hours ashore on Sunday.

While the big-ship men were enjoying a rest in Alexandria, their destroyer colleagues were engaged evacuating British troops from Greece to Crete. Larger ships brought the bulk of the army, except those needed for its defence, from Crete to Alexandria. Athens fell to the Germans on 27 April.

For the next two weeks *Barham* was in and out of harbour for short periods, subjected to air attacks at sea and in port, the ack-ack gunnere were kept on their toes. Opportunity was taken to pass two convoys into Malta. Heavy enemy air activity took place at night on 10 May but the barrage put up by the fleet is best described by a pressman who had joined *Barham* earlier. His despatch was published on 14 May, two days after the battle fleet had returned to Alexandria.

'The heaviest and most spectacular night barrage yet seen was put up by more than thirty warships in the central Mediterranean when for the first time in the war enemy aeroplanes attempted a night torpedo attack at sea against the British Eastern Mediterranean Forces. The firing continued almost ceaselessly for 45 minutes. Two days previously the enemy had failed to score during a daylight attack against our Western Forces.

'The full moon was some 20 degrees above the horizon when cruisers, escorting a convoy, were seen to open fire a few miles distant on our starboard quarter, whereupon our heavy units blazed forth with all their armaments, from six-inches downwards, while a strong destroyer screen flung up an umbrella barrage, protecting the battle fleet from a possible high-level bombing attack. When the battle fleet opened fire the raiders apparently abandoned the convoy, and, splitting up into groups, attacked the Fleet from all angles.

'From the *Barham's* compass platform I had a magnificent panoramic view of the Fleet steaming in line ahead, belching flame in all directions as the barrage, comprising 6in and 4in guns, multiple pom-poms, and even Lewis guns, plastered a wide area extending from the sea level to the sky. Each battleship appeared to be aflame from end to end, and was illuminated for seconds at a time. Enveloped by clouds of smoke from the guns it looked like a giant set-piece during a gargantuan firework display.

'The whole ship shuddered violently under terrific blast as the shells whistled away into the distance. Gun flashes temporarily blinded one as the high-angle barrage passed the bridge, with the reflection on the halyards giving the impression of masses of tracers being hurled vertically to the mast. Speech was impossible, and shouted orders were drowned by the indescribable violence of the barrage.

'Meanwhile the sea, which was lit up by the blaze of the guns, periodically became a mass of small and large waterspouts, as splinters from the destroyers' protective barrage fell all around us. During brief lulls to ascertain the enemy's line of approach the water-cooled pom-poms below the bridge could be heard hissing fiercely, and there was a tremendous clatter of thousands of empty shell cases of all calibres being hastily swept aside before the next barrage opened.

'The cease-fire was given after 45 minutes, and a thick wet fog suddenly descended on the whole sea for the rest of the night, necessitating the use of stern lights to avoid collisions. Darkness prevented the ascertaining of the results of the barrage, but we did not suffer any casualties or damage.

'During seven days' routine operations extending to the Central Mediterranean, in addition to beating off the night torpedo attack, convoys were successfully covered in various directions, light forces bombarded Benghazi harbour, and the Fleet Air Arm shot down seven enemy planes. The weather proved most helpful in obscuring our movements, beginning with a violent sandstorm extending as far as Crete. Afterwards there was a succession of rain, low clouds, fogs, and extensive haze for the remaining days.

'Although convoy figures were not generally released, up to the beginning of April 1941 551 ships, representing about 2,750,000 tons of shipping, had been successfully convoyed by the Mediterranean Fleet.'

It was obvious the enemy intended to try to invade Crete and a naval force was kept at sea to intercept any invasion armada. Part of the battle fleet was at sea to the west of the island as cover to the light forces. When the invasion came it came from the air, from parachutists and gliders on 20 May, by nightfall the German force was secure on the island.

While *Warspite* and *Valiant* were in the thick of things, *Barham* was still in Alexandria for on 20 May while one watch was ashore the duty watch turned to and refuelled from the oiler *Cherryleaf* alongside. For the next two days there was an exodus and influx of staff as experienced ratings were taken from the battleship to be replaced by newcomers from the pool at Alexandria.

On 22 May *Warspite* was hit by a bomb. Operating off Crete the force was subjected to heavy air attacks and although *Warspite* had successfully avoided previous bombs, one, probably a 500 lb armour piercing bomb, penetrated the starboard side of the fo'c's'le deck, and exploded in the 6-inch battery on the upper deck. The bomb caused considerable damage, killing over thirty of the crew and injuring a similar number. Among the dead was the former *Barham* telegraphist who changed ships with Ernie Rowles earlier. *Valiant* was also damaged and both battleships returned to Alexandria on 24 May. This was a black day in British naval history as *Hood* had been sunk in seconds by *Bismarck* some hours earlier.

Barham was still at Alexandria but on the next day, Sunday 25 May, orders were given at 1030 to revert to two hours' notice for steam and at midday she weighed anchor, passed the boom and proceeded to sea with *Queen Elizabeth*. By 1330 *Barham* had increased to 17 knots and in the next two hours was joined by *Formidable*, *Hasty*, *Hereward*, *Janus*, *Kandahar* and *Voyager*. There was an air raid warning as darkness fell. The Swordfish from

Barham was flown off at first light next morning, then *Barham* resumed course and assumed guide of the Fleet.

The object of the sortie was to attack the airfield at Scarpanto, fifty miles from Crete, from which enemy aircraft were raiding the Greek Island and menacing the British Fleet. The attacking force were now joined by *Ajax* and *Dido*. The aircraft from *Formidable* took off for the airfield from a position one hundred miles to the south-south-west. The four Albacores and four Fulmars achieved complete surprise as they raided the airfield between 0500 and 0600. Enemy aircraft were caught on the ground and destroyed or damaged. Unfortunately, due to the small number of attackers, there was no lasting effect.

The enemy soon discovered the presence of the British force and varying degrees of attacks were carried out although *Barham* did not open fire until 0840 and then it was only against a single attacker. An hour later a Fulmar from *Formidable* crashed. In the early afternoon, while withdrawing, the force was subjected to a dive bombing attack by twenty aircraft which flew in from the direction of North Africa, *Formidable* was badly damaged. In the evening the aircraft carrier and escorting destroyers parted company.

Next day, Tuesday, an air raid warning Red was sounded at 0831 and at 0851 the fleet was attacked by dive bombers and near misses holed the bulge and port bow of *Barham*. At 0858 a bomb scored a direct hit on 'X' turret, which in turn caused a cordite ignition and killed three occupants instantly. Two others were mortally wounded and six others injured. The damage control parties cleared up as best as possible and at 1545 the five dead, a chief petty officer, two ordinance articifers and two able seamen were buried at sea with naval honours. An hour later *Barham* was steaming at 14 knots, at 2000 the stern anchor was dropped in 9½ fathoms and 45 minutes later five cot cases were discharged to the hospital ship *Maine*.

In the Atlantic, the Royal Navy detachments which had been heavily committed the past few days, had at last located and sunk *Bismarck*, thereby avenging the *Hood*.

Back in Alexandria leave was granted to both watches over the next two days. The drafting officer was also busy again as 78 men left the ship and 75 joined. On 31 May *Barham* was de-ammunitioned; it was realised that the major repairs necessary could not be carried out locally. *Malaya* had earlier damaged the dry dock in Alexandria and it could not take any ship larger than 29,000 tons; *Barham* displaced 31,350 tons.

Barham was sent through the Suez Canal with the original idea of following *Warspite* to an American shipyard, she sailed through the Canal at a very slow speed, the wash formed from the ragged hole in her side caused the banks of the Canal to collapse. *Barham* stopped at Aden where in a temperature of 120 degrees hoses had to be played on the decks to stop the plates buckling; she crossed the line on 12 June 1941 in the Indian Ocean off the coast of British Somaliland.

From Aden *Barham* proceeded at slow speed, at times down to four knots, to Mombasa where Naval divers examined the underwater damage and surfaced to report that a London trolleybus could be driven through the hole. It was decided that the battleship would never be able to cross the Atlantic in that condition so Durban was selected as an alternative. On arrival at the South African port *Barham* entered Umberto graving dock for repairs. During the six weeks *Barham* was in dock the local people lavished hospitality on the British crew, with many being invited to stay at private homes until the ship was ready for sea again.

While at Durban Jack Rowles was involved in a car accident the day before *Barham* was due to sail and so badly injured that he was unable to leave with the ship. Jack remained ashore in hospital until he eventually recovered and was then posted locally, married, was demobbed in South Africa and did not return to England again, and then only for a holiday, until 36 years later in 1977. This accident undoubtedly also saved his brother's life, for at the end of October while *Barham* was in Alexandria a telegraphist was urgently needed on one of the trawlers still supplying Tobruk. Ernie Rowles, a Chatham rating on a Portsmouth manned ship, now with no brother aboard, was the obvious choice and fortunately for him the move probably saved his life.

Things had been happening while *Barham* was away. On 1 June the War Office announced that the Allied troops had evacuated Crete. Allied losses were very heavy, and the failure was due to lack of air support. This was the first conquest of an island from the air. Unfortunately the part the Royal Navy played in this campaign did not receive much publicity.

On Sunday 22 June Germany invaded Russia at dawn, attacking along a 1,500 mile front from the Arctic to the Black Sea. On 1 July General Sir Claud Auchinleck succeeded General Wavell as Commander-in-Chief of the land forces in the Middle East. On 26 July an attack on the Grand Harbour at Malta by Italian E-boats and other torpedo craft was defeated.

Barham arrived back at Alexandria to find the situation much changed. Enemy bombers could now operate from Crete and Cyrenaica, Alexandria and the Suez Canal were well within range and the replenishment of Malta from the east was virtually impracticable.

While *Barham* had been out of action the Mediterranean Fleet consisted of only two battleships, two cruisers and a dozen destroyers. Despite the British weakness the Italian Navy had not left port in force. However, the Germans built up their air striking force and pushed more U-boats into the Mediterranean.

A new Allied offensive in the Western Desert was scheduled for 18 November. Tobruk, then Benghazi and beyond, was the objective. It was important for the fleet to deny the Axis more reinforcements and supplies that had been reaching Benghazi by sea from Italy.

Admiral Cunningham received messages from the Admiralty and from the Prime Minister himself reminding him of the necessity to intercept tankers carrying fuel to the Libyan port. If the petrol supply to the Afrika Korps could be halted their vehicles would be also and the Eighth Army could continue on the offensive.

On 24 November the Commander-in-Chief Mediterranean despatched a force of cruisers and destroyers to intercept two reported convoys en route to Benghazi. At the time it was thought that heavy units of the Italian Fleet could be at sea as distant cover for the convoy. If the Italians had in fact put to sea Admiral Cunningham did not intend to be caught napping and so sailed in *Queen Elizabeth*, accompanied by *Barham* and *Valiant* from Alexandria at 1600.

Dawn on 25 November 1941, the last day in this world for many fine sailors, broke over a calm azure Mediterranean sea. The destroyer *Hotspur*, returning from patrol, was ordered to join the other eight screening the battleships; she took her position on the extreme port side. The day was spent zig-zagging between Egypt and Crete, waiting for action; when it came it came as a total surprise and from a totally unexpected quarter. Unknowingly the battleships had run into the path of *U-331*, which was one of twenty German submarines in the Mediterranean, at position 32.34N 26.24E.

CHAPTER TWELVE

Between Crete and Cyrenaica

Between 1940 and 1944 more than 600 Type VII U-boats were built in Germany, far more than any other type of submarine ever. The boats carried twelve to fourteen torpedoes for their five 21-inch tubes, four for'ard and one aft. The submarine that sank *Barham* was *U-331*, a Type VIIC boat, and the very first one to be built at the privately owned Nordsee Werke at Emden. Her crew of 44, under the command of Oberleutnant zur See Hans Dietrich Freiherr (Baron) von Tiesenhausen, were to be very grateful to the yard for the high standard of workmanship. This was the first command for the captain who had trained in the Kriegsmarine officers class of 1934; he served under Kapitänleutnant Otto Kretschmer, the most illustrious U-boat commander of World War II, aboard *U-23* before moving on in the same capacity as First Lieutenant under Kapitänleutnant Korth in *U-93*. By coincidence he had been aboard *Nürnberg* at the time of its near collision with *Barham* before the war.

The boat was launched on 20 December 1940 and commissioned at the end of March 1941; working up trials in the Baltic lasted until the beginning of June when the boat was declared operational. After returning to the builder's yard for final adjustments *U-331* proceeded to Kiel for fitting out before sailing on its first patrol.

The submarine completed its patrol off Cape St Vincent before making Lorient on the French Atlantic coast where she joined the 2nd U-boat flotilla, the patrol lasted from the beginning of July until mid-August.

After a spell ashore at the well appointed French base the crew were pleased to get back to sea on their second patrol which commenced at the end of September. The submarine successfully negotiated the dangerous waters of the Bay of Biscay and remained at sea, passing through the tricky passage of the Straits of Gibraltar one night early in October and entered the Mediterranean unobserved. The U-boat patrolled the Eastern Mediterranean until putting in to Salamis, an island to the south of Greece, which had been newly prepared as the headquarters of the 23rd U-boat flotilla under the command of Kapitänleutnant Fritz Frauenheim.

It was the end of October that *U-331* arrived at its new base, but before continuing its story we must put the clocks back to an incident that happened two months earlier. The Eighth Army in Libya were attacking the German and Italian armies on all fronts and the Germans made provision for a small party to attack the supply routes of the Allies. At the beginning of August seven men, under the command of Leutnant Josef Kiefer, were sent to the headquarters of the Lehrregiment Brandenburg in Berlin and practised for a week laying demolition charges beneath a railway line. They drew tropical kit and on 28 August left Berlin by air for Athens where they reported to Hauptmann Schiffbauer, an officer attached to Abwehr II, Secret Service Sabotage.

The party attempted to leave Athens by air three days later but their Dornier 24, a three-engined flying-boat, crashed into the quay and the attempt was abandoned.

Meanwhile, the small commando party were impatiently waiting to get to Africa to assist General Rommel's Afrika Korps. On 12 November they were ordered to take their equipment aboard a submarine at Salamis, *U-331*. The embarkation of the sabotage party had been kept secret from the crew of the submarine until the very last minute. Conditions on board were far from ideal with seven extra passengers and all their equipment.

The cramped U-boat left Salamis on her third patrol at 1900 on 12 November for the North African coast. On arrival at the given point the commando party was duly landed with a wireless operator, Wolfgang Ebertz, detailed to assist the navigation of the rubber dinghy. Ebertz, who by chance was wearing one of von Tiesenhausen's captured British Army shirts with the commander's name on it, was ordered to wait until the party re-embarked. The spot where the saboteurs landed was between Ras Gibeisa and Ras el Schaqiq and their mission was to place demolition charges beneath the coastal railway line.

The army party boarded the rubber dinghy with their equipment which consisted of one light machine gun, 5 machine pistols, 9 stick hand grenades, 2 Very pistols, a signalling lamp, 4 pairs of field glasses, 3 compasses, 3 knapsacks, 3 demolition mines, food and British money. A wireless transmitter, consisting of a laryngeal microphone enabling softly-voiced sounds to be transmitted, was left behind as it was considered too heavy and clumsy.

It was agreed that *U-331* should return to the same position offshore the following night, when a green light would be shone to indicate her presence. The party ashore was to reply with a red light.

The party landed safely and set about its work, leaving two men to stand by the dinghy. These two were later surprised by sentries but overpowered them. On the night of 17 November, after waiting offshore for twenty-four hours, owing to the heavy sea, *U-331* approached to within one mile of the coast railway line. The commando party tried to re-embark this same night but their dinghy capsized in the surf, the gear was lost and the Very cartridges were put out of action by the sea water. The party therefore returned to the shore, where they were all captured a few hours later. Meanwhile, out at sea *U-331* waited all night for the party to make themselves known again the following night but at daybreak abandoned hope and proceeded towards Sollum.

Between 16 and 25 November *U-331* carried out the second half of its mission, patrolling off the North African coast in the neighbourhood of Sollum and Mersa Matruh. The submarine remained submerged during the day and surfaced during the night. At the time Tobruk was being held by the Allies although surrounded by enemy forces and the U-boat was ordered to prevent any supplies reaching the garrison by sea. The supplies had been arriving from Alexandria in small, heavily protected, convoys but all *U-331* saw every time she gingerly surfaced during the day was aircraft, which forced it down again.

At 0800 on 25 November the faint sound of propellers in a northerly direction was picked up by the radio operator on the hydrophone aboard the submarine. The captain ordered the boat to periscope depth and cautiously swept round the horizon, making sure first of all that there were no aircraft around that could pick up the submarine on radar or see the feather wake caused by the periscope. The surface of the sea was empty, the

HMS *Griffin*

HMS *Jervis*

commander could see nothing. He surfaced, saw an aircraft near by and crash-dived right away. There were no bombs but in that short moment he had also searched the horizon in the direction where the propellers had last been heard. Nothing could be seen. The submarine was ordered down again to 50 metres, which was considered to be the best depth for HE listening, so as to check up on the sounds. The submarine carried on the hunt under water and her commander carries on with the story:

After the first unsuccessful surfacing, the boat stayed submerged until shortly after noon. Then there were two aircraft; the first one at a safe distance but later a second approached too close for the submarine to stay on the surface.

The wide band of faint propeller noises was now in a north-easterly direction. We didn't stay down too long and after surfacing again we proceeded in the direction of the last bearing with high speed, but still nothing could be seen for some time. Suddenly a yellowish thickening over the horizon was made out and some needlelike masts could be distinguished. This group of ships moved in a southerly direction and then seemed to disappear to the east altogether, only to grow again after turning west. It became quite clear that this was a fleet of warships. We approached each other on a reciprocal course and from now on things happened in a rather quick succession: by some inexplicably intuitive order the boat turned around full circle and dived. This delay later turned out to be of crucial importance.

There were three battleships steaming west in a line ahead formation with a protective screen of eight destroyers. The three were Queen Elizabeth class ships but it was not possible to establish names.

On the submarine the crew had closed up to full action stations. The time was just after 1600. The late afternoon sun was shining in a south-westerly direction behind the U-boat, perfect weather for an attack.

Tension inside the submarine rose tangibly in the next few moments as unknowingly the British formation approached fast on a collision course. In his periscope the U-boat commander could now see three battleships steaming in line astern, flanked by four destroyers on each side.

Unsuspectingly *Queen Elizabeth* led her two sister ships directly toward the submerged submarine; they were on a reciprocal course, and von Tiesenhausen could hardly have found himself in a better position to attack. He saw flags at the yard-arm of the battleships, which obviously heralded a change in formation. Two destroyers, *Jervis* and *Griffin*, leading the formation, moved forward.

On board *Jervis* the second Asdic operator, an able seaman, had been qualified in his trade for nine months and spent this time in the destroyer. He had practised three or four times with the British submarine *Rorqual*. This operator took over his duties at the start of the first dog-watch at 1600. His able seaman companion on watch had qualified in the destroyer at the beginning of 1940 and in the past year had been aboard the depot ship *Woolwich* on the contact attack teacher and performed operations with a friendly submarine three months earlier. At 1615 this operator picked up an echo and the second operator put the phones over. The second operator's job was to take the range and listen from the bridge and to put down all that happened in the log. The range was between 1,000 and 1,100 yards and the nearest range was just over 800 yards.

The first operator picked up the contact on the edge of the port sweep at approximately 220 degrees and on the second echo reported to the bridge and swept forward until he had the correct right cut on. He swept aft in 2½ degree steps and was still on the echo at about 30 degrees and altered to 5 degree steps. He was still on the echo at 60 degrees so reported to the bridge 'non-sub'.

The lieutenant Asdic officer aboard *Jervis* received a three-week course before joining the destroyer in 1939. In June of that year in the working-up period and later in the Mediterranean he performed exercises with British submarines. He said the destroyer was steering a mean course of 290 degrees at 1615. Two minutes later the anti-submarine cabinet reported an echo bearing 220 degrees, range 900 yards. The echo was loud, rather raucous and sharp. Because the extensive target was between 40 and 60 degrees he considered it to be 'non-sub' and told the A/S cabinet to disregard and carry on the sweep by which time the range was

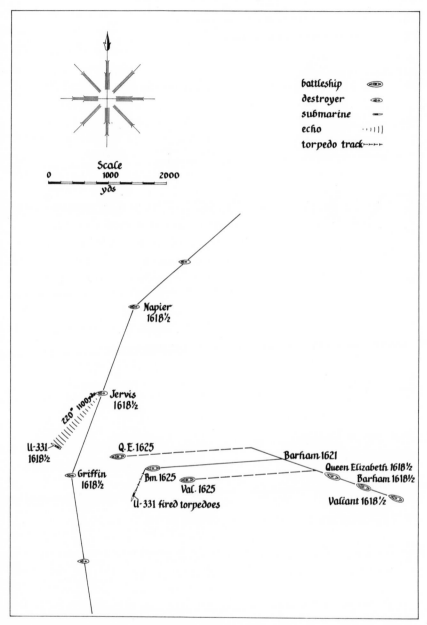

Sketch showing how *U-331* penetrated the destroyer screen to torpedo *Barham*

The view through the periscope of *U-331* (bottom centre right) as the Battle Fleet approach. Part of a painting by H. D. Frhr von Tiesenhausen

400—500 yards on the port beam.

The lieutenant-commander on the bridge of *Jervis* said that when the report was received the Asdic officer switched on the loudspeaker so that they could hear it. He thought the cabinet reported a contact bearing 245 degrees on the port bow and quite extensive. The contact was quite loud and passed down the port side. The original range was given as 1,100 yards. His opinion, after the Asdic officer had told the A/S cabinet to disregard, was that the echo must have been some form of water layer or difference in temperature of water which one found, particularly on warm days. He thought this because of the extent of the target and the ping similar to that received from those layers.

The captain of *Jervis* had left the bridge at 1615 at the completion of the commander-in-chief's night intentions signal and was in his sea cabin. Normally he heard every time the loudspeaker was switched on through his voice pipe, but did not on this occasion and he was not informed of the echo.

The U-boat slipped through between *Jervis* and *Griffin* at periscope depth and now found itself on the port side of the battleships. The first was already too close as it took up more space than the periscope's field of vision could accommodate, then the second battleship in line, *Barham*, appeared. A quick glance showed the prospective target growing bigger and bigger in the cross-wires.

The torpedo men were ready but the angle of over 90 degrees was still too great. The forward torpedo room reported '*Hart-lage*', through the speaking tube but the button could not be pressed as the U-boat was lying almost broadside on to the target which was so close that the periscope could only accommodate part of the battleship.

Strong action had to be taken to overcome the 90 degrees: one engine stopped, the other full speed ahead and the rudder hard to port was a delicate situation in itself. In addition four torpedoes now left their tubes in proper sequence. The distance to the target was 375 metres. Unknown to von Tiesenhausen all the battleships had turned to port, that is, toward him. After the torpedoes had been fired *U-331* came very close to the third battleship, *Valiant*. In fact, in a quick sweep with the periscope von Tiesenhausen had seen a huge mass of grey steel approaching and was sure that his boat would be rammed any moment. Especially so, as a report came from the engineering officer in the control room that the conning tower had broken surface. In addition to these difficulties, the submarine was probably forced out of the water by the movement of *Valiant* so close by. The captain was the only one to realize the dangerous situation. There had been no time to inform the crew of the happenings. He ordered the room in the conning tower to be abandoned quickly; Obersteuermann Walther closed the watertight hatch. After having been visible on the surface for 45 seconds and disappearing only 30 yards off the starboard side of *Valiant*, too close even to be hit by pom-pom fire, *U-331* submerged down deep into the dark safety of the sea. The expected ramming never happened.

As the submarine began sinking like a brick, three detonations were heard, and shortly afterwards a fourth; these were incidental at this time to the submariners, but at least they knew a target had been hit. The elation turned to tension at the speed of the rapid descent of the Emden-built boat, loose articles crashed about and the needle of the depth gauge registered increasing depths. At 70 metres there was a slow down and an evening out at 80 metres. However, since the boat was bow heavy and the screws were still turning, *U-331* continued to go deeper. Going deeper gave the submariners a better chance of escaping the explosions of depth charges, the crew were mystified why none had so far rained down on them.

The submarine continued plummeting toward the bottom; it was indeed fortunate for the crew that they were in deep water, otherwise they would have been in deep trouble. The forward depth gauge showed 265 metres and the captain knew this was the deepest any U-boat in action had ever recorded and survived to make the claim. The submarine was designed for a depth of 150 metres, but with a safety factor of 2.5. The commander continues:

> Finally compressed air blew water out of the tanks and the involuntary descent was halted. The boat was brought up higher, but still was 150 metres below the surface.
>
> This experience gave the crew great confidence in the structure of the boat. No damage was found, although the temporary deformation of the hull at such tremendous pressure — 26 kilograms on every square centimetre — caused sparks at the propeller shafts.

Slowly the boat rose as it crept away northward. There was no SBT fitted to *U-331* which could have left a false echo for the Asdic operators on the destroyers above to attack. This submarine bubble target was a device introduced later that ejected chemical pills which activated on contact with sea water and created an echo to Asdic transmission and so created a disturbance which effected a false target of approximately the same extent as a U-boat. The pill started to operate two minutes after ejection and lasted for the six minutes considered necessary for the U-boat to escape. However the *Pillenwerfer*, as the Germans called it, was in the future; von Tiesenhausen risked the problems of the present. As soon as he felt certain he was clear he signalled Headquarters of his success and his intention of returning to Salamis. He arrived on 3 December.

The initial report of the attack at 32.34N, 26.24E was not over optimistic and on the following day the German radio reported that a U-boat commanded by von Tiesenhausen had attacked a British battleship off Sollum, scoring a direct hit with one torpedo.

It is now time to go back to see what was happening on the

British side at the time *U-331* attacked. The captain of *Valiant* reported:

'The battle fleet was formed in single line ahead, course 290 degrees, speed 17 knots and carrying out zig-zag number 10. In accordance with the instructions for this zig-zag, course was altered together 22 degrees to port to 268 degrees at 1621. *Valiant* was steady on the new course by 1623, and at this time was on the correct bearing from *Barham*, the distance being just under three cables. At 1625 the officer of the watch was taking the distance of *Barham* with the Stewart's distance meter, when he observed a large explosion on the port side of *Barham* abreast the mainmast. He realised immediately that *Barham* had been struck by a torpedo fired from somewhere on the port side and quite correctly ordered "Hard-a-port". I was not on the compass platform at the moment of the explosion, but on reaching the front of it ten seconds later, I observed a very large column of water and smoke alongside *Barham*, only the after end of the quarterdeck being then visible. I immediately ordered "Full speed ahead together"; at the same time the officer of the watch informed me that the wheel was hard-a-port, and I observed that the ship was just beginning to swing to port under the influence of full port rudder.

'About fifteen seconds later a submarine broke surface between five and ten degrees on the port bow at a distance of approximately 150 yards and moving from left to right. By then *Valiant* had swung about eight degrees to port, and was therefore heading approximately 260 degrees. The submarine was steering between 050 and 060 degrees, and her speed appeared to be about 4 knots.

'Immediately on sighting the submarine I ordered "Amidships", and then "hard-a-starboard" in an endeavour to ram her, but before the rudder was hard over it was obvious that it would not be possible to check the swing to port before she was across the bow. Actually the swing was just about checked when the submarine passed down the starboard side, and she submerged again when abreast *Valiant's* bridge at a distance of about fifty yards. As she appeared on the starboard side S.1 pom-pom fired 19 rounds at her with the maximum depression, but all rounds appeared to pass over her. The wheel was then again reversed so as to keep clear of *Barham*. The only portion of the submarine which appeared above water was the periscope and about two to three feet of the conning tower which was flat-topped. A certain amount of disturbed water before and abaft the conning tower indicated the fore and after ends of the hull, and enabled an accurate estimate of her course to be made.'

G. Lovell was serving in *Valiant* as a regulating petty officer when the battleships left Alexandria. He remembers:

'Soon after midday we were spotted by the Luftwaffe and they kept us in view for quite a while, carefully keeping outside the range of our guns; we fired a few rounds at them and they disappeared at around 1330. Later in the afternoon one of the destroyers on the screen hoisted the signal for submarine contact; after investigation Captain (D) signalled disregard as we were in an area where wrecks were numerous. In the first dog-watch I opened a dead light and port hole to let in some fresh air, having spent a couple of hours in the regulating office where we had all been smoking and I had enjoyed a nap. The battleships had just come into line abreast, as part of their zig-zag and this put *Barham* immediately abreast of us, about two cable lengths distant. I then saw a huge column of water rise abreast *Barham*'s forward turrets; and I thought it was a bomb dropped without any air-raid warning. I changed my mind when I saw a couple more huge water spouts along her side and realised that they were torpedo hits. I immediately closed the port, but before I had pulled the dead light down *Barham* was completely on her port side with her funnel touching the water. I went quickly up on to the upper deck, and as I looked at *Barham* there was a terrific explosion and I thought that obviously a magazine had gone up. I actually saw a twin 4-inch AA gun hundreds of feet up in the air and then bits and pieces began falling all around us. Probably as the result of having fired a salvo of torpedoes the conning tower of the U-boat shot up quite close to our bows and one of the forward pom-poms opened up on it but couldn't depress enough to obtain any hits. We altered course in an attempt to ram, but a battleship doesn't alter all that quickly. I don't know what action was taken to try and catch the submarine, but fortunately no depth charges were dropped otherwise the casualty list would have been worse.'

Lieutenant J.A. Hopking was on the after end of the compass platform on HMS *Queen Elizabeth*: he said:

'I was looking at *Barham* through my glasses when on her port side I suddenly saw three columns of water shoot up. I thought it was a stick of bombs and a near miss. I then looked up to see if I could see any aircraft. I looked back at *Barham* who by then had taken on a list to port of, I think, 12 degrees. I then saw a submarine surface on her port quarter. The submarine was just clear of *Barham* when she surfaced. *Barham* continued to list and she was almost on her beam end when I saw this explosion take place. I saw her continue to get a heavier list to port. She was almost on her beam end. I was waiting to see her finally disappear in the water when an enormous column of black smoke and wreckage was blown in the air. I did not see her again because of the smoke. As the explosion actually started I saw a dull red flame, there didn't appear to be much flame but there was a large amount of smoke.'

Paymaster Commander A. d'Orville Morse also of *Queen Elizabeth* said:

'I happened to be looking at *Barham* when I saw a large burst of water appear from behind. I said, "Hello, there's something up in *Barham*". Another splash appeared and another one then we heard the explosion and *Barham* listed over quickly. She turned away to port and as far as I can remember we turned to starboard. We saw a large crowd of men collect on the upper deck about abreast the bridge and superstructure, fo'c's'le and aft. Men were climbing down the ship's side and jumping into the water. Suddenly about four minutes after the original burst there was a terrific explosion abaft midships, I estimate about the level of the mainmast. The whole place was enveloped in smoke, debris flew high in the air and after that there was nothing but a pall of smoke. I did see something on the port bow of *Barham* which I think now was the after end of the submarine; the whole of it could not have been visible. Others say they saw the conning tower but it must have been hidden from me by the bow of *Barham*, it was only there for a second. A little later there was a final explosion and I saw flame a little for'ard of X turret, there was a tremendous amount of smoke with the flame.'

The torpedoed *Barham* listing to port . . .

. . . before she finally explodes

Leading Seaman S.F. Paris was captain of the pom-pom on board HMS *Kipling*, a destroyer on the starboard screen of *Barham*; he says:

'One of my gun's crew suddenly called out that *Barham* had been bombed, and when I looked at her I could see a great water-spout appearing above her upperworks. We instinctively looked skywards, thinking that it was an attack by Italian high-level bombers, but a few minutes later the captain informed the ship's company that the battleship had been torpedoed on the port side. We had, in fact, at that time a suspected submarine contact on our starboard side and hoisted the relevant signal up to the yardarm. As I watched, the battleship started to roll over, and I remember saying to my crew, "She's going down". When she was laying over on her beam ends, I could see some of the crew running over the side and jumping into the sea, then suddenly she blew up and all that could be seen was a huge pillar of smoke. *Queen Elizabeth* and *Valiant* increased speed and we were one of the destroyers detailed to carry on with them as escort. As the others commenced to hunt for the submarine we had warning of an air-attack, but when it came it was directed against the destroyers carrying out the search. After the smoke had cleared and there were only bodies and survivors floating on the water amidst the wreckage, I remember thinking to myself that from the time the torpedoes struck until the time when she had completely gone only about four and a half minutes had elapsed and I then understood how quickly the *Hood* had disappeared. Up until this time I had not thought that such a great ship could vanish from the face of the waters in such a short time.'

Captain Philip John Mack of HMS *Jervis* reported:

'I had been on the bridge until about 1615 and then went down to my sea cabin and the next thing was a report from, I think, the Gunnery officer who shouted down my voice pipe, "*Barham* has been torpedoed". I went up on the bridge and saw her listing over. I told the officer of the watch to put the helm hard a'port, telegraphs to full speed ahead and to house the Asdic dome. I hoisted a signal to the 7th Flotilla to form a circling screen round *Barham* and to the 2nd Flotilla to screen the battle fleet.

'When I was about 1,500 yards from *Barham* she heeled over

and blew up. I reduced speed to Asdic sweeping speed and received a signal from *Valiant* saying the submarine was astern of me. I asked *Valiant* for bearing of submarine and her reply was 050 degrees.

'I saw the final explosion; it appeared to be between the funnel and the mainmast. I definitely saw the bridge and the fore part of the ship clear of the explosion. The starboard side of *Barham* was toward me at the time. It was not a detonation but an explosion. It was not such a violent one — there was a kind of red glow fairly well aft but not as far as X or Y magazines.'

Captain H.S.L. Nicholson of the destroyer HMS *Griffin* reported:

'At about 1624 I was informed by voice pipe that bombs had fallen close to *Barham*. Lookouts simultaneously reported aircraft overhead and an alarm signal to this effect was made by flags. On reaching the bridge I saw that *Barham* had been hit by a large bomb or torpedo and had taken a heavy list. The aircraft overhead proved to be a daylight sighting of the planet Venus so the alarm signal was negatived.

'Captain (D) at once turned towards *Barham* flying the signal "7th destroyer flotilla join me". As senior officer of the remaining four ships on the screen, who were all my own flotilla, I at once hoisted the signal to form screening on *Queen Elizabeth* and *Valiant* with *Griffin*, *Decoy*, *Hasty* and *Hotspur*. After *Barham* blew up, various destroyers including *Hotspur* had been detailed by the Commander-in-Chief to pick up survivors. Captain (D) of the 7th Flotilla in *Napier*, with *Kipling*; and myself in *Griffin*, with *Decoy* and *Hasty* screened the battleships, *Valiant* having formed astern of *Queen Elizabeth* after the initial avoiding turn in the opposite direction. During this period no anti-submarine contact of any sort was made.'

Lieutenant-Commander Hugh Hodgkinson of HMS *Hotspur* was on the bridge for the first dog watch when he heard an underwater explosion amplified by a hydrophone loudspeaker on the bridge, he said it was the usual noise as when a depth charge explodes so he looked round to see which destroyer had turned off the screen to attack. They all seemed in station so he glanced back at the battle fleet on his starboard quarter and saw a great tower of water leap up amidships from *Barham*, leaving only her bows and stern in sight. He called to his captain below in his sea cabin as he yelled orders for the boat to swing round and increase speed to seek out the attacker. At the time *Hotspur* was outside ship of the screen on the port side. Hodgkinson was searching for tell-tale torpedo tracks and was amazed when he heard someone say, 'God, she's going', glancing quickly at her he saw the heavy list. The captain arrived on the bridge to see *Valiant* hoist 'Submarine Astern', but by that time she was in the smoke of *Barham*'s explosion and few saw the signal. *Hotspur* and *Jervis* turned in from the centre of the screen and at this moment the battleship started heeling over quickly, but before she had got far she was rent by a colossal explosion and completely disappeared in a vast puff of smoke.

The Commander-in-Chief ordered the destroyers to screen the battleships but at the same time Captain (D) 14th Destroyer Flotilla ordered *Hotspur* to pick up survivors. Hugh Hodgkinson continues:

'I had anticipated the order, already the crew were cutting the stowage lines of the rescue nets. All rafts were being manhandled to the side. The whaler was manned, and I sent down the young midshipman to cox her. The captain had slowed down, and we were nosing into what looked like a London fog, and smelled worse.

'I ran up on to the fo'c'sle to ascertain the best moment to slip the whaler and Carley floats. We passed into and through the thick fog, which had by now drifted to leeward, and suddenly it cleared. There around and ahead of us was the living aftermath of that tragedy. It was now 1643, dozens of heads bobbed in the water, far more than I expected. The captain steered up for a large clump, who were clinging to *Barham*'s mast. I shouted final instructions to the midshipman: "Go for the far and solitary ones, or those in distress. Leave the rest for us." Then I lowered the whaler to the waterline, and slipped her.

'As soon as we stopped the little bobbing heads moved slowly in towards us and the men were heaved on board. Some men from *Hotspur* jumped overboard to board the Carley floats to paddle them out to more distant groups.

'Great episodes always bring latent greatness to the surface

Survivors being picked up. Picture taken from . . .

. . . HMS *Hotspur*

where one never expected it. A stoker saw a raft on our windward side with no paddles to propel it towards us. Grabbing one end of a heaving line, he was over the side and swimming towards it, before anyone knew he could swim. Others paid out the line from aft, until he reached his objective and secured his end to the raft. Then the whole outfit was heaved up to the rope rescue ladders. Each one of our own rafts had a grass line paid out behind it, so that as soon as it was full we could heave it back at high speed to the ship. The remainder of those on deck hurled life-buoys on lines, and heaved dripping individuals back to life.

'Each man, as he came over the side, was black with oil. Bales of waste were brought up from the store to clean them off. The whole upper deck became layered with oil, so that one could hardly stand up. The whaler came alongside with men too badly wounded to climb out, so Neil Robertson stretchers were lowered, and the men hoisted out, groaning, by tackles slung over the torpedo davit. The sick-bay was soon full.

'Winston talked of blood and toil; this was blood and oil, you couldn't tell which. The captain moved the ship slowly towards the group clinging to the mast. Here the oil was thickest. It was solid, and the men could hardly swim, or hardly cling to the great spar. It touched alongside, just by our foremost net, and men started clambering limply up. There was a Carley raft there, too, from which men were climbing. One seemed to be in charge, and was exhorting each to make his utmost effort. He was too thickly covered with oil to recognize, and he was swimming by the raft and holding on, to give the weaker ones a chance to lie in the raft. When all were up he started too. He put up his arm to a helping hand. It seemed to be nothing but gold stripe, and I realised who it was. I never expected to receive an admiral on board in such circumstances, but this was Admiral Pridham-Wippell.'

At about 1730 *Jervis* and *Jackal* opened fire on an unidentified aircraft to southward. Between 1740 and 1820 *Hotspur* was engaged with more unidentified aircraft. No bombs were dropped and no aircraft appeared within one mile. By 1754 all the survivors were picked up, so the whaler and one Carley float were hoisted and the captain went slow ahead through the oil and wreckage to make sure there were no men left. Two Carley floats had to be

left as aircraft were being engaged at the time. At 1830 course
was shaped to join the Commander-in-Chief, the speed of the
destroyer was 29 knots.

Lieutenant-Commander Hodgkinson continues:

'While we were rejoining the battle fleet I went round the wardroom and mess-decks to see that everyone was being well looked
after. It was a sorry sight. Many of the men had swallowed oil
and were trying to vomit it up. Dozens of them had their hands
torn from clambering over the barnacle-crusted sides as the battleship rolled over; *Barham* had only been back in service a few
months but the warm waters of Alexandria had played havoc
with her bottom. There were many badly wounded, and all
covered in oil from head to foot, and partly blinded by getting
it in their eyes.

'Many of the older ones were mentally numbed from the whole
experience but the younger ones were soon cheerfully yarning
once again. I went up on deck from the wardroom, and found a
stoker lying among a crowd of others round the hatch down to
our cabins. His leg was shattered at the ankle and the bone sticking out. He never asked for treatment or morphia. He just lay
there quietly until his turn came along. On the mess-decks it was
hard to move, the doctor was going round dealing with all he
could. His only assistant was a sick-berth 'tiffy', who had only
served six months.'

Altogether *Hotspur* rescued 337 survivors, 14 officers including
the Vice-Admiral, 12 serious and 12 fairly minor cases of wounded,
all cot cases and there were numerous men with superficial cuts.

Nizam, arriving at the scene a little later, had also rescued some
150 men. At 1906 the battle fleet were sighted on the port beam
and course was altered to close. On joining the company *Hotspur*
was stationed on the port wing of the screen and remained in
company. One of the men rescued by the whaler was found to be
dead on arrival on board the destroyer and another died during
the night. They were buried at sea at 0830 the next morning when
the service was read by Lieutenant-Commander C.R. Stratton-
Brown of *Barham*.

Lieutenant-Commander Stratton-Brown has been mentioned
before, when taking a party of gunners from *Barham* to *Iron*

Duke, at the time she was immobilised in Liverpool. Now as senior surviving officer from *Barham* he takes up the story followed by others, of what happened aboard the battleship.

'I was on duty during the first dog-watch, the battleship had just completed a leg of the zig-zag as I went to the chart house. Soon after I entered I heard and felt a violent explosion. I was just outside the chart house on the port side of the bridge when I felt two more explosions about half a second apart. I was looking up for aircraft so did not see where the explosions took place, the 6-inch director fouled my view aft. I continued my course and had reached the after end of the bridge when I felt the fourth explosion and saw a column of water and wreckage thrown up abreast the mainmast on the port side. When I reached the ADP I observed from the mainmast that the ship had a list of seven or eight degrees to port. Then a submarine broke surface bearing Red 120 about 150–200 yards away, pointing towards our stern. I could not communicate with the 6-inch armament from the ADP and before I could get through to the 4-inch armament the submarine had dived. *Valiant* fired a burst of pom-pom at the swirl where the submarine dived and made good shooting but the overs reached *Barham*'s side.

'I looked aft again and saw that the list had increased slightly in spite of the fact that the ship was altering course rapidly to port. I then gave the order 'On lifebelts' and this was passed by SP telephone to all quarters although we could not know whether the orders were received. I then told the director's crew to come down and sent the ADP's crew down to the starboard side. At this time the port side of the boat deck aft was under water and the ship was slowly turning over. All traffic from aloft had ceased and I was left in the ADP with a midshipman and one rating. We were not able to go down so hauled ourselves up to the starboard side and waited for the sea to take us out, our lifebelts were on and inflated.

'We watched the water swirling over the port side of the ADP and come up to us in about one second. I had no control over my movements in this swirling water and expected soon to be clear. Soon I felt three or four ropes foul me round my stomach and I was drawn down. Whilst I was trying to decide the best means of escape these ropes, which must have been the signal halyards, parted and I started swimming for the surface.

'I could see that I was going towards the light but it looked a long way. I touched two or three bound in the same direction but do not know who they were. After some time I thought of taking off my clothes but decided not to as I should have to take off the lifebelt first. I still seemed to have a very long way to go when I took my first mouthful of water and spat it out. Then came complete darkness and silence. I couldn't remember anything of this type in the various stories I have read so I opened my mouth and took in three good deep breaths of air. I had no time to think any further before I was in water again and could see the light a long, long way above. I went on towards the light. Eventually I came to a mass of feet — it was quite dark and I had great difficulty in finding a space to get through. However, I broke surface in time and was seized by the left arm by a rating who tried to hold me up. I persuaded him to let go and find my own wreckage. The general behaviour of the men was of the highest standard. In the ship they were cheerful, quiet and tried to help each other, and in the water too this was so. They talked to each other quietly and waited patiently for the rescue boats.

'There was no rushing the whaler from *Hotspur* which was nearest to me but an orderly queue of men waiting their turn. When the boat filled, a number of us held on to the life-lines at the sides and were towed to the destroyer where we were welcomed with every possible attention and kindness.'

Lieutenant-Commander A.J. Cobham was relaxing as *U-331* came through the destroyer screen. He recalls:

'There were about ten to us in the wardroom and I think I am right in saying there were four explosions within a space of three seconds of which the second and third were very close. We went out on the half deck, which was full of dust, and it appeared, some smoke. There was a smell of cordite which I assumed to be from the explosion. At that time I did not know whether it was bombs or torpedoes. I went out on the quarter-deck, where I met two officers coming up from the port side. One of them told me he had seen a track and the submarine. I went up on the boat deck to get floats and rafts cleared away. Work was proceeding satisfactorily so I went forward to the group around

the funnel abreast No 1 HA gun where three men were cutting
Carley floats adrift on the superstructure. A few men were climbing down the side of the superstructure from the signal bridge;
at this time the ship was listing to 45 degrees. Four men remained
on the superstructure until the ship turned over and I think they
were blown off by the explosion. The ship started to go very
rapidly. I pulled myself up the deck by No 1 gun and climbed
over the splinter shield. I had reached the railing when she was
afloat on her side and was just climbing over when the ship blew
up aft. I could see flame and black smoke and much flying
material. I was struck on the legs by some of this. I tried to jump
clear and must have cleared the splinter shield of No 1 gun.

'I was sucked down for a considerable period but managed to
get some breaths in two air bubbles. At this time I seemed to be
striking through a large number of bodies and a lot of wreckage.
When I eventually came to the surface it was completely dark but
I was trapped under the ship in a pocket of air, but gradually it
lightened and I realised that it was a pall of smoke. There was
some wooden wreckage near me and a Denton raft with a number
of men about ten yards away.

'I feel certain the final explosion was "X" magazine because
it was that area where 'X' magazine was. I can definitely say that
it came from abaft the main mast. The explosion came through
the side, it appeared to be through the centre of the lower bulge;
here the 4-inch magazine was right alongside, outboard between
"X" and "Y" magazines.'

P.J. Setchell was reading the Night Intentions when the explosion
occurred. He said:

'The explosion resembled a bomb explosion, it was on the port
side. While proceeding to investigate there were two more hits
but I could not see where they hit as they were under No 4
four inch mounting and aft. During this time the ship was listing
well to port but appeared to steady herself for a short while, then
carried on listing.

'Captain Cooke was investigating the proceeding on the starboard wings of the bridge; Lieutenant Lochome reported that
both engines were stopped. The captain ordered on life belts,
this was the last I saw of them both. Owing to the failure of the

broadcast system I gave the life belt order over the wings of the bridge.

'By this time people were realising that she was going and began to clamber onto the starboard bulges; many were leaving the top and director. It was now that I told my lookouts to get away the best they could, and was about to leave myself when the submarine broke the surface. It was exceedingly close, well under a hundred yards distant; the conning tower was well visible, and the nose by the tubes. *Valiant* opened fire on her by pom-pom.

'My way of escape was by jumping from the Admiral's bridge onto the flag deck, then by climbing over M3 pom-pom starboard side onto B gundeck. By this time there was great difficulty in climbing across the decks. From here I slid down onto the lower bulge. Here I waited and adjusted my lifebelt, blowing it well up. Several men jumped at this point. I was about to go when a little persuasive force behind me helped me on my way; this may have been the beginning of the great explosion. In the water I had time to recover my wind before being sucked down. It was very worrying going down because every gulp was nothing but water. I had given up all hope of recovering when I took in a breath of air. Opening my eyes I saw that it was exceedingly dark all about me and that I was being forced upwards. This I put down to an air bubble caused by the explosion. It was some time after breaking surface that the smoke and fumes cleared away. The sea was covered with oil and wreckage. Several seamen and myself grabbed two spars and by placing them under either armpit we managed to propel ourselves along towards the destroyers. Several people made attempts to get hold of the spars but after a while had to leave go. It was about three-quarters of an hour to an hour before we were picked up by *Hotspur*.'

Midshipman P.B. Edwards remembers:
'At 1626 I was sitting reading in my armchair at the far side of the gunroom. There were three or possibly four explosions all within a few seconds and the ship lurched over to port taking a list of eleven degrees. All the lights went out, cordite fumes and water came in from somewhere. There were about twelve altogether in the mess, all of whom rushed out onto the halfdeck. I was, I think, the last through the door. I did not stop to pick

up my lifebelt. The halfdeck was flooded and it is possible that the first few out of the gunroom door may have been swept for'ard by the initial rush of water, it was about a foot deep when I waded through it. I went up the ladder past the gunroom heads and so onto the boatdeck. I climbed up to the starboard side where I waited for about twenty or thirty seconds. I found three midshipmen and a large number of ratings there. At this time several men were freeing PB seats so they would float off and I saw Lieutenant-Commander Cobham walking for'ard along the boatdeck. The ship now started to roll over to port again instead of righting herself as I expected.

'A lot of men were now going over the side and several attempted to jump from the boatdeck itself and landed on the bulge breaking various limbs and thus standing little chance of surviving. One of the midshipmen did this and hit the lower bulge with both his legs; others, including myself, ran and slipped down to the lower bulge and then jumped from there. By the time I got there the ship was nearly on its beam. I kicked off my shoes and jumped with about a 50 foot drop. I was sucked down and seemed to stay under her for a considerable period, during which time I had a breath of air from what was probably an air bubble as it was still pitch black. When I came to the surface smoke was hanging low over the surface and it was impossible to see the ship. The flag lieutenant was the only person anywhere near me and we clung to part of a writing desk, changed to a PB seat, followed by a broken Carley float and were eventually picked up by *Hotspur*'s whaler. The surface was covered with oil fuel and wreckage. I have no recollection of the magazines or any boilers blowing up.'

Midshipman D. McNeill was in the foremast HA director when the first explosion occurred; he remembers:

'The first torpedo hit us on the port side just abaft the bridge; the other two followed practically at once. They hit just a little further aft.

'After the first hit the ship instantly took a list of about eleven degrees to port. She then steadied up a little and it seemed as if she was going to remain there. But after a few seconds she continued listing to port. After she had reached a list of about eighteen degrees there was no doubt that she was going as the port battery was flooded.

'When this all happened I was in the foremast HA director, when we were hit it shuddered and rattled so much that her training broke down, so that the director was now useless. So I told the crew to go down to the ADP. When we reached there the ship had taken on a list of about 45 degrees. I looked out on the port side and practically on our port beam I saw the submarine which was partially on the surface. It was of medium size and it reminded me of a Greek submarine.

'By this time the ship was nearly over to 90 degrees so I scrambled down on the upper deck where I took my shoes and jacket off. I then climbed down the ship's side to the bulges and was just about to jump into the water when a minor explosion occurred aft on the port side. I think it must have been a 4-inch magazine. This was followed by a much louder explosion, and I think the blast from this blew me into the water.

'When I reached the water I was sucked down and when nearly out of breath I was able to get one gasp of air, before I was drawn down again. After about a minute I broke surface and all I could see was a great cloud of smoke. I saw the destroyers stop to pick us up so I swam to *Hotspur* and climbed aboard.'

Midshipman A.E.H. Sladen had just relieved the schoolmaster and was in the plot when the torpedoes struck the ship. He continues:

'Under the impression that the first was a bomb I automatically glanced at the Deck Watch and noted the time as 1626. Two other explosions followed in quick succession within the space of three or four seconds all appearing to strike aft.

'The port door to the plot was open and I was amazed to see first the periscope and then the complete conning tower of a submarine, within a cable, and on an opposite course to the ship. I automatically noted that *Valiant* was in a position to ram and an officer yelled "For God's sake, open fire", before it dived. A somewhat tardy burst of fire from one of *Valiant*'s close range weapons marked the spot. The conning tower was fairly small and open and reminded me both on account of its shape and colour, of the Greek and Yugoslav submarines lying in Alexandria.

'Upon the torpedoes striking, the ship immediately heeled to about ten degrees and then although still heeling, appeared to steady up. After about 1½ minutes however the heel rapidly increased. I seized and inflated my lifebelt and went out onto the admiral's bridge. The end was now a matter of time and on reaching the flag deck, I forsook the ladder and walked down the now almost horizontal superstructure to the upper deck. By seizing the forward 4-inch gun shield I managed to reach the guard rails and so onto the ship's side. I had not reached the water line when first one and then a larger explosion shook the ship.

'I found myself under water and a breath of air I managed to get in complete darkness left me with the impression that I was trapped inside the ship. However after further underwater acrobatics I found I could again breathe and as the smoke cleared I found myself on the surface. The battered but still buoyant remains of a Carley raft was at hand and soon about 25 ratings joined me. In spite of their experience and the fact that several were wounded all were remarkably cheerful. When we were picked up by *Hotspur* about an hour later we had already sung a number of songs.'

At the time of the first explosion Instructor Lieutenant G.M. Wolfe was just outside his office which was on the port side of the ADC Flat, that is, the first deck above the boat deck on the bridge structure. He continues:

'Since I was leaving the office, I was facing aft, and saw the flash of the explosion which appeared to be immediately abaft the funnel. After a slight pause, two further explosions occurred, both slightly further aft. I crossed immediately to the starboard side, where a crowd was already gathering on the upper deck, and gave my pocket knife to a petty officer who was trying to unlash two Carley floats which were secured at the bottom of the ladder up to the pom-pom deck.

'I went rapidly back to my office for my Burberry, and then returned to the starboard side with some difficulty as there was already an appreciable list. I descended to the upper deck, where the ship's company was already going over the side. I shouted to all near me to follow their example, rather unnecessarily as there was little panic and the men were not wasting any time. The list was steadily increasing and as everyone about me was over the guard rail, I went over also at a point level with the forward end of the bridge, and slipped down to the bilge keel. By now she was going over fast, and I reached the bottom of the ship, now an almost vertical wall. Here I hesitated, owing to the difficulty of keeping my balance because the final jump appeared hazardous with the bottom coming up to meet me.

'It was then that a big explosion took place aft, and the ship plunged over so rapidly that I was flung backwards into the water with many others. After being sucked down, we eventually surfaced and I swam over to a Carley float which appeared close at hand. All trace of the ship had vanished. I discarded my Burberry, blew up my lifebelt, and held on to the side of the float with many more until picked up by *Hotspur* an hour later.'

Warrant Ordinance Officer P.E. Wilson was working in his office at the time of the first explosion. He says:

'I felt the first impact followed by two others about one second intervals, respectively. I waited for a few seconds to see what developed and as the ship took a violent list I passed from there along the half deck through the screen door on to the starboard side of the quarterdeck. By that time the water was coming in on the outer screen door. There was quite a crowd gathered at the foot of the gangway leading up to the boat deck. I remained there for a further period; about half a minute or a minute. It was almost impossible to keep one's footing on the deck at that time. We had to hang on to the guard rails. With two other officers I dragged myself along to the stern and went off the edge. I was followed by two other officers. At the time the explosion took place I was about fifty yards away. The only thing I saw was a huge column of debris and smoke blown in the air. When the explosion happened I looked round; I noticed a plate dropping which looked like a ship's side plate. It fell quite close. Following it there was one or two heavy waves such as I had seen at Stanley Bay, and then it subsided. My life saving belt would not inflate as I found I could not get any air into it. Eventually I was picked up by *Nizam*.'

Horace Cowley served on *Barham* for less than a month, being drafted aboard at Alexandria after his previous ship had been bombed in the Crete evacuation. Seaman Horace continues:

'My first big ship: I hardly had time to get to know my mess-mates and part of ship before she got hit. I remember coming off the afternoon watch on the 4-inch HA port side. I arrived down at the mess and started to prepare supper as I was duty cook. Until I joined *Barham* I thought only destroyers and small ships had canteen messing! My other cook of the mess was missing as usual, and I had to fetch the meat from the butcher, we were on steak and onions for supper. With tears streaming from my eyes from peeling the onions I was having a natter to the killick of the mess about the missing cook when we felt and heard the dull thud of torpedoes as they hit us. The general opinion on the messdeck seemed to be that we had received a near miss from a bomber. Naturally we made for the upper deck to find out what it was, but before I had reached the second gangway the old ship was taking a list to port. I then went on to the upper deck, getting on to the starboard side as she was almost on her beam end, then in to the water as she went up with the biggest bang I've ever heard.'

To conclude the representative selection of survivor's stories is that of the oldest man aboard, Vice-Admiral H. Pridham-Wippell. He was on the starboard side of the 4-inch gun deck as the torpedo struck:

'I personally was knocked down by the first explosion, which was not a very large one. Immediately thereafter I got over the berthing rails on to the 6-inch glacis but the ship was heeling to port at an appreciable speed and I failed to get any further. I have no further recollection of what happened until finding myself floating on my back in the water about ten to fifteen yards clear of the port side of the ship. The smoke cloud from, presumably, the main explosion enveloped me almost at once though I neither heard nor felt the explosion.

'The behaviour of the ship's company was exemplary both while abandoning ship and in the water. There was no noise or panic and all hands took to the water in an orderly manner.'

As soon as the extent of the disaster had been realised there was an immediate order that wireless silence had to be maintained. The pilot of the Walrus aircraft from *Queen Elizabeth* was there-

H. D. Frhr von Tiesenhausen wearing the *Ritterkreuz* he was awarded for sinking *Barham* . . .

. . . with (below) *U-331*, photographed in Salamis in February 1942. The big flag indicates the sinking of *Barham*.

fore launched at dawn the following morning to carry the news to Alexandria so that arrangements could be made at the Naval Headquarters ashore for the survivors. After carrying out his orders the pilot repaired to the Cecil Hotel for a drink, only to find that the sinking of *Barham* was the main topic of conversation!

On board the rescue destroyers officers and men provided cigarettes and refreshment and gave up blankets and clothes for the benefit of the survivors. It was in this borrowed kit that the *Barham* men landed with the rest of the force at Alexandria, at midday. Buses and ambulances were already waiting to hurry them away. A car arrived for the Admiral.

The unwounded were taken to HMS *Resource*, a depot ship, where they bathed and were fed and given a Red Cross shipwreck bag. As far as possible the men were kitted up in the clothing store and all received a very welcome two Egyptian pounds with which to buy such little necessities and comforts as could be obtained from the canteen; this was greatly appreciated.

It was on this day that the German radio reported that a U-boat commanded by von Tiesenhausen had attacked a British battleship off Sollum, scoring a direct hit with one torpedo.

Admiral Cunningham visited many of the rescued later in hospital and commented on the injuries many of them sustained through sliding down the ship's bottom. Despite not long being out of dock in Durban barnacles had grown to an enormous size in the warm water of Alexandria.

Of the crew lost in the sinking Frank Loy particularly remembers some of the larger than life characters: Able Seaman Sid Hyde, three-badgeman and outstanding seaman, ever ready with good advice, help and genuine concern for young seamen; Regulating Petty Officer 'Reggie' Strickland, public enemy number one to the younger set who hounded them from stem to stern and yet helped make boys into men — he was posthumously awarded the Conspicuous Gallantry Medal; Ted Spacey, handsome two badge leading seaman, killick of 10 Mess, port side topman's messdeck; super-efficient, straight as a die, an example to all and the finest man Frank has known.

Frank also remembers particularly two of the survivors as the old firm of 'Thommo and Caxton', the tottering tailors who had a jewing firm in 'B' turret. Able Seamen Walter Claxton and Thomson, QO's and bespoke tailory. The 30/- tailors measured at 0900, had first fittings at 1030 and collection at 1330 when the finished product was always a perfect fit. They were two very rare characters, of many, that made *Barham* the happy ship she was.

CHAPTER THIRTEEN

Board of Enquiry

It was obviously in the interests of all, as well as a matter of procedure that a Board of Enquiry be immediately set up to look into
the sinking of *Barham*.

The enquiry was held aboard the depot ship HMS *Woolwich*
in mid-December, when the commanding officers of all ships in
the immediate vicinity of *Barham* were questioned, as were several of the survivors. Written statements were taken from those
not well enough to attend.

Vice-Admiral H. Pridham-Wippell was definitely of the opinion
that the ship was hit by four torpedoes, with a slight interval
before the first and the other three. Lieutenant-Commander
C.R. Stratton-Brown, the senior surviving officer of *Barham*,
produced a stop watch showing 4.31.32; he was of the opinion
that four torpedoes struck the ship all abaft the bridge. He was the
only survivor who claimed to see a torpedo track, he thought it
was a direct shot, as opposed to angle gyros, because he saw the
whole of the U-boat's conning tower and said at this time *Barham*
had moved on. He told the Enquiry that life-saving belts were
carried by all men – not necessarily worn, but they had to be
on hand, usually slung on one shoulder. There were no special
satchels for this purpose. Water-tight doors were closed for cruising; this meant that doors and hatches on the main deck and
below were closed and fully clipped except to machinery compartments in use and down to the magazines, down to 'A' space and
'AB' space. 'X' and 'Y' spaces were left open. The armoured doors
leading to 'A' space and 'B' space were half open. 'X' and 'Y' space
were half open for communication. The ventilation to compartments which were closed was shut and ventilation valves closed
including mushroom heads. He told the Enquiry the only explosion he saw was abreast the mainmast.

Lieutenant-Commander A.J. Cobham, the next most senior

officer to survive from *Barham*, was asked about men getting away from the ship; he said:

'The Carley floats aft had ropes crossed over them, holding them to the deck, the for'ard had a toggle strap. I did not consider this a satisfactory method of securing the rafts and had repeatedly tried to get slips, but was always informed that they were unavailable.

'I heard no order to abandon ship or indeed any order from start to finish. The upper deck lights were on and I have also been told that they were on for'ard until she was literally on her side. I think she was slightly down by the stern when I came out on the quarterdeck.'

Part of the evidence the captain of *Valiant* gave to the Enquiry was as follows:

'As soon as the smoke and spray had cleared away and *Barham* became visible again, it was seen that she had developed a very heavy list to port, probably 20 to 30 degrees, as it was observed that the water was level with the after screen door into the lobby as the fore end of the quarterdeck. She appeared to hang in this position for about a minute, then she began to roll over on approximately an even keel.

'She continued to roll over and sink deeper in the water until the sea was seen to be entering the funnel. A moment or two after this there was a loud explosion amidships, and a very large column of black and brown smoke with flame from the explosion in the middle of it shot into the air. This explosion occurred at 1630, or five minutes after the torpedoes hit, when *Barham* was just abaft beam from *Valiant*'s bridge.

'All observers are agreed that, as the torpedoes hit, there were three explosions, a first, followed about one or two seconds later by two in quick succession, and that the explosions all occurred between funnel and mainmast. It is not certain what caused the final explosion but the general opinion was that it was the 6-inch magazine. It did not appear large enough, nor loud enough, for a 15-inch magazine, and it was certainly not "A" or "B" magazines, as the centre of the explosion was abaft the bridge, and I am of the opinion that it was not as far as "X" magazine. The final point of the whole explosion seemed to be just abaft the funnel as the ship was then lying over at 90 degrees. Although it was

impossible to see exactly at what point the explosion occurred
I think it came through the ship's side because the explosion was
upward. At the time of the explosion *Valiant* was one or two
cables ahead of *Barham* on the main line of advance.'

The commanding officer of *Jervis*, Captain Philip J. Mack, Captain
(D) of the 14th Flotilla told the Enquiry:

'It was not until 2100 that I first realised *Jervis* had established
A/S contact. The echo was reported from the A/S cabinet to the
bridge as bearing 220 degrees and a range of about 1,200 yards.
Asdic working conditions were fair to good with a working range
of eighteen hundred yards. I understand it was a very loud echo
and gave an extensive target of about 60 degrees. I think no left
cut on was ever obtained. I was in my sea cabin and was not
informed of this echo. The officer of the watch, taking into consideration the enormous extent of the target considered it to be
"non-sub".

'HMS *Griffin* was next on screen to port of *Jervis*, 1,500 yards,
bearing 200 degrees. The bridge repeater was not in use until
the echo was reported. I normally hear every time the loud
speaker is switched on, through my voice-pipe; their employment
is left to the discretion of each commanding officer of the flotilla.
I would have been doubtful of the large extent of target experienced being a submarine. The operators continued working on
that echo for two minutes and still continued to report large
extent of target. There was every possibility that *Griffin*'s wake
would have been included in it. The range and echo was about
400 yards with *Griffin*'s wake but there was no hydrophone effect
although this might have been muddled with *Griffin*.'

The Board of Enquiry was told that in *Griffin* no contact or
hydrophone effect was heard throughout the watch by operators
or on the bridge where the loudspeaker was switched on at maximum. The first operator had just joined the ship after an A/S
course in *Woolwich* and had very little experience, the second
operator had been in the ship some time and was very experienced.

*Statement on enquiry into sinking of Barham — from HMS Wool-
wich 18 December 1941*
At 1625 approximately, the fleet being then on the port leg of

a zig-zag from 1621, *Barham* was attacked by a submarine which passed through the destroyer screen. The submarine obtained a very close range of probably about 400 yds. or less from *Barham* and so was able to fire a concentrated bow salvo of three or four torpedoes. The submarine broke surface very close to *Barham*, probably as a result of firing the rapid salvo. She then had to alter course to starboard to make sure of not ramming *Barham*. All torpedoes appear to have struck *Barham* on the port side between the funnel and the after turrets. Allowing for discrepancies in times taken we consider that four minutes was the period between *Barham* being struck and a heavy explosion aft, by which time the ship was on her beam ends to port. The final explosion undoubtedly took place in the after part of the ship and there is reasonable evidence to show that it was abaft the mainmast. The still photographs from *Valiant*'s film show the explosion to have been a very heavy one, in spite of the small concussion it caused. From study of these photographs it appears probable that the explosion vented itself in two directions; approximately at right angles through the upper deck and by blowing away a portion of the starboard side of the vessel. Evidence from witnesses who were leaving *Barham* down her starboard side and from witnesses in *Queen Elizabeth* establish the seat of the explosion as probably being abreast the magazines of 'X' and 'Y' 15in. turrets. We are unable to establish the reason for the explosion, but in *Barham* 4-inch HA magazines had been fitted between the outboard sides of the 15-inch magazines and the ship's sides, so that the only protection for these 4-inch magazines from a torpedo was the ship's side and the narrow after portion of the bulge protection. It therefore may have been possible that, as a result of the torpedoes, a fire was started in the port 4-inch magazine which spread to the adjoining 15-inch magazines, with the resultant explosion. This supposition is supported by the fact that there are no magazines before 'X' and 'Y' until forward of the boiler rooms. The still photographs make it clear that the effect of the explosion spread well forward. Although this explosion undoubtedly accelerated the rate at which the vessel sank, it is our opinion that it was not the primary cause of the foundering of HMS *Barham*.

There was insufficient evidence upon which to reconstruct events within the ship, but we believe that the ship's side over a considerable length of hull was blown in, thus opening her vitals to the sea, causing her to list heavily to port immediately upon being hit, and with a slight pause at an angle of heel of about 40 degrees to continue the list until in about four minutes time the beam end position was reached.

The internal lighting and communication system failed rapidly.

The vessel was in a recognised state for cruising and the degree of water-tight subdivision appears to have been satisfactory. The damage was so considerable and the rapidity with which she heeled over so great, as to preclude any effective measures to save the ship.

The conditions for launching boats or rafts were extremely severe, but the fact that certain rafts were secured with lashings which had to be cut, as stated by one witness, was an unsatisfactory feature.

No general orders for the conduct of the ship were heard subsequent to her being struck. This was probably due to the broadcast system failing. The behaviour of the ship's company was throughout calm and collected.

From the evidence of *Jervis*, it appears that the submarine passed the destroyer screen submerged and at high speed through a position between *Jervis* and *Griffin*. Evidence showed that stress of operational work had resulted in only one practice A/S attack being carried out by *Jervis* during the preceding year. No A/S contact whatever was obtained by *Griffin* but a contact of wide extent of target, 60 degrees, was obtained by *Jervis* at 1618½ on a bearing 220 degrees range 1,100yds. This contact on being classified as non-sub was disregarded and the anti-submarine sweep continued.

The Director of Anti-submarine Warfare concurred in the findings of the Board of Enquiry and recorded with regret, his opinion that the primary cause of the loss of *Barham* was an A/S failure of two destroyers. His summary read:

'The facts were as follows: Asdic conditions are described as 'fair to good' but were sufficiently poor to cut the Asdic working range of the day from 2,500 yards to 1,800 yards. A working range of 1,800 yards is approaching the limit at which 'reliance can be placed on Asdics'; it is not clear if this working range was reported by signal to the Commander-in-Chief. The U-boat passed through the screen, apparently at comparatively high speed on opposite courses, between *Jervis* and *Griffin*, closer to the latter than the former.

'Captain (D), 2nd Flotilla, reports that no A/S contact of any sort was made by *Griffin*. It is noted that a newly-joined, newly-rated and inexperienced man was first operator on watch in *Griffin*.

'The U-boat was probably just outside the working range of *Jervis*'s previous sweep on the port side. After sweeping starboard side *Jervis* obtained a 'loud, raucous and sharp' echo on her first transmission on a bearing of Red 70 on the port sweep. This echo may well have been from the U-boat herself but the operator, sweeping forward, obtained a series of echoes off the wake and reported a wide extent of target. He never trained aft far enough to get the 'left-cut-on' of the target and was ordered by the Officer-of-the-Watch to 'disregard and carry on with the sweep'. No hydrophone effect was heard. This operator had been qualified for two years and had 12 months experience in his ship. A quicker appreciation by either the operator or officer would have shown the necessity of finding the "left-cut-on" and this would almost undoubtedly have led to the detection of the U-boat and to a counter-attack in time to save the situation. On the other hand, the possibilities of this particular situation are not emphasised in the hand-books and action is being taken to do this, and to draw attention to this point in the A/S schools.

'The fact that *Jervis* had had so little opportunity for A/S exercises undoubtedly militated against efficiency on this occasion. The need of adequate A/S training is fully recognised, but there are no submarines for purely training duties in the Mediterranean, and operational submarines have to be detailed when possible. The Board of Enquiry finds that stress of operational work resulted in only one exercise being carried out by *Jervis* during the preceding year. It is important that A/S vessels employed on fleet screening duties should have regular training in screening detection at high speeds of advance in addition to the normal hunting practices. The failure of the screen on this occasion emphasises the danger of sending capital ships into U-boat waters without this training. It is assumed that, having achieved an ideal firing position, the U-boat fired a full salvo of four torpedoes from her bow tubes and that all four hit. This probably caused her subsequent break-surface. No details are given in these papers to show why the U-boat was able to make good her escape and this must remain a matter for profound regret.

*

The Director of Training and Staff Duties division said of the Board of Enquiry's report:

> The evidence as to happenings inside the ship after the torpedoes struck is very slender; that power and lighting quickly failed is supported by the apparent failure of the broadcasting system. The probability is that there was an immediate partial failure owing to damage, and that this became worse as compartments flooded. The Director of Training and Staff Duties feels that in this, as in every other form of Naval activity, the use of units which are not fully worked up and kept in practice is an unprofitable method of waging war.

After all the relevant statements had been made and questions asked, and answered, Admiral Cunningham withdrew the submarine *Otus* from operations to act as a practice target for the instruction of A/S ratings.

The loss of *Barham* was a big enough blow but more bad news was to follow. On 10 December *Repulse* and *Prince of Wales* were sunk off Malaya, and the day after the Board of Enquiry had issued their report of the sinking of *Barham*, her two sister ships *Queen Elizabeth* and *Valiant* were badly damaged by charges from human torpedoes in Alexandria harbour.

While on leave in Berlin Oberleutnant von Tiesenhausen broadcast a description of the attack over the German radio.

Gradually the former crew of *Barham*, recovering from their ordeal, were drafted to different ships; never again would they sail together as a crew. One person, however, was determined that they would not be forgotten.

Mrs Constance Cooke, widow of *Barham*'s 51-year-old Captain Geoffrey Cooke, devoted the rest of her life to his memory by doing everything in her power for the parents, widows and sweethearts of the men who died with him. One of these men was Ian

Jones, director controller of guns, off duty at the time of the sinking. His brother Rodney Vernon Jones had served on the same ship for eighteen months in 1921–22.

On 27 January 1942 the Admiralty issued the following communique to the Press:

> The Board of Admiralty regrets to announce that HMS *Barham* (Captain G.C. Cooke RN), flying the flag of Vice-Admiral H.D. Pridham-Wippell, KCB, CVO, Second-in-Command of the Mediterranean Fleet has been sunk.
>
> Vice-Admiral Pridham-Wippell is safe, but Captain Cooke lost his life.
>
> *Barham* was sunk on 25 November, 1941. The next of kin of casualties were informed, but the loss of the ship was not announced, since it was clear at that time that the enemy did not know that she had been sunk, and it was important to make certain dispositions before the loss of this ship was made public.
>
> The German radio has, from time to time, made statements with the obvious intention of endeavouring to discover whether a battleship of the Queen Elizabeth class, which they claimed to have hit with torpedoes, had in fact sunk.
>
> This information has been denied to the enemy for the reason given above, but as it is clear that they are now aware that *Barham* was sunk, her loss can be announced.

Later that same day the German radio announced that the *Ritterkreuz* had been awarded to H. D. Freiherr von Tiesenhausen, commander of *U-331*, for this exploit.

The Times published a casualty list on 23 February 1942; 861 men lost their lives. Since most of the crew had been from the Portsmouth Division Mrs Cooke spent the rest of the war years in an hotel near there to look after all the wives and mothers in that area; she distributed gifts of food and clothing personally along with any financial help needed. For years she looked after two orphans whose mother died shortly after the disaster.

In 1943 a pair of standard candlesticks were given to Westminster Abbey in memory of the crew of *Barham*, from a fund largely raised by Mrs Cooke. One of the sailors had lived in Barham, Huntingdonshire, so Mrs Cooke presented a memorial plaque and chalice to the church there, in his memory.

Each year, on the anniversary of the ship's sinking, she organised and financed a meeting of the dependents at her London flat and a memorial service at Westminster Abbey. After the service she would invite as many as a hundred people back to tea; she made it her life's work to help all those whose relatives died on *Barham*.

Mrs Cooke was in her eighties when she died in May 1966; her dying wish was that relatives of the seamen who lost their lives with her husband should not be forgotten. To this end she left a large sum of money to help them should they be in need. Today there is still a flourishing Barham Survivors Association, with close links with Training Ship *Barham* for sea cadets. The annual service is still held at Westminster Abbey on the Saturday nearest to 25 November. The author was privileged to attend this moving ceremony in 1977 and enjoy a convivial evening with the survivors at the Union Jack Club.

It was as well that the gunnery of *Barham* had not been too inaccurate fifty years earlier, for in 1978 the memorial dinner was held aboard HMS *Chrysanthemum*, moored at the Thames Embankment — the same ship that towed the target for *Barham*'s gunners to practise on in the twenties! These survivors, and their predecessors certainly knew the difference between a strong breeze and a full gale, for they served aboard *Battleship Barham*.

*Admirals who served aboard HMS Barham —
with date of appointment*

Rear-Admiral Hugh Evan-Thomas KCB MVO   25th August 1915
Vice-Admiral Sir Arthur C. Leveson KCB   1st October 1918
Vice-Admiral Sir William C.M. Nicholson KCB   1921
Vice-Admiral Edwyn S. Alexander-Sinclair
   KCB MVO   14th October 1922
Rear-Admiral W.W. Fisher CB MVO   14th September 1924
Rear-Admiral C.M. Steveley CB CMG   7th September 1925
Vice-Admiral Sir Michael H. Hodges
   KCB CMG MVO   9th March 1926
Vice-Admiral John D. Kelly CB   30th April 1927
Rear-Admiral The Hon. R.A.R. Plunkett-Ernle-Erle-Drax
   CB DSO   12th April 1929
Rear-Admiral Max K. Horton CB DSO   12th December 1933
Rear-Admiral T.H. Binney CB DSO   25th July 1936
Rear-Admiral R. Latham CB   14th August 1938
Vice-Admiral G. Layton CB DSO   23rd July 1939
Vice-Admiral H.D. Pridham-Wippell KCB CVO   12th May 1941

*Captains who served aboard HMS Barham —
with date of appointment*

Arthur W. Craig	June 1915
Henry T. Buller MVO	18th April 1918
Richard Horne DSO	1st October 1918
Robin C. Dalglish	1st October 1920
Percy L.H. Noble	14th October 1922
R.A.S. Hill	27th September 1924
F.A. Marten CB CMG	14th October 1925
J.C.W. Henley CB	9th March 1926
H.S. Monroe DSO	1st December 1927
James F. Somerville DSO	1st December 1928
J.C. Hamilton	16th March 1929
R.J.T. Scott	15th December 1933
N.A. Woodhouse	30th August 1935
H.E. Horan DSC	28th July 1937
Algernon U. Willis DSO	22nd April 1938
H.T.C. Walker	31st January 1939
Geoffrey C. Cooke	25th March 1940

Index